GERMAN SCIENCE READER

AN ANALYTICAL APPROACH TO TRANSLATION PROBLEMS

By

GEORGE WM. RADIMERSKY

ASSOCIATE PROFESSOR OF FOREIGN LANGUAGES
MICHIGAN STATE COLLEGE

THE RONALD PRESS COMPANY , NEW YORK

3

Library of Congress Catalog Card Number: 50-8071
PRINTED IN THE UNITED STATES OF AMERICA

PREFACE

This book is the outgrowth of an effort which the author has made for a number of years to understand and analyze the difficulties which the student of scientific German meets during the period of transition from the first to the second year in his study of the language. Further, it sets forth in considerable detail a method of proved usefulness for obviating these difficulties, thus lightening the learner's effort in overcoming the basic obstacles that are inherent in his task. From first to last the principles and methods here presented have been developed by means of actual classroom practice.

The present volume treats the various outstanding problems of translation as they confront the student, and not at all as they are merely observed and noted by the instructor. Though claims to completeness of treatment are by no means made, nevertheless the author believes that all major aspects of translating technical German have been carefully analyzed and adequately presented. The wide range of subject matter here offered will suffice, it is believed, to acquaint the student with such a fund of technical terminology that any reading he may do in fields that are here not touched upon will be greatly facilitated. The author therefore hopes that this book may constitute a concrete contribution to the field of language pedagogy as it applies to teaching and learning to read scientific German.

An expression of gratitude is hereby extended to Mrs. George Wm. Radimersky, whose merit it is to have made the original suggestion for this type of reader. She felt that the author's knowledge of translation problems and his acquaintance with the difficulties that students encounter should receive tangible expression. The result is this present volume.

G. W. R.

East Lansing, Michigan
1950

ACKNOWLEDGMENTS

The author wishes to acknowledge permission extended to him by the publishing houses mentioned below for the use of factual and background material for the following essays:

"Der Gedanke des menschlichen Fortschritts." From *The History of Human Society* by Frank W. Blackmar, Chas. W. Scribner's Sons, New York, 1926. The chapter on "Essentials of Progress."

"Die Entwicklung der Wissenschaften." *Ibid.* The chapter on "The Evolution of Science."

"Die Geschichte und das Wesen der Psychologie." From *Psychology* by E. G. Boring, H. S. Langfeld, and H. D. Weld, John Wiley & Sons, Inc., New York, 1935. The chapter on "The Nature of Psychology."

"Seelenheilkunde in Kriege." From *Psychiatry in Modern Warfare* by E. A. Stecker and K. E. Appel, The Macmillan Company, New York, 1945.

"Ursachen und Verhütung des Verbrechens." From *Principles of Criminology* by E. H. Sutherland, J. B. Lippincott Company, New York, 1947, The chapters on "Causes of Crime" and "Prevention of Crime."

"Der Fingerabdruck, Geschichte und Anwendung." From *Fingerprinting: A Manuel of Identification* by Charles E. Chapel, Coward-McCann, Inc., New York, 1941.

"Die Bevölkerung und die Einwanderung." From *Everyday Problems of American Democracy* by J. T. Greenan and A. B. Meredith, Houghton, Mifflin, and Company, New York, 1943. The chapter on "Population and Immigration."

"Die Tuberkulose." From *Tuberculosis* by H. E. Kleinschmidt, M.D., The National Health Series edited by the National Health Council, Funk and Wagnalls Company, New York, 1937.

"Der Krebs." From *Cancer* by F. C. Wood, M.D., D.Sc., *ibid.*

"Radar." From *Radar* by O. E. Dunlap, Jr., Harper & Bros., New York, 1946.

CONTENTS

PART I

PROBLEMS OF TRANSLATION

PART II

GERMAN SCIENCE READER

INTRODUCTION

This science reader is not intended to teach either science or the sciences. Rather, its purpose is to supply a book which teaches how to read technical German and which is suitable for the first semester or term of the second year. As its title indicates, it is designed to fulfill definite functions. These may be succinctly stated as being those of bridging the wide gap which exists in the attainments of first-year students when they begin their second year's work. It is an almost universal experience that the period of adjustment at the beginning of the second year is a painful one. Therefore it is with the view in mind of making this period of adjustment less severe that this book has been written. The methods involved and presented are based on more than fifteen years of teaching experience in the field of scientific German, and on many years of tutoring. The requirements of the latter, especially when met effectively, are such that any method employed must be more than idle play. The author has therefore selected methods for this reader which experience shows will yield the best results.

With this view in mind, the general make-up of this volume includes, besides the introduction, an essay addressed to the student, entitled, "How to Master the Reading of Scientific German," and the body of the reading material which is divided into parts according to the division of sciences into philosophical, individual, and applied. Although a closer analysis of the reading material will show that the principle of adjustment is carried to the last page, it is especially the first part of the book which is of greatest strategic value. Thus Part I consists of a series of ten problem readings. These are designed to develop an effective translation technique by singling out the most important difficulties encountered by the student and by analyzing them *from the practical angle of translation.* Each reading in Part I thus becomes an illustration of a major problem. These are the following:

1. Principles of the simple statement or main clause.
2. Principles of the dependent clause.
3. Multiple-clause constructions.
4. The absolute participial constructions.
5. The relative clause.
6. The participial modifier.
7. The infinitive.
8. Certain features of verbs.
9. The subjunctive.
10. Orientation for translation.

Analysis of any one of these problem readings shows the following organization: First there appears an anlaysis of the problem as seen from the translator's viewpoint, and illustrated, when necessary, by diagrams. This analysis includes exercise material, which is, in turn, followed by a series of review questions for oral discussion. Finally, there follows the reading selection, which includes a basic vocabulary at the bottom of the pages.

Part II presents general readings intended to accustom the student to face any or all the translation problems in one continuous essay. It has not been the author's intention, however, to make the style more difficult than is to be found in comparatively simple research material. In other words, he does not approve of the involved style of technical readings such as prevailed twenty-five and more years ago. On the basis of proved methods, the introductory essay, "How to Master the Reading of Scientific German," contains many suggestions concerning the correct attitude on the part of the student, and also suggestions as to how to go about doing effective work. The book concludes with a list of abbreviations and the customary German-English vocabulary.

A few words should be said about the vocabulary. Throughout the text it is presented at the bottom of the pages, and is composed of those items that have basic scientific value. Thus entries that appear at the bottom of the page are to be learned by the student. This is especially true of Part I. In the second part the student should stress the mastery of idiomatic phrases that are important to the reading of scientific texts. Only a few of these appear in each reading selection; on the whole, they usually comprise only about thirty to forty items.

It is hoped that the entire procedure that was followed in the composition of this book will be found to present a unified and practical approach to the art of reading scientific German, such as has been proved effective in actual classroom work.

HOW TO MASTER THE READING OF SCIENTIFIC GERMAN

The student who begins the second year of German usually passes through a period of rather difficult adjustment. Experience has borne out that this is especially true in the case of scientific German because, it seems, the technical aspects involved require the application of a greater degree of discipline than does literary German. On the other hand, it has also been found that once the student has acquired the mastery of technical German, actual reading is by no means the problem which it seemed to be at the outset. In view of these experiences, it appears reasonable to supply the student with sufficient guidance material. The following is not meant to convey the idea that the procedures suggested here are the only practicable ones. On the contrary, there are many other ways of mastering language skills. Every student has his own preferred procedure. It is true, however, that many students never develop an effective approach to technical reading. Years of experience have shown the type of approach outlined below to be highly effective.

The problem can be circumscribed by saying that the student must have at his command (1) a sufficient vocabulary, (2) a mastery of the various types of clauses and clause constructions, and (3) the ability to attain a reasonable speed. All this can be achieved only by means of adequate tools.

The Tools. These can be enumerated very briefly. First of all is the text chosen by the instructor for classroom use. Ordinarily this will have a suitable vocabulary near the end. Such a vocabulary will often be insufficient, however, because many so-called simple words may not be included in it. It behooves the student, therefore, to have a dictionary. A number of good ones are on the market. Recommended for the beginner are

A German-English Dictionary for Chemists, by A. M. Patterson, published by John Wiley and Sons, Inc., and *German–English Science Dictionary for Students in the Agricultural, Biological, and Physical Sciences*, by Louis De Vries, published by The McGraw-Hill Book Company, Inc. Other dictionaries are listed in each of those mentioned above.

The student should also have a separate notebook for the orderly and classified entry of such points as may be brought up during class discussions. At least two thirds of this notebook should be assigned to vocabulary entries; all but about four or five pages at the end, to the entry of idiomatic technical expressions; the remainder should be reserved for special points. The vocabulary portion may well be subdivided into four sections of equal length, except for the last which may be about half as large as the others. Section 1 should receive all nouns; Section 2, all verbs; Section 3, all adjectives and adverbs; and Section 4, all miscellaneous words. Such a division of the notebook will facilitate learning and also save much time and effort.

The Vocabulary. Mastery of the basic technical vocabulary is the first requirement for effective reading of technical German. It is not our intention to furnish the student with specific methods as to how to acquire his vocabulary. Any method that functions adequately is satisfactory. We have, however, already indicated a general plan for subdivision. This may be further reduced by gradually striking out all words which have been mastered, and others which have some clear resemblance to their English equivalents. By this means only a relatively few words will remain to take up the student's time. At any rate the instructor should, at all times and regularly, point out those words which are to be learned. Since technical German tends to make use of many stock words and expressions, the student will find that the amount of vocabulary to be mastered gradually becomes less and less.

Mastery of the Various Types of Clauses and Clause Constructions. This is as important as the acquisition of a vocabulary.

Moreover, it assumes a number of other skills on the part of the student. First of all, he must know certain facts of grammar. He must have clearly in mind the fundamentals of German. If he does not, then it is absolutely necessary that he review these fundamentals at once. He must also have a correct estimate of his own knowledge of English. If he has not, and if, let us say, understanding the meaning of grammatical terms causes him difficulty, he should by all means make use of an English review grammar to be recommended to him by his instructor. During his work in technical German it is not so much a matter of the student's being able to analyze grammatical constructions; rather, his entire approach should be a practical one: "What do these forms mean in my English?" Thus the student will still have to know the function of a preposition, the form of adverbs as compared with those of adjectives, and such matters. All this can best be acquired when he comes to appreciate the fact that, after all, English and German are very much alike. The basic differences are, of course, matters of syntax and inflection.

But now to come to the point: The student must absolutely be able to recognize the two types of clauses and the several types of clause constructions, e.g., the absolute participial construction, the participial modifier, and the extended appositive. In order to master the clause he must be familiar with verbal constructions and with the function of coordinating as well as of subordinating conjunctions. These can best be memorized. When all this has been achieved, it is merely a matter of correct procedure, i.e., of knowing how to move along in the kind of clause or clause construction at hand. And inasmuch as each of these has its own individual make-up, the instructor should analyze, or preferably diagram, the manner in which each is to be translated.

The Ability to Attain a Reasonable Speed. Application of this ability should be the main source of a student's satisfaction to be derived from his study of technical German. Necessarily it rests on the first two points discussed above: mastery of a technical vocabulary and of the various clauses and clause constructions. The basic assumption that underlies a satisfactory rate of progress may be considered to be the element of orientation. By this we mean that the student should familiarize himself with the entire sentence unit before he begins the actual translation. He should never work blindly. He should know how long a sentence is, how many clauses it contains, and what kind of clauses these are. He should also know what constructions other than clauses the sentence contains. It will usually take only about half a minute per sentence to make such an estimate; practice will presently reduce this to only a few seconds; mastery will make of it an almost subconscious step which will require only a negligible amount of time. It may be said that since technical German can be read only in a systematic and efficient manner, its mastery is based on scientific procedure; it must always be accurate and intelligent. Actual quantitative achievements are here beside the point. Both the instructor's requirements and the student's degree of mastery are the determinants for this. The last and perfect stage in the reading of technical German is, of course, reading and not translating. If the student adheres to the suggestions that have been set out here, or to any other set of rules of procedure that suits him better, and if he adheres to them faithfully and intelligently, he will soon have arrived at the point where the reading of his assignments will no longer be drudgery, but rather a pleasant and profitable experience.

PART I

PROBLEMS OF TRANSLATION

This section of the book is designed to enable the student to accomplish two ends.

1. To master a basic general vocabulary suitable for reading technical material. These words appear at the bottom of the page, below the selections. The number preceding each word refers to the number of the line in which the word occurs.

2. To master translation procedure. The essential principles are presented in the introductory portion of each chapter.

CHAPTER 1

PRINCIPLE OF THE SIMPLE STATEMENT OR MAIN CLAUSE

The grammatical principle of a simple statement also applies to the main clause of a complex sentence. This principle is readily mastered. It has to do chiefly with the position of the verb under various conditions. It is characterized by the partial transposition of the verb when there is a compound verb form in the statement and by the element of inversion. Let us study this system by first examining the statement that contains a simple verb form. We shall follow that by considering a statement that contains a compound verb. Following that we shall study inversion.

A. The Statement that Contains a Simple Verb Form

When a statement contains a simple verb form, its treatment in translation does not differ from the corresponding English construction.

Wir sehen die andere Seite in einer speziellen Bedeutung.
We see the other side in a special significance.

B. The Statement that Contains a Compound Verb Form

1. When a simple statement contains a compound verb form, we usually find that the finite verb remains with or near the subject and that all other verb forms are placed at the end of the statement. The student will sometimes find this latter rule violated in modern, and especially in recent, writings. Various authors remove the verb forms from their end position to a place nearer the finite verb. Occasionally such end or terminal verb forms appear directly after the finite verb. For the sake of cor-

rect translation procedure we must here distinguish between a compound verb form that consists of two words and one that consists of more than two. For example:

Wir werden . . . sehen.
We shall . . . see.

Wir werden . . . gesehen haben.
We shall . . . seen have.

TRANSLATION PROCEDURE I

The proper method for translating such a construction may be expressed by a rule and illustrated by a diagram. Since the following diagram is basic to several others, the student is urged to learn it well. The rule may be stated as follows: When a simple statement (or main clause) contains a compound verb form, translate past the finite verb, go to the end to complete the verbal construction, return to the point where you left off, and finish as usual. Illustrated by a diagram, the translation

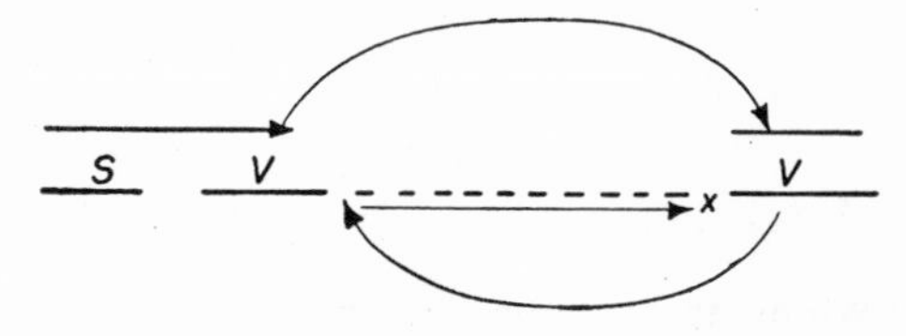

procedure appears as follows, with V being the verb and S the subject. The arrows indicate the progress through the construction.

This translation procedure also applies to compound verb forms that contain either a simple tense modal auxiliary, a simple tense passive, or the simple tense of a separable verb.

Wir wollen . . . sehen.
We want to . . . see.

Die andere Seite wird . . . gesehen.
The other side is . . . seen.

Wir stellen uns darunter geordnete Wissensgebiete vor.
We imagine in them orderly fields of knowledge.

2. If the verb form contains more than two words, the finite verb form remains with or near the subject and all others are

found at the end of the statement. Here again the same limitation exists that was previously indicated.

TRANSLATION PROCEDURE II

The translation procedure in this case is similar to the one given above, except that the terminal verb forms are translated backwards, as shown by the following diagram, where **S** is the subject and **V ⌒ V** is the verb.

Wir würden . . . gesehen haben.
We would . . . seen have.

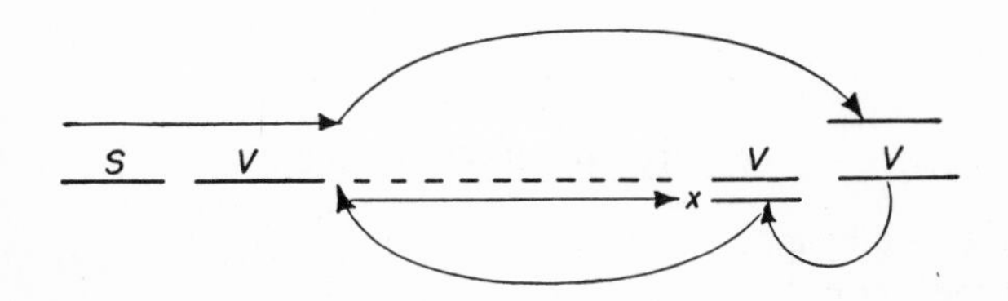

This translation procedure also applies to compound verbs that contain either a compound tense modal auxiliary or a compound tense passive construction.

Wir haben . . . sehen können.
We have . . . see been able to.

Die andere Seite würde . . . gesehen werden.
The other side would . . . seen be.

C. The Statement that Contains the Element of Inversion

In German inversion occurs when a statement begins with a unit of speech which is neither the subject nor a coordinating conjunction. Usually only one such unit appears as the inversion-causing element; however, even a scientific style tends to show individual traits and sometimes the student will find two such elements at the beginning of a statement. More than two are extremely rare. This construction is characterized by the initial use of the inversion-causing element **X,** which in its turn is directly followed by the *finite verb-subject* arrangement. The usual translation procedure is to rearrange the entire inverted construction into the smoother English subject-verb-X sequence as shown below.

Aus vielen Erfindungen (X) **entwickelte sich** (V) **Radar.** (S)

Radar (S) developed from (V) many inventions. (X)

It is frequently possible, however, to insert the word *there* directly after the element X and then to proceed normally. If, on the other hand, the verbal construction should be a compound verb, the sentence must be completely reconstructed in English. The student will find that the use of the word *there* will eliminate at least one step in the translation process.

D. Translation Exercise

1. Ganz allgemein gesprochen bedeutet das Wort „Wissenschaft" w i s s e n, k e n n e n oder auch e r k e n n e n. 2. Das ist die eine Seite der Definition des Wortes. 3. Eine jede Einzelwissenschaft kann wieder in andere, engere Felder eingeteilt werden. 4. Das gesamte Gebiet der Wissenschaften ist eingeteilt in eine immer mehr wachsende Anzahl von kleinen Einzelfeldern. 5. So wurden im Laufe der Jahrhunderte bestimmte Vorgänge entwickelt. 6. Deshalb mußte die geschichtliche Entwicklung der Technik als Instrument des Denkens auch universale Wege gehen. 7. Im Laufe ihrer geschichtlichen Entwicklung ist die Technik oft geändert worden. 8. Ein genaues Datum kann nicht angegeben werden. 9. So konnte Erfahrung zum Ziel werden zwischen kirchlicher und säkularer Philosophie. 10. Jede Wissenschaft hat ihr eigenes Feld.

E. Practical Review Questions

Answer the following questions concisely: 1. What is the position of a simple verb in a simple statement? 2. Of a compound verb? 3. How can a question be begun, and what is the position of a simple verb in it? 4. Of a compound verb? 5. What is inversion, and how do you treat it in translation? 6. How does a modal auxiliary change the position of an accompanying infinitive? 7. What if the modal auxiliary appears in a compound tense? 8. In what form does the main verb in the passive voice always appear? 9. What is the characteristic of a passive construction that appears in a perfect tense? 10. Diagram one sentence each for the questions numbered 1, 2, and 4.

F. Die Wissenschaften

Was sind die Wissenschaften? Oder besser gesagt, was ist Wissenschaft? Ganz allgemein gesprochen bedeutet das Wort „Wissenschaft" wissen, kennen, erkennen und bezieht sich so auf einen allgemeinen Zustand. In dieser Bedeutung erstreckt sich dieses Wort nicht nur auf Gebiete wie z.B. die Physik oder die Zoologie, sondern auch auf abstraktes Denken wie in der Logik oder der Philosophie. Dazu kann man sogar noch das weite Gebiet des Könnens hinzufügen wie z.B. manche Seiten der Industrie. Das Wort „Wissenschaft" erstreckt sich also auf konkrete, abstrakte und angewandte Dinge. Das ist die eine Seite der Definition dieses Wortes. Die andere Seite sehen wir in seiner speziellen oder besonderen Bedeutung. So stellen wir uns speziell unter „Wissenschaft" geordnete und folgerichtig entwickelte Sondergebiete des allgemeinen Wissens vor wie z.B. die Physik, Chemie, Medizin, u.a.m. Ja, in neuerer Zeit ist man sogar daran gegangen, solche Einzelgebiete noch mehr einzuteilen. So sprechen wir im allgemeinen Gebiet der Chemie, z.B. von den Teilgebieten der physikalischen und organischen Chemie. Und eine jede dieser Einzelwissenschaften kann wieder in andere ihr untergeordnete Felder eingeteilt werden. Eine solche Einzeleinteilung findet man heutzutage in fast allen Gebieten des Wissens. Das gesamte Gebiet der Wissenschaften ist in eine immer mehr wachsende Anzahl von kleinen Einzelfeldern eingeteilt als Folge der außerordentlich weitverzweigten Spezialisierung. Wir sind an-

1 **Wissenschaft** science
2 **allgemein** general
3 **sich beziehen auf** to refer to
4 **Zustand** condition
5 **Gebiet** field
8 **hinzufügen** to add
9 **sich erstrecken auf** to extend to
10 **angewandt** applied
12 **Bedeutung** significance
13 **folgerichtig** logical
16 **einteilen** to divide
19 **unterordnen** to subordinate
23 **Anzahl** number
23 **Folge** consequence
24 **anscheinend** seemingly

scheinend auch heute noch nicht am Ende dieser mannigfaltigen Verzweigung angelangt. 25

Für unsere Betrachtungen ist es zunächst wichtig, in wenigstens einigen Worten die Geschichte der Entwicklung der Wissenschaften anzudeuten. So hat man im Laufe der Jahrhunderte bestimmte Vorgänge entwickelt, um mit deren Hilfe die vielen Erscheinungen 30 und Tatsachen zu untersuchen. Wohlbekannt ist z.B. die Fragemethode des großen Altertumslehrers Sokrates oder auch die der Analyse und Synthese des französischen Philosophen Descartes. Solche Vorgänge nennen wir Technik. Nun ist aber das Wissen, d.h. die vielen Tatsachen und Erscheinungen in der Natur und 35 dem menschlichen Wesen, universal. Deshalb ist die geschichtliche Entwicklung der Technik als Instrument des Denkens auch universale Wege gegangen. Natürlich kann man nicht sagen, das ist überall und immer der Fall. Im Laufe ihrer wissenschaftlichen Entwicklung ist die Technik oft abgeändert worden. Besondere 40 Aufgaben mußten auf besondere Art und Weise gelöst werden, und man hat dazu besondere Wege gewählt, d.h. man hat besondere Vorgänge oder Methoden entwickelt. Ein bekanntes Beispiel hierzu liefert uns die Kernphysik. Diese hat sich den Atomzertrümmerer, das Zyklotron, erfunden, um in die Geheimnisse des 45 Wesens der Materie einzudringen. Im allgemeinen aber beruht alle wissenschaftliche Technik auf dem Grund der Rationalisierung der Arbeitsweise. Und diese Rationalisierung stellt eben das Universale in der Wissenschaft dar. Soweit bezüglich einer allgemeinen Aussage über die Natur des Wissens und unserer 50 Annäherung an sie.

Der Gedanke der Wissenschaft zeigt sich schon sehr früh in der Geschichte der menschlichen Gesellschaft. Ein genaues Datum kann nicht angegeben werden; ja, man kann nicht einmal ein

27 **Betrachtung** consideration
28 **Entwicklung** development
29 **andeuten** to indicate
30 **Vorgang** procedure
31 **Tatsache** fact
32 **Altertum** antiquity
35 **Erscheinung** phenomenon
36 **Wesen** being, nature
39 **Fall** case
40 **abändern** to change
41 **Aufgabe** task, problem
43 **Beispiel** example
44 **liefern** to furnish
45 **erfinden** to invent
46 **beruhen auf** to rest on
47 **Grund** basis, reason
48 **Arbeit** work
49 **bezüglich** as concerns
50 **Aussage** statement
53 **Gesellschaft** society
54 **angeben** to cite

bestimmtes Jahrhundert dafür zitieren. Der Beginn der Wissenschaften verliert sich in grauer Vorzeit und hat sich im Laufe der Zeit durch geschichtliche, geographische und philosophische Einflüsse weitgehend verändert. Jedenfalls sprach die Antike schon von Wissenschaften. So unterschied sie schon zwischen Wissenschaften auf Grund von Ursachen und Prinzipien einerseits (Aristoteles) und andererseits auf Grund von Erfahrungen, d.h. Tatsachen. Das ist schon eine ganz bestimmte und zudem hochentwickelte Anschauungsweise. Sie enthält die Grundlage unserer modernen Definition. Im Mittelalter erhob sich dann der kirchliche Gedanke immer mehr und beherrschte dann großenteils das ganze menschliche Leben. Das Fragen nach allgemeinen und speziellen Ursachen in der natürlichen Umgebung des Menschen kam ins Stocken, und man bezog sich immer mehr auf das übernatürliche Element, um aus ihm die Antworten auf die vielen Fragen zu ziehen. Mit anderen Worten, man entwickelte immer mehr das Metaphysische zu einer allgemeinen Anschauungsweise und unterwarf ihr auch die Wissenschaften. So blieb es bis ins 17. Jahrhundert. Dann aber beginnt, wissenschaftlich gesprochen, die Moderne, oder Neuzeit, wie der Deutsche sagt. Im 17. Jahrhundert begann sich der Gedanke der exakten Wissenschaften immer mehr herauszuarbeiten. Man entdeckte und folgte dem Prinzip der methodischen Erfahrung, einem beliebten Vorgang in der Philosophie des ebengenannten Jahrhunderts. Erfahrung aber stimmte nicht immer mit kirchlichen Gesetzen überein. So konnte Erfahrung zum Ziel werden zwischen kirchlicher und sekularer Philosophie, und die letztere entfernte sich immer mehr von der ersteren. Die Erfahrung ist auch heute noch ein bedeutendes Instrument in unserem Denken.

Der Gedanke der Methodik und Technik charakterisiert nun einen der bedeutendsten Unterschiede zwischen der abendländi-

55 **Jahrhundert** century
56 **Vorzeit** prehistory
57 **Einfluß** influence
58 **weitgehend** far-reaching
59 **unterscheiden** to distinguish
60 **Ursache** cause
61 **Erfahrung** experience
62 **zudem** at that
63 **Anschauungsweise** attitude
64 **Mittelalter** Middle Ages
65 **beherrschen** to dominate
67 **Umgebung** environment
72 **unterwerfen** to subject
73 **wissenschaftlich** scientific
76 **entdecken** to discover
78 **ebengenannt** just mentioned
79 **übereinstimmen** to agree
80 **Ziel** goal
81 **sich entfernen** to draw away from
85 **Unterschied** difference

schen und anderen Zivilisationen. Wohl hat sich der wissenschaftliche Gedanke in den westlichen Ländern immer höher entwickelt und scheint auch heute noch alle Seiten des menschlichen Lebens zu beherrschen; ja, man könnte sagen, alles Menschendasein ginge im Wissenschaftlichen auf und fände da seine endgültige Bestimmung und Beantwortung. Eine nähere Untersuchung aber ergibt andere Resultate. Schon vor vierzig Jahren, genauer gesprochen um 1910 herum, setzt eine starke Reaktion ein gegen den immer erdrückender werdenden Gedanken einer allesbeherrschenden Wissenschaft. Eines der mächtigsten Ergebnisse wissenschaftlicher Arbeit war im 19. Jahrhundert der Materialismus. Und gerade dieser Materialismus bedingte bestimmte moralische Gegensätze. Und ihnen schloß sich auch der wissenschaftliche Gedanke an, d.h. er wollte sein Endziel nicht mehr im materiellen Aufschwung der menschlichen Gesellschaft sehen. Im Gegenteil, der Gedanke an eine Wissenschaft um ihrer selbst willen breitete sich immer mehr aus. Die Wissenschaft begann, neue Wege zu gehen.

Die ebengenannten geschichtlichen Punkte sind natürlich nicht einschließend. Es ist eigentlich Aufgabe der Philosophie, dies näher zu untersuchen. Untersuchen wir lieber die Systematik der Einteilung unter den vielen heut bestehenden Wissenschaften. Eine der klarsten Darstellungen dieser Art bietet uns Der Große Brockhaus. Darnach hat jede Wissenschaft ihr eigenes Feld von Gegenständen und Tatsachen. Diesen wendet sie sich zu. Jede Wissenschaft hat ihre eigenen Probleme, d.h. ihren Fragenkreis oder ihre Problematik. Und diese Problematik sucht sie zu lösen oder zu beantworten. Außerdem hat jede Wissenschaft ihr eigenes Verfahren, auch Methodik oder Technik genannt. Damit sucht sie, Resultate zu erzielen. So kann man nach diesen allgemeinen Gesichtspunkten die Wissenschaften in die folgenden großen Klassen einteilen: erstens nach ihren Gegenständen, zweitens nach Fragestellungen, d.h. ihren Problemen, drittens

89 **Dasein** existence
89 **aufgehen in** to terminate in
91 **Untersuchung** investigation
91 **ergeben** to yield
95 **Ergebnis** result
97 **bedingen** to cause
98 **sich anschließen** to join
99 **Aufschwung** progress
101 **sich ausbreiten** to spread
104 **einschließend** inclusive
106 **bestehen** to exist
107 **Darstellung** presentation
108 **darnach** according to this
109 **Gegenstand** object
112 **lösen** to solve
112 **außerdem** moreover
114 **erzielen** to obtain
115 **Gesichtspunkt** viewpoint

nach ihren Zielen und viertens nach ihren Methoden. Natürlich ist das nicht die einzige Einteilung. Man hat oft versucht, bessere Einteilungen zu unternehmen. Heutzutage aber vermehren sich die Wissenschaften wegen immer größerer Spezialisierung. Eine allesumfassende Einteilung muß endlich in einer Enzyklopädie ihren Abschluß finden. Den ebengenannten Klassen wollen wir deshalb noch einige weniger wichtige Einteilungen hinzufügen. 120 125

Die erste und am meisten gebrauchte Einteilung ruht auf den behandelten Gegenständen. Wir haben es hiernach mit den sogenannten Ideal- und Realwissenschaften zu tun. Eine Idealwissenschaft befaßt sich gewöhnlich mit den Gedanken in einer Wissenschaft, wie z.B. die Mathematik oder die Logik. Eine Realwissenschaft dagegen befaßt sich mit der konkreten Wirklichkeit, wie z.B. die Zoologie oder die Medizin. Die zweite Einteilung betrifft die Fragestellung des Wissenschaftlers zu einer Wissenschaft, d.h. der Wissenschaftler sucht die Probleme heraus und beantwortet sie, soweit er kann. Die Fragestellung ist immer Problematik und ist somit der Philosophie eng verwandt. Deshalb spricht man auch von philosophischen und Einzelwissenschaften. Die ersteren behandeln allgemeine Probleme, die letzteren spezielle Fragen. Eine solche Einteilung aber hält nicht immer Stich, denn manchmal entwickelt sich aus einer Einzelwissenschaft eine philosophische oder allgemeine. Das ist z.B. der Fall mit dem großen Problemkreis auf Grund des Darwinismus. Auch kann das Umgekehrte der Fall sein: eine Einzelwissenschaft kann sich aus einer allgemeinen entwickeln, wie z.B. seit dem 18. Jahrhundert die Psychologie oder die Soziologie auf Grund der allgemeinen Philosophie. Die dritte Einteilung wird nach den Zielen der verschiedenen Wissenschaften gemacht. Das heißt, man fragt sich: W a s w i l l m a n d u r c h d i e b e t r e f f e n d e n W i s s e n s c h a f t e n e r r e i c h e n ? Will man nur diskutieren und sich so in 130 135 140 145

120 **unternehmen** to undertake
122 **allesumfassend** all-inclusive
123 **Abschluß** conclusion
127 **behandeln** to treat
129 **sich befassen mit** to occupy oneself with
131 **dagegen** on the other hand
133 **betreffen** to refer to
134 **Wissenschaftler** scientist
136 **somit** thus
136 **deshalb** therefore
138 **erstere** former
138 **letztere** latter
142 **Kreis** circle, sphere
143 **umgekehrt** converse
147 **verschieden** different, various
148 **betreffend** respective

der Logik üben, oder vielleicht dadurch Antworten auf gewisse 150
Fragen erhalten? Oder will man irgendwelche praktischen Resultate erzielen? Im ersteren Fall sprechen wir von theoretischen, im letzteren von praktischen Wissenschaften. Im ersteren Fall will man durch folgerichtiges Denken zu neuem Wissen gelangen, wie z.B. in der theoretischen Physik; im letzteren Fall will man 155
irgendwelchen praktischen Nutzen genieszen, wie z.B. in der Medizin. Die letzte große und vierte Einteilung der Wissenschaften kann man nach ihren jeweiligen Verfahren, nach ihren Methoden, unternehmen. In dieser Beziehung sprechen wir von erklärenden und beschreibenden Wissenschaften. Erklärende 160
Wissenschaften behandeln Ursachen und Gründe von Erscheinungen und enthalten oft das Element des Beweises, wie z.B. die Mathematik oder die Physik. Beschreibende Wissenschaften dagegen beschreiben Vorgänge. Das sieht man in der Geschichte oder der Soziologie. 165

Weniger wichtige Einteilungen können nach den folgenden Gesichtspunkten unternommen werden: exakte Wissenschaften können den nicht exakten gegenüber gestellt werden, so z.B. die Mathematik der Geschichte. Ihre Methoden sind einerseits streng logisch entwickelt und deduktiv in ihrem Wesen oder auch experi- 170
mentell und induktiv in ihrer Natur. Andererseits brauchen die Methoden der nicht exakten Wissenschaften nicht logisch sein. Ein Beispiel letzterer Art liefert uns die Geschichte. Eine noch andere Einteilung ist uns von Wilhelm Dilthey (geboren am 19. November 1833 in Biebrich am Rhein; gestorben am 3. Oktober 175
1911 in Seis am Schlern) gegeben worden. Dilthey war ein bedeutender Philosoph des 19. Jahrhunderts und sprach von Geistes- und Naturwissenschaften.

Wie schon gesagt ist die Neuzeit nicht immer zufrieden mit solchen traditionellen Einteilungen oder Klassifizierungen der 180
Wissenschaften wie den obigen. Manchmal tauchen Versuche auf, dem philosophischen Wesen der Wissenschaften neue

150 **gewiß** certain
151 **irgendwelche** some
154 **gelangen** to arrive at
156 **Nutzen** use
158 **jeweilig** respective
162 **enthalten** to contain
162 **Beweis** proof
168 **gegenüber** opposite
169 **einerseits** on the one hand
171 **andererseits** on the other hand
173 **Art** kind, type, species
178 **Geist** mind, intelligence
179 **Neuzeit** modern times
181 **obig** above

Bedeutung zu geben. Besonders klar ist das im Bereich der verschiedenen Sozialwissenschaften zu sehen. Wie bekannt beziehen diese alles auf die gesamte menschliche Gesellschaft, also 185 wird auch Wissenschaft nur als nutzbares Werkzeug der Gesellschaft anerkannt; d.h. Wissenschaften werden den Zielen der Gesellschaft untergeordnet. Und die Ziele der menschlichen Gesellschaft sind oft wenig greifbar, denn sie können verschieden gedeutet werden. Eines dieser Ziele kann z.B. die Freiheit sein. 190 Was aber ist Freiheit? Eine Orientierung der Wissenschaften in der Richtung der Freiheit aber kann kaum zu konkreten Definitionen gelangen, denn sofort spielt der Idealismus oder sogar die Politik mit hinein. Das haben wir zur Genüge während der letzten 25 Jahre unter den verschiedenen großen Regierungs- 195 systemen gesehen. Eine Unterordnung der Wissenschaften unter politische Systeme kann sogar zu verhängnisvollen Resultaten führen. Man hat deshalb versucht, die Wissenschaft als Idealbereich des Gedankens von äußeren Einflüssen rein zu halten, und so sagt man, wie z.B. auch im Falle der Musik, die Wissenschaft 200 ist eine universale Macht.

183 **Bereich** sphere
185 **gesamt** total, all
186 **Werkzeug** tool
189 **greifbar** tangible
190 **deuten** to interpret
190 **Freiheit** liberty
192 **Richtung** direction
195 **Regierung** government
197 **verhängnisvoll** fatal
199 **rein** pure

CHAPTER 2

PRINCIPLES OF THE DEPENDENT CLAUSE

The dependent clause is by far the most important syntactical construction in German. This is especially true from the point of view of translation into another language. Being characterized by an introductory dependent or subordinating conjunction, as well as by the position of its verbal element, it can readily be compared with the main clause. Generally speaking, a main clause may be introduced by its subject, by a prepositional (adverbial) phrase, by its finite verb (if it happens to be a question), or by any one of the following four coordinating conjunctions:

aber	but	**oder**	or
denn	for	**und**	and

Sometimes a so-called correlative conjunction may also introduce a main clause. The two of these that are most used are:

weder . . . noch	neither . . . nor
entweder . . . oder	either . . . or

On the other hand, a dependent clause — and we are at the moment not considering the relative clause — is introduced by one of the following subordinating conjunctions:

als	when	**obgleich**	although
wann	when (interrogative)	**wenngleich**	although
da	since, because	**seitdem**	since that time
seit	since, because	**ehe**	before
weil	since, because	**nachdem**	after
		ob	whether, if
damit	so that	**sobald**	as soon as
daß	that, in order that	**wenn**	if, whenever
sodaß	so that	**bis**	until, till
indem	while		
während	while		

Since the subordinating conjunctions are signs by means of which one can instantly recognize dependent clauses, it is highly important that the student commit them to memory. There are, of course, other subordinating conjunctions besides those given above.

The second feature that characterizes a dependent clause is the position of its verbal construction. The student will usually find it at the end of the clause, and since German almost invariably uses commas to separate dependent clauses from each other and from main clauses, it is a relatively easy matter to determine the length of a dependent clause. The verb at the end always occurs in an order which is the reverse of the English (see Chapter I, B, 2). The dependent clause, which is a very stable construction in German, cannot be influenced in its syntactical make-up by any features outside it. It may occur either before or after a main clause. If it is the introductory clause of the sentence, it causes inversion. The translation procedure is basically that of the simple statement. Thus, beginning with the dependent conjunction and continuing with the subject, the student must then go to the end of the clause, which will be indicated by either a period or a comma, complete the verbal construction, return exactly to the place where he left off, and continue from there in the usual manner.

Obgleich wir . . . sehen.
Although we . . . see.

Obgleich wir . . . { sehen werden. / sehen können.

Although we . . . { see shall. / see can.

Separable verbs are not separated in a dependent clause. It should also be stated that any verbal adjuncts are considered as part of the verb and are usually found directly in front of the verbal construction.

Obgleich es . . . ganz anders aussieht.
Although it . . . very much different looks.

In the translation procedure, a dependent clause may be represented by the following diagram in which **S⁀C** is the subordinating conjunction, **S** is the subject, **V⁀A** is the verbal adjunct, and **V⁀V** is the verb.

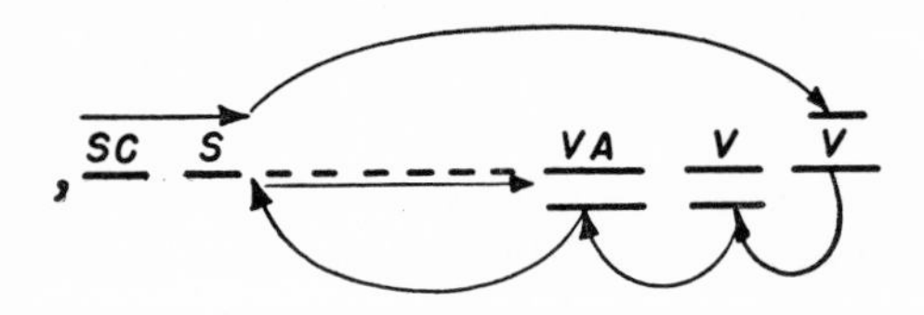

A. Translation Exercise

1. Als man die Wissenschaften immer weiter entwickelte, vermehrten sich dieselben auch sehr. 2. Die Anzahl der Wissenschaften vermehrte sich immer mehr, als man sie immer weiter entwickelte. 3. Obgleich das die eine Seite einer folgerichtigen Systematik ist, kann man sich des Eindrucks nicht erwehren, daß die anderen ebenso wichtig sind. 4. Seit jede Einzelwissenschaft wieder in kleine Einzelfelder eingeteilt werden kann, ist es fast unmöglich, das gesamte Gebiet der vielen Wissenschaften zu übersehen. 5. Während man bestimmte Vorgänge entwikkelte, setzte auch schon die Reaktion ein. 6. Weil ein genaues Datum nicht angegeben werden kann, kann man auch nicht sagen, daß dieser Wissenschaftler an der Entwicklung teilnahm. 7. Daß das Wort „Wissenschaft" *wissen* oder auch *kennen* heißt, weiß man. 8. Es bleibt nur noch die Frage, *wann* und *warum* sich solche Einzelfelder entwickelt haben.

B. The *wenn*-Clause

German technical writers frequently omit the dependent conjunction **wenn** when its clause introduces the sentence. (Compare such an English statement as: Were I at home now, (then) I could easily do it. In such a case the finite verb is so placed that the clause begins with it. Thus the translator has to restore the complete normal statement in English. The student should memorize the following rule: If a sentence begins with a verb, and if there is no question mark nor exclamation point at the end, the translation must be begun by saying *if* . . . . The translation diagram appears below. Here **V⁀V** is the verb, **S** is the subject, and **V⁀A** is the verbal adjunct.

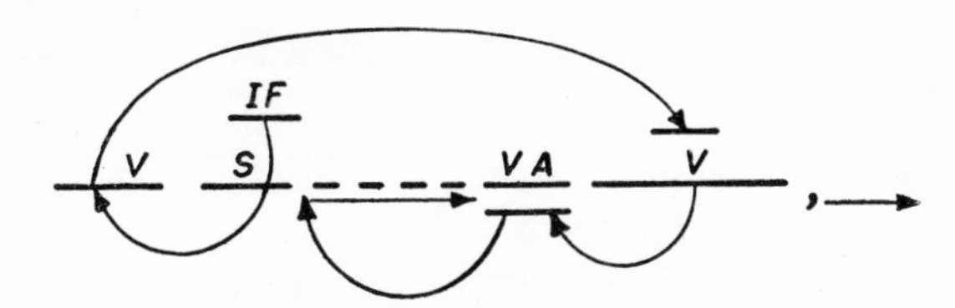

C. Translation Exercise

1. Erweist sich diese Bestimmung für richtig, so ist der Fall damit auch entschieden. 2. Überblickt man seine physikalisch-chemischen Arbeiten, so kann man nur staunen. 3. Erwähnt man die Erscheinung der Phosphoreszenz, so muß man auch die der Fluoreszenz nennen. 4. Gelingt dieser Nachweis, so kann man die Wellenlänge auch zahlenmäßig erfassen. 5. Sollten von diesen Schwingungen die transversalen Wellen ausgehen, so ist die Wellenlänge auch berechenbar. 6. Waren diese Wellen herstellbar und auch nachweisbar, so konnte man an der Theorie nicht mehr zweifeln. 7. Sind seine Veröffentlichungen gerade nicht sehr zahlreich, so hat er doch einen wichtigen Beitrag zur Geschichte der Wissenschaft geliefert. 8. Liest man heute seine Hauptschriften, so ist man immer wieder von dem Reichtum seiner Gedanken ergriffen.

D. Practical Review Questions

1. How do you recognize a dependent clause? 2. What are its characteristics? 3. Name fifteen of the common subordinating conjunctions. 4. Compare the position of the verbal constructions of a simple statement and of a dependent clause when (a) the verb is a simple verb, (b) when the verb is compound. 5. How will a separable verb appear in a dependent clause? 6. Diagram the translation procedure of a dependent clause that contains a compound verb. 7. Where would you ordinarily find

such constructions as verbal adjuncts in a dependent clause? 8. Is inversion possible in a dependent clause? 9. Analyze a present perfect tense modal construction that contains an accompanying infinitive in a dependent clause.

E. Der Gedanke des menschlichen Fortschritts

Wie alt der Gedanke einer Philosophie des menschlichen Fortschritts ist, kann mit Genauigkeit nicht gesagt werden. Ebenso kann man nicht annehmen, daß solch ein Gedanke allen oder doch wenigstens den wichtigsten der vergangenen und gegenwärtigen Kulturen gemeinsam war oder noch ist. So ist es verhältnismäßig ein Leichtes zu fragen, ob z.B. die Chinesen oder Hindu unter „Fortschritt" dasselbe verstehen wie wir. Sobald wir aber versuchen, diese Frage zu beantworten, stoßen wir sofort auf große Schwierigkeiten. Obgleich wir nämlich alle eine Idee haben, was dieses Wort bedeutet, können wir wohl kaum sagen, was Fortschritt eigentlich ist. Das heißt, es ist äußerst schwierig, eine Definition für dieses Wort zu liefern. Der eine denkt an materielle Erscheinungen als Inhalt einer Kultur, wie z.B. Industrien, Waarenmengen, und die Anzahl und Größe von Gebäuden; der andere richtet sich nach den verschiedenen Errungenschaften der Künste: der Malerei, Bildhauerei, Musik, Literatur oder vielleicht sogar nach der herrschenden Philosophie. Wer will z.B. leugnen, daß der Neanderthaler Mensch keinen Fortschritt verzeichnete, als er zum erstenmal ein Mammut mit einem neugeschaffenen Steinspeer tötete und sich so eine Waffe für den Angriff so wohl als auch für die Verteidigung herrichtete? Wer wollte ebenso leugnen, daß die erste Höhlenmalerei als primitive Übersetzung eines Schönheitsgedankens nicht zu den vollkommenen Wandmalereien der italienischen Meister des späteren Mittelalters führte? Ein anderer Gedanke leitet uns dahin zu fragen, warum wir allein, d.h. die neuzeitliche menschliche Gesell-

1 **Gedanke** thought
2 **Fortschritt** progress
3 **annehmen** to assume
4 **gegenwärtig** present
5 **verhältnismäßig** relatively
9 **Schwierigkeit** difficulty
10 **bedeuten** to mean
11 **eigentlich** really
13 **Inhalt** content
15 **sich richten nach** to orient
19 **verzeichnen** to register
20 **schaffen** to work, to create
22 **leugnen** to deny
23 **Übersetzung** translation
25 **leiten** to guide
26 **menschlich** human

schaft und besonders die weiße Rasse, die Dynamik des Lebens als geordnete Erscheinung empfinden sollten. Wie dem auch sein möge, der Gedanke einer fließenden Dynamik in der menschlichen Gesellschaft ist in seiner heutigen Deutung noch ver- 30 hältnismäßig jung. Und doch kennzeichnet er unser Denken, Tun und Lassen; er färbt unsere Geschichte und unser heutiges geschichtliches Verhalten; er unterliegt unserer gesamten Philosophie und scheint sich augenblicklich sogar als Gestaltungskraft unseres Schicksals zu offenbaren. Alles in allem ist es unmöglich, das 35 Wort „Fortschritt" als solches und als Gedanken zu definieren. Unmöglich aber ist es nicht, diesen Gedanken in seinem Wesentlichen so zu umreißen, daß wir feste und genaue Eindrücke davon erhalten.

Die Anthropologen unterrichten uns, daß es eine Zeit gab, als 40 die Menschen ohne jegliche Waffe, ohne jegliches Werkzeug und irgendwelche Hilfsmittel ihr Dasein verbrachten. Sie erzählen uns, wie es in grauer Vorzeit der Stein war, welcher Waffe und Werkzeug wurde, wie der Mensch sich das Feuer dienstbar machte und von da an sich langsam immer höher schwang. Gemein- 45 schaften erstanden, Arbeitsverteilung fand statt, Organisation erschien und gemeinsame Anstrengungen zeitigten Resultate, welche einen gewissen Grad von Geborgenheit und Sicherheit nach sich zogen. Eines der klarsten Beispiele dieser Art soll ein großes Negerreich an der Westküste Afrikas gewesen sein. In dieser 50 großen und weitverzweigten Gemeinschaft waren das Erwerbswesen, die Industrie, der Transport und die Staatssicherheit so hoch spezialisiert, daß bestimmte Dörfer nur gewisse Pflichten hatten; d.h. ein Dorf stellte nur Körbe her, ein anderes Feldharken, ein drittes lieferte Soldaten, ein viertes Trommler für die großen 55 Nachrichtentrommeln, usw. Das Wesentliche an allem jedoch ist die Tatsache, daß der so verzeichnete Fortschritt das Resultat

30 **heutig** present
31 **kennzeichnen** to characterize
32 **färben** to color
32 **geschichtlich** historical
34 **Gestaltungskraft** formative power
37 **wesentlich** essential
38 **umreißen** to sketch
40 **unterrichten** to teach
44 **dienstbar** serviceable
46 **erstehen** to arise
46 **stattfinden** to take place
47 **zeitigen** to produce
48 **Sicherheit** certainty
51 **Gemeinschaft** community
52 **Staat** state
53 **gewiß** certain
56 **Nachricht** news
56 **Trommel** drum

des reflektierenden Menschen, vielleicht Einzelmenschen war, mit anderen Worten, daß es keinen Fortschritt ohne Gedankenkraft gibt. Dies ist der Beginn unseres Begriffsumrisses. Ist 60 Fortschritt aber nicht an Gegenstände und konkrete Wirklichkeit gebunden, sondern mit dem Gedankengang des Beobachters identisch, möge der Beobachter nun der passive oder aktive Faktor sein, so liegt es nahe, das Wort „Fortschritt" mit den dynamischen Geisteskräften des denkenden Menschen zu identifizieren. Wie 65 wissen wir das? Nun, erstens ziehen wir als Anthropologen Schlüsse auf Grund von früh- und vorgeschichtlichen Ausgrabungen und Funden, und zweitens rationalisieren wir, indem wir die Bedeutung solcher Funde und Entdeckungen mit gegenwärtigen, heutigen Kulturen vergleichen. Das ist wissenschaftlicher Vor- 70 gang. Wohl mögen darin Fehler enthalten sein, doch man hat der Analogie volle Berechtigung als wissenschaftliches Werkzeug gegeben.

Ein anderes Merkmal des Fortschritts kann in der sogenannten Differenzierung des Einzelnen und der Verallgemeinerung des 75 Ganzen gesehen werden. Mit der Differenzierung des Einzelnen meinen wir, daß ein Einzelmensch oder eine Einzelgruppe oder auch ein Einzelvolk sich je nach seinen oder ihren besonderen Charaktereigenschaften entwickelt. Obwohl solch eine Entwicklung weitgehend an das geographische oder klimatische Element 80 gebunden ist, liegen hier die Hauptkräfte dennoch im Einzelnen selbst. Man denke z.B. an die antiken Griechen und ihre hohen Kunsterrungenschaften auf Grund ihres religiösen Empfindens; oder man erinnere sich an die Entwicklung der Regierung, d.h. der Verwaltung, unter den Germanen, oder an die ungeheure 85 gegenwärtige Entfaltung des Transportwesens in den Vereinigten Staaten. Die Verallgemeinerung dieser Züge kann man ebensogut beobachten. Alle Einzeleigenschaften tragen etwas Universales in sich, d.h. sie neigen dazu hin, Allgemeingut zu werden. Das

60 **Kraft** force
60 **Begriff** concept
62 **Beobachter** observer
67 **Ausgrabung** excavation
70 **vergleichen** to compare
71 **Fehler** mistake
72 **Berechtigung** justification
74 **Merkmal** characteristic
75 **Verallgemeinerung** generalization
79 **Eigenschaft** quality, attribute
83 **Errungenschaft** achievement
86 **Entfaltung** development
87 **Zug** trait
89 **neigen** to incline

kann auf verschiedenen Wegen geschehen wie durch Borgen, 90
Entlehnen, einfaches Nehmen oder sonstwie. Es sei hier an den
medizinischen Fortschritt erinnert, der sich durch die Internationalisierung des Bayer Aspirin kund tut oder an die des
Dieselmotors.

Oberflächlich betrachtet scheint es, als ob der Fortschritt am 95
klarsten durch die Gewalt der Änderung gekennzeichnet würde.
Das braucht aber durchaus nicht der Fall zu sein, denn Änderung
in Verhältnissen und Zuständen geschieht meistens gewaltsam,
plötzlich und in ihren Folgen unvorhersehbar. Die Menschheit
ist konservativ und begenügt sich mit dem, was sie hat. Krieg, 100
Revolution, Hungersnot, Krankheit und äußerliche Naturereignisse wecken die Menschheit auf und hämmern auf den
menschlichen Geist, bis dieser sich an die neuen Verhältnisse
gewöhnt, zu ihnen positive Stellung nimmt und ihnen zu begegnen
sucht. Sobald das aber geschehen ist, geht der Mensch wieder 105
seine alten Bahnen. Aber nur scheinbar so, denn etwas ist ihm
durch das vorangegangene Ereignis mitgegeben worden; etwas
hat seinen Geist bereichert. Das ist Erfahrung, und im Laufe
der Zeit sammelt Erfahrung sich so an, daß sie zu Wissen wird.
Es ist nun nicht so sehr Erfahrung an sich, welche fortschrittlich 110
wirkt, sondern der langsame Vorgang der Anpassung des Menschen an die neuen Verhältnisse. Wendet er nun die Erfahrung
zu seinem Nutzen an, so sagen wir, er ist fortschrittlich. Das
heißt, so würde der Soziologe sprechen. Denn als Volkswissenschaftler bezieht er ja doch das gesamte Daseinsphenomen in 115
letzter Hinsicht nur auf die konstruktiven Beiträge des Einzelnen
zur Gesellschaft. Nur wenn zur Besserung der menschlichen
Gesellschaft beigetragen wird, läßt er den Gedanken des Fortschritts gelten. Nehmen wir z.B. an, jemand erfindet eine Maschine oder einen Mechanismus und verwertet seine Errungen- 120
schaft zur Zerstörung des Menschen und seiner Erzeugnisse, so

90 **geschehen** to happen
93 **kund tun** to manifest oneself
95 **oberflächlich** superficial
96 **Gewalt** force
96 **Änderung** change
101 **äußerlich** external
103 **Verhältnis** circumstance
107 **Ereignis** event
110 **fortschrittlich** progressive
111 **Anpassung** adaptation
112 **anwenden** to apply
116 **Beitrag** contribution
119 **gelten** to hold true
120 **verwerten** to utilize
121 **Erzeugnis** product

kann solch eine Erfindung nicht als Fortschritt angesehen werden. Deshalb haben wir augenblicklich auch das berechtigte Bedenken, ob das Ereignis der Atombombe wirklich als Fortschritt bezeichnet werden kann. Moralische Philosophen haben oft mit einem entschiedenen Nein geantwortet. Es kann aber auch nicht geleugnet werden, daß gewisse Erfindungen, wie z.B. das Auto oder das Radio mehr das Segensreiche in sich tragen als das Unheilvolle. Sehen wir uns solche Errungenschaften ein wenig näher an, so kommen wir einem weiteren Merkmal des Fortschritts auf die Spur. Manche von ihnen sind aus ganz kleinen Anfängen hervorgegangen. Manche haben sich zu großen Beiträgen entwickelt, viele andere wieder nicht. Mit anderen Worten: Fortschritt braucht nicht an große Dinge gebunden zu sein, obwohl das auch oft genug vorkommt. Im Großen und Ganzen aber ist Fortschritt das Gesamtresultat unzähliger wesentlicher Beiträge zum Wohl einer Gruppe oder eines Volkes; und, wenn er sich über andere Völker ausbreitet, auch zum Wohl der ganzen Menschheit.

Wir können auch sagen, daß Fortschritt sich in vielen Richtungen hin auf einmal bemerkbar macht, so z.B. in biologischer Hinsicht, wenn wir von vermehrtem Gebrauch des Gehirns sprechen oder von der Fähigkeit des Menschen, sich an seine Umgebung anzupassen. Oft ist solcher Fortschritt rein sozial in seinem Wesen, wie z.B. bezüglich der Ausbildung der gesellschaftlichen Organisation, die in der Regierung ihre Spitze findet. So hat es einerseits die Erfindung des Autos mit sich gebracht, daß das Volk sich neuen Regeln des Verhaltens unterwarf, so bei Straßenkreuzungen, vor Verkehrslichtern, bei Unfällen, usw. Anderseits aber hat die Entwicklung unseres Transportwesens in allen Richtungen hin der Gesellschaft solch große Probleme aufgegeben, daß dieselben nur durch Vermehrung und Spezialisierung des Verwaltungsapparats gelöst werden können.

Wir haben so weit gesehen, daß Fortschritt an Ideen gebunden ist, daß er durch Wissen, Können und Willenskraft getragen wird

122 **ansehen** to look upon
123 **augenblicklich** momentarily
126 **entschieden** decisive
131 **hervorgehen** to start, to come from
135 **vorkommen** to occur
142 **Hinsicht** respect
143 **Fähigkeit** ability
145 **Ausbildung** formation
145 **gesellschaftlich** social
148 **Regel** rule

und gleichsam durch segensreiche Anwendung dieses Wissens ans Gesamtwohl der Gruppe gemessen werden kann. Und dennoch besteht ein bedeutender Unterschied zwischen dem, was wir heute Fortschritt nennen und dem, was wir in früh- und vorgeschichtlichen Zeiten als solchen zu erkennen glauben. Früher, und das 160 braucht gar nicht lange her zu sein, war Fortschritt meistens an das Zufällige und Reflektive des Einzelnen gebunden, manchmal auch an die Willenskraft des Einzelnen, sagen wir eines Herrschers oder eines Diplomaten. Es sei hier an die ersten Anfänge der chinesischen Kultur erinnert, an die Zähmung des Feuers, die 165 Erfindung, oder sollen wir sagen die Entdeckung, des Rades. Viele andere Einzelmomente können noch angeführt werden. Heutzutage dagegen scheint sich der Gedanke des Fortschritts fast zu einer grundlegenden Philosophie unserer gesamten Kultur entwickelt zu haben. Wir glauben an Fortschritt, als ob dies fast 170 eine religiöse Überzeugung wäre. Und das ist bei weitem noch nicht alles. Der Gedanke des Fortschritts hat bei uns ein programmatisches, rationelles Kollektivgepräge angenommen. Als Philosophie unseres Volkes und als Ethos unserer Kultur wird er systematisch in den Schulen gelehrt und zwar so, daß unser 175 ganzes Bewußtsein, unsere Kraftanstrengungen und Bewertungen sich nach dem Maßstabe des Fortschritts richten. Angenommen es gibt so etwas wie Fortschritt, ist es wünschenswert, daß er bewußt beschleunigt wird? Gibt es ein Ende des Fortschritts, und wenn, was könnte es sein? 180

162 **zufällig** accidental
168 **heutzutage** nowadays
169 **grundlegend** basic
171 **Überzeugung** conviction
173 **Gepräge** aspect
176 **Bewußtsein** consciousness
176 **Bewertung** evaluation
179 **beschleunigen** to accelerate

CHAPTER 3

MULTIPLE-CLAUSE CONSTRUCTIONS

A construction may occur which contains a series of two or more simple statements or main clauses. In fact, the student will often find two or more entirely separate short statements arranged in a series either with or without commas between them. Translation procedure for such a multiple-clause series consists in merely repeating the procedure which applies to a simple statement. A similar construction that consists of a series of two or more dependent clauses may be handled in the same fashion. The situation is different, however, when either construction contains a finite verb that is common to two or more successive clauses. The following example and analysis will serve to guide the student.

A. The Multiple Main-Clause Construction

Zwei Jahre mußte er in einem unbekannten Laboratorium arbeiten und sich dadurch allerhand Einschränkungen auferlegen.

For two years he had to work in a strange laboratory and endure all sorts of limitations when doing so.

An examination of the sentence above reveals several significant features. (1) The sentence consists of two clauses that are not separated by a comma because both have the same subject. (2) The finite verb common to both clauses is a modal auxiliary (**mußte**). (3) Each clause ends with an accompanying infinitive. The translation procedure is as follows: (1) As usual, begin with either the inversion-causing element or the subject. (2) Translate the finite verb at the beginning of the sentence. (3) Continue with the first accompanying infinitive (**arbeiten**). (4) Proceed to the conjunction, the second accompanying infinitive (**sich auferlegen**), and so on.

It should be noted (1) that the finite verb may not always be a modal auxiliary but rather it may be any other verb that is suitable for this function; (2) that the accompanying infinitives may be replaced by future infinitives or by past participles. In the translation diagram shown below, **S** is the subject, **AV** is the auxiliary verb, **I:P** is the infinitive or participle, and **CC** is the coordinating conjunction.

B. The Multiple Dependent-Clause Construction

Er mußte sich entscheiden, ob er unter diesem bekannten Arzt Medizin studieren oder sich für den Lehrerberuf vorbereiten wollte.

He had to decide whether he wanted to study medicine under this well-known physician or prepare himself for the teaching profession.

An examination of the sentence above reveals several features: (1) The sentence consists of three clauses — a main clause and two dependent clauses. (2) The dependent clauses are coordinate in nature, being connected by the coordinating conjunction **oder.** (3) There is no comma between the dependent clauses because they have a common subject. (4) Both dependent clauses are **ob**-clauses. (5) The finite verb (**wollte**), which is common to both accompanying infinitives (**studieren** and **sich vorbereiten**), is at the end of the entire dependent construction. The translation procedure is similar to that for the multiple main-clause construction, except for the necessity of going to the end of the entire dependent construction for the finite verb.

Again, the finite verb may be other than a modal auxiliary, and the accompanying infinitives may be future infinitives or past participles. In the translation diagram shown below, **SC** is the subordinating conjunction, **S** is the subject, **I:P** is the infinitive

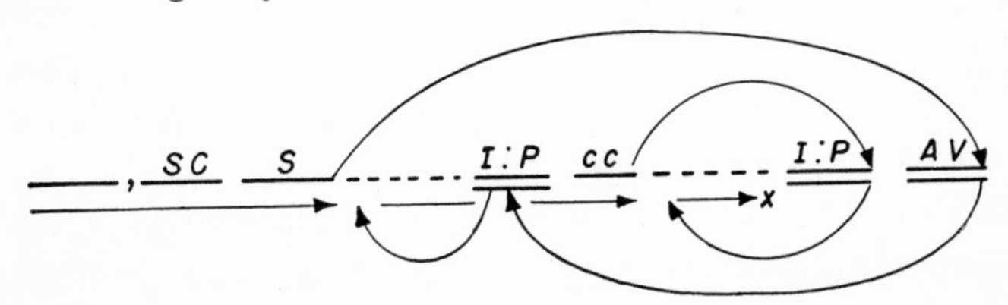

or past participle, **CC** is the coordinating conjunction, and **AV** is the auxiliary verb.

C. Translation Exercise

1. Das Ergebnis hängt davon ab, ob man die einzelnen Kräfte genau messen und ihre Abhängigkeit voneinander erfassen kann. 2. Da diese Arbeiten ganz bestimmte Begrenzungen haben und ihre Ergebnisse von ganz besonderer Wichtigkeit sind, muß man äußerst sorgfältig vorgehen. 3. Hier ist ein Mann, der das Ideal seiner Wissenschaft verkörpert und mehr als irgend ein anderer zu ihrem Fortschritt beigetragen hatte. 4. Er verdient es wohl, daß wir seiner öfters gedacht oder doch wenigstens mehr von seinen Schriften gelesen hätten. 5. Nachdem er das Experiment Hunderte von Malen unternommen aber niemals etwas Konkretes dadurch erreicht hatte, bat er seine Kollegen um Beistand (*assistance*). 6. Jahrelang hatte er seine embryologischen Studien betrieben und viel zum Fortschritt dieser Wissenschaft beigetragen. 7. Auf diese Weise würde es sich ins Gesamtbild eingliedern und vielleicht auch den Schlüssel (*key*) zur Deutung bieten. 8. Die Verbreitung der Spezie ist dadurch scharf umgrenzt oder doch wenigstens effektiv eingeschränkt. 9. Sie werden eine ganz andere Mission zu erfüllen und deshalb ihre Pläne zu ändern haben. 10. Er hat keine Entdeckungen gemacht aber doch durch seine Persönlichkeit viel für seine Mitmenschen (*fellow men*) getan.

D. Practical Review Questions

1. What are the various translation procedures for a simple statement? 2. When do you find a comma between two or more successive simple statements? When do you find none? 3. What is the translation procedure for a compound sentence having two coordinate clauses and only one common finite verb? 4. What is the translation procedure for a dependent clause? 5. How does it affect the translation procedure of a following main clause? 6. When is the comma absent between two successive dependent clauses? 7. What is the translation

procedure for two successive dependent clauses that have a finite verb in common?

E. Die Entwicklung der Wissenschaften

Wenn wir uns mit dem Gedanken der geschichtlichen Entwicklung der Wissenschaften befassen und deren Bedeutung für das Gesamtwohl der Menschheit genügend verstehen wollen, so ist es ohne weiteres einleuchtend, daß wir sofort auf erhebliche Schwierigkeiten stoßen. Wir müssen uns klar werden, welchen Standpunkt wir in dieser Hinsicht einnehmen; denn einerseits ist es uns möglich, daß wir uns mit dem gedanklichen Fortschritt beschäftigen und so die philosophische Seite unseres Problems betonen, oder wir können anderseits versuchen, das Bild des wissenschaftlichen Werdegangs im Lichte einzelner Persönlichkeiten zu malen. In jedem Fall aber müssen wir uns vor Augen behalten, daß, je weiter wir in die Vergangenheit zurückgreifen, Persönlichkeiten immer mehr verschwinden und einzelnen Errungenschaften Platz machen. So denke man daran, daß solch wichtige Erfindungen und Entdeckungen wie das Rad, der Speer oder der Bogen, das Schiff oder die Nutzbarmachung des Feuers an gar keine bestimmten Persönlichkeiten gebunden werden können. Noch kann man sie mit ganz bestimmten Zivilisationen oder Völkern verknüpfen. Ja, man muß sich sogar ernstlich die Frage vorlegen, ob jene Urväter je den Gedanken hatten, daß sie mit ihren Erfindungen und Verbesserungen zu einem kontinuierlichen geschichtlichen Strom beigetragen haben; ob sie die Vorstellung eines fortschrittlichen Gedankens überhaupt haben konnten. Denn wir unterscheiden ja bekanntlich zwischen statischen und dynamischen Zivilisationen. Um einer Lösung dieser Frage nahezukommen, hat man gesagt, daß jede Zivilisation, ob sie nun groß oder klein war, Elemente des Fortschrittes besitzt, diese aber nicht immer

3 **Menschheit** mankind
3 **genügend** sufficient(ly)
4 **erheblich** considerable
5 **Standpunkt** standpoint
6 **einnehmen** to occupy
7 **sich beschäftigen** to occupy oneself
8 **betonen** to emphasize
10 **Werdegang** development
12 **Vergangenheit** past
13 **einzeln** single
14 **wichtig** important
16 **Nutzbarmachung** utilization
16 **bestimmt** definite
18 **verknüpfen** to connect
21 **Verbesserung** improvement
22 **beitragen** to contribute
24 **bekanntlich** as is known
25 **Lösung** solution
27 **besitzen** to possess

bewußt entwickeln kann. Ausgeprägteste Eigenschaften, wie z.B. in religiöser Hinsicht, können die Entwicklung anderer Begleiteigenschaften im Gefolge haben. Das war der Fall bei den Ägyptern und ihren hochentwickelten Künsten der Architektur, Schrift, und Kleidung. Ferner hat man gesagt, daß eine Änderung, sei sie nun langsam oder plötzlich, an sich nicht Fortschritt zu bedeuten habe; im Gegenteil, eine Änderung an sich kann einen Rückgang andeuten. Ganz allgemein gesprochen drückt der Fortschritt sich in verschiedener Weise aus. So kann man ihn auf dem Gebiete der Biologie suchen und z.B. das langsame aber dennoch merkliche Wachstum des menschlichen Gehirns betrachten. Oder man könnte auch die Ausbildung und Leistungsfähigkeit des Körpers oder einzelner Teile desselben verfolgen. Fortschritt drückt sich auch in dem Maße der Naturbeherrschung aus. Die Bewältigung der Erdoberfläche muß der des Erdinneren gleichgestellt oder wenigstens mit ihr günstig verglichen werden. Die Bewältigung des Luftraumes ist nicht weniger Fortschritt als die Erkenntnis des Wesens der Materie. In der Tat, es gibt wenige Seiten des menschlichen Daseins, die der Macht des Fortschrittes nicht unterworfen sind. Um den Ursprüngen der menschlichen Kultur nahezukommen, hat man versucht, in zwei Richtungen vorzugehen: Ausgrabungen der Reste alter und vergangener Zivilisationen vorzunehmen und noch bestehende Zivilisationsgruppen in ihren verschiedenen Fortschrittsstadien zu untersuchen. Beide haben erfreuliche Resultate zur Folge gehabt.

Ganz anders aber verhält es sich, wenn wir mit Zivilisationen und Zeitaltern arbeiten, welche sich nicht nur einer bestimmten Einstellung zum Wissen als solches bewußt sondern auch der Künste verschiedenartiger Aufzeichnungen bemächtigt waren,

28 **bewußt** conscious
28 **ausgeprägt** pronounced
29 **begleiten** to accompany
31 **Kunst** art
34 **Gegenteil** contrast
35 **Rückgang** recession
35 **ausdrücken** to express
38 **merklich** noticeable
38 **betrachten** to consider
39 **Leistungsfähigkeit** capacity
40 **verfolgen** to trace
41 **Maß** degree
45 **Erkenntnis** knowledge
47 **Ursprung** origin
49 **vorgehen** to proceed
49 **Rest** remains
50 **vornehmen** to undertake
52 **untersuchen** to investigate
56 **Einstellung** attitude
56 **Wissen** knowledge
57 **Aufzeichnung** record

wie z.B. die alten Griechen es waren. Wir verdanken ihnen und ihren philosophischen Methoden mehr, als wir uns oft eingestehen wollen; denn es ist vor allem die Einstellung oder Annäherung des Menschen zum und an das Unbekannte, die aus ihm entweder einen Träumer, Wissenschaftler, Philosophen oder einen Unwissenden macht. So waren die alten Griechen wohl Philosophen aber kaum Wissenschaftler. Dasselbe kann auch von den Völkern der abendländischen Kultur gesagt und bewiesen werden, wenn wir uns auf die mittelalterliche Zeit beschränken. Und dennoch hat sich schon das mittelalterliche Abendland in dieser Beziehung geändert; denn es war Roger Bacon (1214–1294), der sich von dem rein Spekulativen fort und dem ernstlichen Betrachten der konkreten Natur mittels Beobachtung und Versuchs zugewandt hat. Eines der ersten und wichtigsten Werkzeuge allen wissenschaftlichen Untersuchens war somit gegeben: das Unbekannte soll nur auf Grund seiner eigenen Eigenschaften untersucht werden ohne Rücksicht darauf, was Andere und andere Wissenschaften schon darüber gesagt haben. Roger Bacon's Namensvetter, Francis Bacon (1561–1626), fügte dem Gebilde der Wissenschaften einen weiteren Baustein hinzu. Er beschäftigte sich nämlich mit der Klassifizierung des Wissens und lieferte dadurch die Grundlage aller noch kommenden Wissenschaften. Dadurch, daß Kopernikus die Aufmerksamkeit des Menschen von der Erde als dem Mittelpunkt des Universums hinweg und auf die Unendlichkeit unseres Sonnensystems zulenkte, trug er nicht wenig zur Ausgestaltung der so notwendigen, objektiven wissenschaftlichen Einstellung bei. Der Mensch lernte endlich erkennen, daß er ein weit weniger wichtiges Geschöpf ist, als er es bisher geglaubt hatte. Der Schwerpunkt des menschlichen Lebens begann, sich allmählich aus dem Menschen hinaus und in die ihn umgebende Natur zu verlegen. Das objektive Interesse war erwacht. Es galt nun, bestimmte Methoden zu erfinden und entwickeln, um

65 **abendländisch** occidental
65 **beweisen** to prove
66 **beschränken** to limit
67 **Beziehung** respect
70 **Beobachtung** observation
70 **Versuch** experiment
73 **Grund** basis
76 **weiter** further, additional
77 **Baustein** building stone
78 **nämlich** namely
79 **Grundlage** basis
80 **Aufmerksamkeit** attention
83 **Ausgestaltung** formation
86 **Schwerpunkt** center of gravity
87 **umgebend** surrounding
88 **verlegen** to shift
89 **entwickeln** to develop

dem Warum auf den Grund zu kommen. Die erste Methode dazu 90
gab uns Descartes in seinem System deduktiver Analyse
und Synthese. Die Betonung mathematischer Werte läßt ihn
als Newton's Vorläufer erscheinen.

Je mehr wir uns der Neuzeit nähern, desto klarer erkennen wir
auch die allmähliche Differenzierung des Wissens. Die Wissen- 95
schaften aller elektrischen Erscheinungen gehen auf Gilbert
(1540–1603) zurück; die moderne Anatomie kann bis zur Entdeckung des Blutkreislaufes durch Harvey (1578–1657) verfolgt
werden. Möglich gemacht wurde dies durch die Anwendung von
mathematischen Maßstäben d.h. Messungen und Wertbestimmun- 100
gen. Die Mathematik, die selbst ihren Ursprung in der Astronomie hat, wurde so allmählich zum Werkzeug aller anderen
Wissenschaften. Es kann wohl kaum daran gezweifelt werden,
daß Ticho Brahe und sein berühmter Schwiegersohn Kepler der
Nachwelt den Wert von mathematischen Messungen demonstriert 105
und bewiesen haben. So ist z.B. die Physik als Wissenschaft nur
durch Anwendung von mathematischen Messungen möglich und
dadurch auch zum Helfer der modernen Astronomie geworden.
Jede Wissenschaft bedient sich heutzutage der Mathematik, und
durch dieselbe Mathematik werden wiederum neue Wissen- 110
schaften von schon bestehenden abgespaltet, um sich dann selbstständig weiter zu entwickeln.

Eine interessante Begleiterscheinung des heutigen Bildes der
Wissenschaften ist die Tatsache, daß sich Wissenschaftsmittel-
punkte herausgebildet haben. Das ist in den verschiedenen 115
wissenschaftlichen Akademieen und Universitäten oder technischen Hochschulen zu sehen. Neuerdings haben die einzelnen
Regierungen sogar den Wert der Wissenschaften im Kampf ums
Dasein erkannt und unterstützen Institute und Einzelwissen-
schaftler in jeder Hinsicht. Es scheint also, als ob die Wissen- 120
schaft an sich zum Instrument des menschlichen Daseins geworden

92 **Betonung** emphasis
93 **erscheinen** to appear
94 **erkennen** to recognize
97 **Entdeckung** discovery
99 **Anwendung** application
100 **Maßstab** value
100 **Wert** value
102 **allmählich** gradually
105 **Messung** measurement
109 **sich bedienen** to use
111 **spalten** to split
115 **herausbilden** to develop
117 **neuerdings** recently
119 **unterstützen** to support

ist, und zwar von solcher ungemeinen Bedeutung, daß sie universale Beachtung findet. Sie ist nicht mehr Vorliebe des Einzelnen, sie ist Notwendigkeit der Allgemeinheit.

Natürlich haben das neunzehnte und bisher auch das zwanzigste 125 Jahrhundert die Entwicklung besonderer Wissenschaften gesehen: die Geologie, Zoologie, Botanik, Chemie, Physik und besonders die Atomanalyse, Elektrizität und die Radioaktivität, um nur einige zu nennen. Das Bewußtsein der Notwendigkeit ist wohl in den meisten Fällen der stärkste Anstoß für solch moderne Entwick- 130 lungen gewesen. Man denke nur an die Entstehung und Verbreitung der schweren Seuchen, und wie sie zum unmittelbaren Anlaß zur Entdeckung der Bakterien und deren Bekämpfung wurden. Koch, Pasteur, Lister und andere Bakteriologen bauten am Ende des neunzehnten Jahrhunderts und am Anfang des 135 zwanzigsten die Wissenschaft der Bakteriologie aus. Praktische Anwendung allergrößten Ausmaßes aber findet die Wissenschaft in der Erscheinung der modernen Industrie. Diese, ein junger Riese, bedient sich wiederum der Wissenschaft und ihrer Methoden, um immer größer und mächtiger zu werden. Wenn man 140 sich nun vorstellt, daß beide, Wissenschaft und Industrie, nicht nur fast ganz den Schwerpunkt des menschlichen Lebens enthalten sondern diesem den weitaus größten Teil des Inhalts verleihen, so ist es schwer, sich das gesamte Problem des geschichtlichen wissenschaftlichen Werdegangs zu vergegenwärtigen. Mit Recht 145 fragen wir uns, wohin die Wissenschaft uns noch führen und wieweit sie uns noch beglücken kann. Mit Recht zweifeln wir daran, ob die allmähliche Verschmelzung der wissenschaftlichen Einstellung mit fast allen anderen Seiten des Lebens so hätte sein müssen. Das ist aber Aufgabe des Philosophen. Und den- 150 noch können wir letzten Endes solch einer Frage nicht entgehen, denn sie ist ja auch aus rein objektiver Einstellung heraus gewachsen.

123 **Beachtung** attention
124 **Notwendigkeit** necessity
129 **Bewußtsein** consciousness
130 **Anstoß** impetus
131 **Entstehung** origin
132 **unmittelbar** direct
133 **Anlaß** cause
137 **Ausmaß** degree
139 **wiederum** again
143 **verleihen** to furnish
145 **sich vergegenwärtigen** to realize
148 **Verschmelzung** fusion
150 **Aufgabe** task

Hier können wir nicht umhin, uns an manchen deutschen Wissenschaftler zu erinnern, der endlich Philosoph geworden ist. 155 Denn alle Wissenschaft ist Fragestellung und Suche nach Beantwortung. Ist aber die Antwort gegeben, so ist immer noch die Frage vor uns: Und was ist die Ursache dazu? Die letzte Antwort wird nie gegeben werden.

CHAPTER 4

THE ABSOLUTE PARTICIPIAL CONSTRUCTIONS

Among the dependent adverbial clauses, two give rise to special constructions. These are the so-called absolute participial constructions. Thus a **während**-clause may also be rendered by an absolute present participial construction, and a **nachdem**-clause by an absolute past participial construction. This, however, can happen only when both, the dependent clause and the main clause, have the same subject. It is used frequently enough to warrant special attention.

Nach den Gründen menschlicher Handlung suchend, vertiefte er sich immer mehr in die Philosophie.

While he was seeking the reasons for human actions, he plunged more and more deeply into philosophy.

OR

Seeking the reasons for human actions, he plunged more and more deeply into philosophy.

Einmal die Gründe für solche abnormale Handlung bestimmt, fand er auch die richtige Behandlung dafür.

After he had once found the reasons for such abnormal behavior, he also found the correct treatment for it.

OR

Having once determined the reasons for such abnormal behavior, he also found the correct treatment for it.

Several features of this sentence arrangement should be noted. The absolute construction has neither finite verb nor subject; its subject is also the subject of the main clause. If the construction is a relatively short one, no comma separates it from the main clause. E.g., **Die Gründe bestimmt ging er sofort zur Behandlung über.** *Having determined the causes, he proceeded at once with the treatment.* If, on the contrary, the construction is of some length, a comma is usually present. The examples given above illustrate this.

Translation must always begin with the participle or with a reconstructed dependent clause. Thus the present participle will either remain as such or be translated by a tense that will indicate the present time element. The past participle will either remain a past participle or be turned into a tense that will indicate the correct past time element in relation to the action that follows. Study the examples given above.

Observing the presence or absence of the comma is of special importance because, if it is present, the starting place of the translation is easily seen. On the contrary, if the comma is absent, the starting place may easily be overlooked. In the latter case the student will do well to practice orientation in such manner that, beginning with the first word of the sentence, he will notice that either participle is followed directly by the finite verb of the main clause. Once having found the proper location, he should place a comma after the participle and then proceed according to the pattern set out above.

A. Translation Exercise

1. In einer Sprache geschrieben, die an Deutlichkeit nichts zu wünschen übrig ließ, erregte das Buch bald großes Aufsehen. 2. Das Beweismaterial in gemessener Sprache vorführend, umriß er das Krankheitsbild immer klarer. 3. Eine glänzende Idee verfechtend, sprach er bald in allen Hauptstädten Europas. 4. In der Physik und der Chemie gut bewandert, wandte er sich nun der Medizin zu. 5. Im Jahre 1874 nach seiner Heimat zurückgekehrt, begann er sein letztes und größtes Werk. 6. Den Schnitt andeutend beobachtete er seinen Gehilfen scharf. 7. Mit Bändern versehen werden die Tücher dem Patienten aufgelegt. 8. Alle bekannten Tatsachen beleuchtet, wenden wir uns nun deren Deutung zu. 9. In Boston geboren, und zwar als siebentes Kind in einer kinderreichen Familie, wurde er zuerst Lehrling in einer Apotheke. 10. Sein Werk beendet, zog er sich in seine Vaterstadt zurück.

B. Practical Review Questions

1. How can an absolute present participial construction be equivalent to a **während** clause? 2. Establish the same relationships for the absolute past participial construction. 3. Under what condition only may such an abbreviated construction be used? 4. What is the translation procedure for each?

C. Die Geschichte und das Wesen der Psychologie

Nach dem Ursprung und der Bedeutung des Wortes Psychologie fragend, ist es uns ein Leichtes, auf die griechischen Formen psyche: Seele und logos: Lehre hinzuweisen. Das Bestehen dieser Wörter im Griechischen läßt uns auch vermuten, daß die Griechen, die beiden Begriffe einmal klar umrissen, ebenfalls so etwas wie Seelenkunde betrieben. Das ist, wie wir noch weiter unten sehen werden, auch wahr. Jedenfalls ist das gesamte große Gebiet der Seelenkunde ein allgemeiner Gegenstand gewesen, und erst mit dem Erscheinen Christian Wolffs (1679–1754) ist man der näheren Erforschung des menschlichen Geistes einsichtlich geworden. Viele Regelmäßigkeiten des Verhaltens zu Gesetzen zusammenfassend, kam man bald zu dem Bewußtsein, daß es sich hier nicht nur um vereinzelte Erscheinungen des menschlichen Geistes handelte, sondern daß man es mit einer ganzen Wissenschaft zu tun hatte. Heutzutage ist die Psychologie zu einer selbstständigen Wissenschaft herangewachsen und bedient sich nicht nur ihrer eigenen Fragestellung sondern auch ihrer eigenen Methoden. Sie hat sich zur Aufgabe gestellt, das gesamte seelische Leben mittels ihrer Methoden durch Beschreibung seiner Erscheinungen und Vorgänge zu erforschen. Uns mit einer kurzen Wiedergabe ihres Wesens befassend, können wir nicht umhin, auch etwas über ihre Geschichte zu erwähnen. Wie schon oben angedeutet, besaßen die alten Griechen die erste Form einer selbsständigen Wissenschaft, Seelenlehre genannt. Die ersten großen Werke sind von Aristoteles geschrieben worden.

3 **hinweisen** to point out
4 **vermuten** to assume
7 **jedenfalls** in any case
11 **Verhalten** behavior
13 **vereinzelt** single
16 **selbstständig** independent
17 **Fragestellung** problematic
19 **mittels** by means of
20 **erforschen** to investigate
21 **Wiedergabe** reproduction

Es waren die drei Bücher „Über die Seele" genannt. Dieser große Philosoph lehrte, daß es zwei Arten von Deutungen des Seelenlebens gäbe. Zum ersten nimmt er an, die Seele ordne sich alle Lebenserscheinungen unter und gewinne dadurch ihren Inhalt, und das könnte man als den biologischen Standpunkt 30 bezeichnen; zum andern aber beruhe das Seelenleben auch auf Erfahrung. Mit diesen beiden großen Anfangspunkten versehen, tat die Nachwelt aber wenig, denn der erstere Standpunkt wurde später im Mittelalter von der Metaphysik aufgenommen und hinderte so auf mehrere Jahrhunderte die Entwicklung der letz- 35 teren. Zwar hatte man ein wenig Beweismaterial dafür, um Ansätze für eine spekulative Psychologie zu besitzen, man erkannte solche Selbstbeobachtungen aber nicht als das an, was sie eigentlich waren.

Mit dem Wesen der Metaphysik lange eng verbunden, konnte 40 sich die Psychologie im engen Sinn des Wortes nicht davon ablösen; und so waren es erst die philosophischen Richtungen des 17. und 18. Jahrhunderts, die der weiteren Entwicklung der Psychologie einen Anstoß gaben. Die klassische Auffassung, die Seele sei mit dem Organischen des Lebens verbunden, wurde von 45 Descartes beiseite geschoben. Es gelang ihm, das rein Seelische von dem Organischen zu trennen und beide Seiten des Lebens enger zu umschreiben. So wurde das Seelische eingeengt durch den Begriff, daß es sich nur mit den Tatsachen des Bewußtseins befassen sollte; und mit den organischen Erscheinungen bezog 50 man sich nur auf die mechanischen Lebensvorgänge. Diese klare Zweiteilung wurde, immer mehr in ihrer Bedeutung anerkannt, zum empirischen Ausgangspunkt der modernen Psychologie, obgleich sie sich noch nicht von der Gewalt der mitteialterlichen Metaphysik zu trennen vermochte. Die erste Epoche der moder- 55 nen Entwicklung in der Seelenkunde war aber nicht ohne feste Errungenschaften. Einige Begriffe und Vorgänge wurden dennoch klar erkannt als das, was sie waren und, sich immer wieder in ihrer Wahrheit bewährend, behaupteten sie sich bis in unsere

32 **versehen** to supply
37 **Ansatz** beginning
41 **sich ablösen** to separate
46 **beiseite** aside
48 **umschreiben** to define
53 **empirisch** empirical
55 **vermögen** to be able to
57 **Errungenschaft** achievement
58 **sich bewähren** to prove itself

Zeit hinein. So z.B. der Begriff der Apperzeption, die dreifache Einteilung aller seelischen Vorgänge in Denken, Fühlen und Wollen, sowie auch Leibniz' Lehre vom unbewußten Seelenleben. 60

Eine weit wichtigere Entwicklung erfuhr die Psychologie von Seiten gewisser englischer Forscher. In England hatte sich nämlich die Philosophie des Empirismus immer mehr herausgearbeitet, und es ist nicht schwer, hier den Faden wieder zu Aristoteles' Erfahrungspsychologie zu verfolgen. Der Empirismus beschäftigte sich vornehmlich damit, Tatsachen der Assoziation in den Mittelpunkt des Forschungsverfahrens zu stellen. Ja, man ging sogar so weit, daß z.B. John Locke (1632–1704) annahm, alle seelischen Tätigkeiten würden durch einen eigenen inneren Sinn wahrgenommen, was er Reflexion nannte. Von der Zweispaltung des Lebens in das seelische und organische Element bis zu dieser ersten Gegenstandsbestimmung der neuen Wissenschaft war schon ein großer Schritt getan. Einmal als wesentlich angenommen konnte diese Assoziationsphilosophie sich schnell durch Männer wie Hume, Hartley und Priestley zu einem breiten System ausbreiten. Schließlich wurde sie um die Mitte des 19. Jahrhunderts zur Grundlage der neuen experimentellen Psychologie. Mit dem Entstehen aber der experimentellen Psychologie treten wir schon in das letzte Zeitalter der geschichtlichen Entwicklung dieser Wissenschaft, denn heutzutage stecken wir immer noch drin. 65 70 75 80

Man hatte nämlich mittels naturwissenschaftlichen Experimentierens großartige Erfolge im Bereich der genauen, exakten Wissenschaften erzielt. Nun übertrug man die Messungsmethoden auch auf die Psychologie. Die Folge davon war natürlich, daß die bisher unklar umrissene Wissenschaft nun Gestalt und Klarheit bekam. Einmal anerkannt wurde diese Klarheit so sehr Ziel der Psychologen, daß sich von nun an der Schrei nach einer selbstständigen Wissenschaft immer lauter erhob. Das traf besonders in Deutschland zu. Die ersten Ver- 85 90

62 **Lehre** doctrine
66 **Faden** thread
67 **erfahren** to experience
68 **vornehmlich** especially
69 **Verfahren** procedure
72 **wahrnehmen** to perceive
74 **Bestimmung** determination
82 **stecken** to be
85 **Erfolg** success
85 **Bereich** sphere
86 **übertragen** to carry over
86 **Messung** measurement
92 **zutreffen** to be true

suche in der Anwendung mathematischer Werte an seelisches Geschehen wurden von J. Fr. Herbart unternommen und zwar in seinem Werk „Statik und Mechanik des Geistes" dargelegt. Zwar setzten seine Anschauungen sich nicht durch, dennoch aber waren sie Anregungen für andere Versuche, so z.B. für Th. Fechners Maßmethode für psychische Größen, wodurch dieser zum Begründer der Psychophysik wurde. Wilhelm Wundt hat viel dazu beigetragen, der Psychologie ihre heutige Gestalt zu geben. Ein dreifaches Verdienst ist ihm zuzuschreiben: er hat das ungeheure, zerstreut daliegende Material über Sinnespsychologie organisiert und der Mit- und Nachwelt zugänglich gemacht; er hat das Gebiet der Psychologie erweitert, indem er sie bis zur Völkerpsychologie ausdehnte; er hat viel zur Gründung des ersten psychologischen Instituts (1875 in Leipzig) beigetragen.

Der nächste Abschnitt in der geschichtlichen Entwicklung der Psychologie wird in zweierlei Hinsicht gekennzeichnet: es machte sich eine Richtung nach dem sogenannten höheren Seelenleben hin bemerkbar; es zeigte sich unter dem Einfluß einer immer breiter wachsenden Mannigfaltigkeit des Lebens eine allmähliche Spaltung der allgemeinen Psychologie in kleinere Bereiche. Die Wendung nach dem höheren Seelenleben hin, d.h. dem Gedächtnis, Gefühl, Denken und Willen, ohne Zweifel von der steigenden Kultur der Neunziger des vorigen Jahrhunderts getragen, ist dadurch gekennzeichnet, daß sie vom Experiment guten Gebrauch macht. Hier haben wir den Beginn der angewandten Psychologie. Drei bedeutende Forscher können nun genannt werden: Ebbinghausen, dieser erschloß die Gesetze des Gedächtnisses durch Anwendung von sinnlosen Silben; Stumpf, dieser begründete die sogenannte Tonpsychologie; und A. Lehmann, dieser wendete sich mit Hilfe von Ausdrucksmethoden dem interessanten Gebiet der Gefühlspsychologie zu. Für die Erforschung des Denkens und Wollens war die sog. Würzburger

95 **darlegen** to explain
97 **Anregung** stimulus
98 **Begründer** founder
101 **Verdienst** merit
103 **zugänglich** accessible
104 **erweitern** to enlarge
105 **Gründung** foundation
107 **Abschnitt** section
109 **sogenannt** so-called
110 **bemerkbar** noticeable
111 **Mannigfaltigkeit** variety
117 **Gebrauch** use
119 **erschließen** to determine, to unlock
122 **Ausdruck** expression

Schule, an deren Spitze Oswald Külpes stand, verantwortlich. 125
Diese machten beide genannte Gebiete des menschlichen Geistes
dem Experiment zugänglich und entwickelten die Eigenart und
die gesetzmäßige Weise des Denkens. Geistige Gesetzmäßigkeiten
feststellend trennten sie nun die Welt des Fühlens von der des
rationalen Gedankens und unterschieden diese von der ersteren 130
so scharf, daß sie von nun an nie wieder im Sinne eines einheitlichen Begriffs gebraucht wurden.

Die neueste Entwicklung wird ebenfalls durch zwei Hauptmerkmale gekennzeichnet. Teils haben sich die schon herausgearbeiteten Gegenstände dergestalt vermehrt, daß man immer 135
neue Zweige der Psychologie zu Wissenschaften gemacht hat;
teils aber sind diese vertieft und ausgebreitet worden. Zudem
kann man sagen, daß die moderne Psychologie von zwei Hauptgedanken geleitet wird: dem Bestreben, sie möglichst intensiv
wissenschaftlich auszubeuten und der praktischen Anwendung 140
auf den verschiedenen industriellen und sozialen Gebieten.
Zusammenfassend kann man drei allgemeine Arten der Psychologie unterscheiden: die sog. Ganzheitspsychologie, die objektive
Psychologie und die sog. Tiefenpsychologie. Die erste wird von
F. Krueger geleitet und von der weitbekannten Gestaltpsychologie 145
vertreten. Diese entstand ungefähr um 1912 und bildete in ihrer
Einstellung den deutschen Protest gegen die überlieferte klassische
Psychologie. Der Dualismus, in der Trennung der objektiven
Welt von der Geisteswelt bestehend, wurde in ihr fortgesetzt,
sodaß der sog. Gestaltpsychologe sich vornehmlich mit Sinneser- 150
fahrung des Gegenstandes durch den Menschen beschäftigte und
diese Erfahrung als ganzes Phänomen betrachtete. Die Gesamtgestalt und der Gesamteindruck und nicht nur die einzelnen
Bestandteile bildeten Gegenstand des Studiums. Kennzeichnend
für die Gestaltpsychologie aber ist, daß vorheriges Wissen den 155
Sinneseindruck zu einer neuen Wirklichkeit ändern kann. Unter

125 **Spitze** head
127 **Eigenart** characteristic
128 **gesetzmäßig** regular
131 **einheitlich** uniform
134 **teils** partly
135 **dergestalt** in such a manner
136 **Zweig** branch
137 **vertiefen** to deepen
139 **leiten** to guide
139 **Bestreben** endeavor
140 **ausbeuten** to exploit
142 **zusammenfassen** to summarize
143 **Ganzheit** entity
146 **ungefähr** about
149 **fortsetzen** to continue
154 **Bestandteil** component part
155 **vorherig** previous
156 **Wirklichkeit** reality

dieser Ganzheitspsychologie wurde die Forschung auf die verschiedensten Gebiete übertragen. Noch heute übt diese einen großen Einfluß aus. Daß die alte englische Assoziationspsychologie auch endlich angegriffen wurde, war natürlich zu erwarten. 160
Dies wurde durch die objektive Psychologie erreicht, besonders aber in ihrer Form des in Amerika so stark vertretenen Behaviorismus' und der Reflexpsychologie. Kennzeichen dieser Deutung ist, daß ihre Vertreter nur das objektiv feststellbare Verhalten gelten lassen, d.h. nur die objektive Anregung und der objektive 165
Verlauf einer Handlung oder des Verhaltens wird dem Studium unterworfen. Ganz entgegengesetzt dieser Richtung aber ebenso objektiv veranlagt, ist die sog. geisteswissenschaftliche Psychologie Diltheys, die sich in der Errichtung objektiver Beziehungen des Menschen zu den Gebilden der äußeren Welt zeigt. 170

Ein ganz neues Kapitel in der geschichtlichen Entwicklung der Psychologie wurde mit der Aufstellung und Ausbildung der sog. Tiefenpsychologie geschrieben. Als allgemein bekannt sind Sigmund Freud, Alfred Adlers, C. G. Jungs ihre Hauptvertreter. Es wäre zu weitläufig, auf eine noch so skizzenhafte Erklärung 175
derselben einzugehen. Wir kommen noch später darauf zu sprechen. Kurz erwähnen wollen wir aber im Zusammenhang damit die Kinder- und Jugendpsychologie, die Persönlichkeitsforschung und Verzweigungen derselben, so wie sie uns in der Erziehungs- und Wirtschaftspsychologie begegnen. Auch nicht zu 180
vergessen ist die Anwendung derselben in der modernen Heilkunde.

Einiges soll noch betreffs der amerikanischen Richtung gesagt werden, ehe wir diese Betrachtung abschließen. Wie schon oben gesagt, wird die Psychologie gegenwärtig in Amerika vom Behaviorismus beherrscht. Das heißt, der Mensch wird nur in Ver- 185
bindung mit der ihn umgebenden Welt angesehen, und beide bilden eine Einheit. Verbunden wird der Mensch mit der Umwelt durch die Sinnesanregungen. Diese werden entweder einzeln als

161 **erreichen** to achieve
164 **feststellbar** determinable
166 **Verlauf** course
167 **unterwerfen** to subject
168 **veranlagt** organized
168 **geisteswissenschaftlich** intellectual
171 **Kapitel** chapter
175 **weitläufig** far-reaching
176 **eingehen** to enter
177 **Zusammenhang** connection
179 **Verzweigung** branch
180 **begegnen** to meet
183 **abschließen** to conclude
184 **gegenwärtig** at present
185 **beherrschen** to dominate

solche betrachtet oder in einer Vielheit, Situation genannt. Das behavioristische System ist demgemäß sehr einfach und beschränkt sich auf drei Elemente: die Anregung, das weiterleitende Sinnesorgan und ein sich aus beiden ergebendes Verhalten. Diesen Mechanismus weiter betrachtend wird es uns ohne weiteres klar, daß das Hauptgewicht nicht so sehr in dem sich manifestierenden Resultat eines einzigen Systems dieser Art beruht als auf der Differenzierung vieler Systeme, vieler Individuen; d.h. auf dem Ergebnis, das auf einer solchen Differenzierung ruht. Da nun persönliche Erfahrung von jedermann beobachtet werden kann, wird derselbe Maßstab an das Verhalten vieler zu derselben Situation gelegt, um so zu einem Ergebnis der Erfahrung zu gelangen. Wir sind also damit wieder teilweise bei Aristoteles und seiner wenigbeachteten Erfahrungspsychologie angekommen. Die verschiedenen vorherrschenden Theorien übersehend, erkennen wir deren vier als besonders wichtig. Die beiden ersten, dualistisch in ihrem Wesen, sind die der Interaktion und des psychologischen Parallelismus'; d.h. die erstere sagt aus, daß physiologische Tatsachen geistige Reaktionen veranlassen und umgekehrt; die zweite, daß geistige Tatsachen parallele Vorgänge sind, die an sich Ursache und Wirkung sind gerade so wie die Kette von Anregung und Verhalten. Die beiden letzten Theorien sind monistisch und werden als Doppelaspekt und Identitätstheorie bezeichnet. Die erstere sagt aus, daß Geistestatsachen nur verschiedene Seiten eines und desselben Erscheinens sind, und die letztere, daß die Identität dieses Erscheinens unbekannt ist und daß die beiden verschiedenen Seiten eines solchen Erscheinens dieselbe Tatsache sind, nur durch verschiedene Methoden beobachtet. Die Unterschiede sind natürlich fein, und einmal erwähnt, sollen sie nicht weiter erörtert werden. Die moderne Richtung ist eklektisch, d.h. die besten Theorien werden vor allen anderen ausgewählt und auf ihren Inhalt hin geprüft. Ferner wird der Mensch als Versuchsgegenstand immer mehr in den Hintergrund gedrängt und durch das Tier ersetzt. Die moderne Psychologie ist ganz und gar wissenschaftlich experimentell.

189 **Vielheit** multiplicity
201 **gelangen** to arrive at
201 **teilweise** partly
203 **übersehen** to survey
208 **umgekehrt** vice versa
218 **erörtern** to explain
220 **prüfen** to test

CHAPTER 5

THE RELATIVE CLAUSE

So far as translation is concerned, the relative clause has the same construction and undergoes the same treatment as the dependent clause. The student should, however, keep several points in mind. There is a definite and an indefinite relative pronoun. The definite is **welcher, welche, welches,** *plural* **welche,** or **der, die, das,** *plural* **die.** The indefinite is **wer** or **was.** The relative clause can usually be recognized by the fact that it is an internal one; it is never the principal clause in the sentence. It is always preceded by a comma.

Die Ergebnisse, die (welche) er . . . beschreibt, . . .
The results which he . . . describes . . .

On the contrary, the **wer**-relative clause, or the **was**-relative clause, may often be clause Number 1. In such cases its true nature is easily recognized by the absence of the question mark at the end of the sentence. It then means *whoever, whatever,* or *that which.*

Was er untersuchte, war der Vorgang der Oxydation.
That which he investigated was the process of oxidation.

An important variation of the relative construction occurs when the relative pronoun is accompanied and preceded by a suitable preposition which may be compounded into the well-known **wo**-form if the antecedent is not a human being.

Das Experimentieren, durch das (wodurch) er früher so viele Kenntnisse erworben hatte, wurde nun überflüssig.
The experimenting by means of which he formerly had acquired so much knowledge now became superfluous.

It is clear that in such instances the relative pronoun must be in the case that is required by the preposition.

A. The Use of *indem* and *in dem*

Among the prepositional relative clauses, one assumes major importance. It opens with **in dem** which is often mistaken for **indem.** The difference plainly lies in the fact that the former, which is written as two words, means *in which* or *in whom.* The latter is written as a compound word, **indem,** and is translated by *in that* . . . or *by* . . .*ing.*

Das Buch, in dem er gerade las, war eine Abhandlung über Hormone und Vitamine.

The book in which he was just then reading was a treatise on hormones and vitamins.

Indem er die Elektrolyse des Wassers beobachtete, fand er auch die Werte für die einzelnen Bestandteile.

In that he observed (*or* By observing) the electrolysis of water, he also found values for the individual components.

B. Translation Exercise

1. Er kam dabei zu den Ergebnissen, die (welche) er dann in seinem Hauptwerk beschreibt. 2. Die Erscheinung der Phosphoreszenz, welche (die) er zum erstenmal beschrieb, war nichts Neues. 3. Seine Veröffentlichungen, die nicht gerade zahlreich waren, sind dennoch von größter Bedeutung gewesen. 4. Die Gestalt, um welche sie sich gruppierten, war der größte Physiker seiner Zeit. 5. Er gehört aber auch der Geschichte der Medizin an, an deren Entwicklung er so regen Anteil nahm. 6. Was sich nun ereignete, übertraf alles, was in dieser Zeit darüber bekannt war. 7. Das Erfreulichste, was davon herauskam, war das Gesunden aller seiner Patienten. 8. Die Bücher, woraus er so viel gelernt hatte, wurden nun beiseite gelegt. 9. Der Beweis, in dem er eine neue Methode einführte, war einfach aber klar. 10. Indem er eine neue Methode einführte, sparte er sich und seinen Mitarbeitern viel Zeit. 11. Er erreichte sein Ziel, indem er neue Methoden und bessere Instrumente einführte.

C. Practical Review Questions

1. What are the structural similarities of a dependent clause and a relative clause? 2. What are the structural differences of these two types of clause? 3. What is the difference between the definite relative pronoun and the indefinite? 4. Is it possible to have two or more relative clauses coordinated by a suitable conjunction? 5. If so, what is the difference in translation procedure between such coordinate relative clauses and dependent clauses of the same kind? 6. Sketch such a translation diagram.

D. Aus der Geschichte des Urzeugungsgedankens

Wer die Geschichte der Medizin und besonders die der medizinischen Philosophie bis in die graue Vergangenheit verfolgt, kann nicht umhin, sich die Frage zu stellen, was denn eigentlich mit dem Wort Urzeugung gemeint sei. Zudem wird der, welcher sich mit der heutigen Bedeutung dieses Wortes befaßt, zu dem überraschenden Resultat kommen, daß es sich um die Erschaffung von Leben aus der toten Natur handelt. Ein Vergleich dieser heutigen Auffassung aber mit dem Verständnis, welches man in früheren geschichtlichen Zeiten davon hatte, zeitigt sofort die Tatsache, daß wir unseren Standpunkt betreffs der Definition des Wortes stark geändert haben. Das Überraschendste, was wir bei den Alten in dieser Hinsicht bemerken, ist die Tatsache, daß sie wohl von der Erschaffung von Leben, d.h. Lebewesen wie Insekten, Schlangen und sogar höheren Tieren sprachen und überzeugt waren, daß diese aus Erde, Schlamm oder Staub und Wasser entstehen, daß sie aber niemals den Gedanken vertraten, die Natur sei an sich tot und aus toter Materie zusammengesetzt. Im Gegenteil, überall begegnen wir der Überzeugung, daß die gesamte Natur ein großes lebendiges Gebilde ist, daß folglich

3 **eigentlich** actually
4 **meinen** to mean
7 **Vergleich** comparison
8 **Auffassung** idea
10 **betreffs** in reference to
12 **bemerken** to notice
14 **überzeugen** to convince
16 **entstehen** to arise
16 **vertreten** to represent
17 **zusammensetzen** to compose
18 **überall** everywhere
19 **Gebilde** structure
19 **folglich** consequently

Erde, Schlamm, Staub und Wasser ebenso von einem Lebensprinzip durchdrungen sind. Jegliches Entstehen von Leben geschehe somit aus dem, was schon Leben ist. Es kann also gar keine Rede von Urzeugung im überkommenen Sinn des Wortes sein. 20

Im folgenden wollen wir uns mit einigen wenigen Einzelmomenten dieses Gedankens beschäftigen, so wie er sich in den verschiedenen Zeitaltern und Zivilisationen widerspiegelt. Im Rahmen unserer Aufgabe wäre es ein zu umfangreiches Unternehmen, auch nur die wichtigsten Vertreter anzuführen, welche sich darüber ausgesprochen haben. Von den großen alten Zivilisationen könnte man China, Ägypten und Indien anführen. So glaubte man in China, daß Läuse auf Bambus entstehen, wenn dieser längere Zeit feuchtem und warmem Wetter ausgesetzt war. Schon wenigstens 3000 Jahre v. Ch. bildete man in Ägypten die Göttin Hekat, welche die Auferstehung symbolisiert, mit einem Froschgesicht ab. Das Wesentliche daran ist, daß damals der Glaube lebendig war, wonach der Nilschlamm sich zu Fröschen und Kröten verwandelt. Und auch in den heiligen Büchern Altindiens, den Upanischaden, der Mahabhârata und den Gesetzbüchern des Manu, die alle ihre Entstehung vom 3. Jahrhundert n. Ch. bis zum 8. Jahrhundert v. Ch. haben, finden wir eine Einteilung aller Lebewesen in solche, die Lebend-, Ei-, Sproß- und Schweißgeborene sind. 25 30 35 40

Diejenigen, welche sich besonders mit den Quellen des griechischen Altertums befassen, sind erstaunt über ihre Fülle, Klarheit und über die Tatsache, daß sie nun an bestimmte Persönlichkeiten gebunden werden können. Was einem Schwierigkeiten bereitet, ist zunächst die rechte Auswahl unter ihnen. Sollen wir uns an Thales, den ältesten jener Weisen, richten, der das Wasser als Grundelement betrachtete, oder vielleicht an Anaximander oder Xenophanes oder Parmenides oder die vielen anderen, die See- und Landtiere, Pflanzen und sogar Menschen aus Seeschlamm, 45 50

23 **überkommen** traditional
23 **Sinn** sense
27 **widerspiegeln** to reflect
28 **umfangreich** voluminous
29 **Vertreter** representative
29 **anführen** to cite
33 **aussetzen** to expose
34 **abbilden** to represent
37 **sich verwandeln** to change
42 **Lebewesen** creature
44 **Quelle** source
47 **Schwierigkeit** difficulty
48 **Auswahl** choice

der Erde und Wasser, dem Urschlamm der Erde entstehen sehen? Etwas anders lautet schon Anaxagoras (510–428? v. Chr.), gemäß welchem die Erde von „ätherischen" Keimen befruchtet wird. 55 Und bedenken wir, daß jene Philosophen fast nichts von unserem heutigen Wissen besaßen, wonach sie die verschiedenen Naturerscheinungen beurteilen konnten, so muß man doch staunen, daß ein Mann wie Empedokles (490–444? v. Chr.), der die Pflanzen als „Kinder der Erde" bezeichnete und mehr Philosoph als Natur- 60 forscher war, Feuchtigkeit und Wärme im Boden als Grundbedingung für Pflanzenwuchs annahm. Platon (427–347 v. Chr.) spricht wohl am klarsten aus, was wir schon am Anfang dieses Aufsatzes sagten, nämlich, daß alles Leben aus schon Lebendem käme. Er sagt, alles pflanzliche und tierische Leben kommt nicht 65 aus sich selbst, sondern wird durch die Psyche belebt. Was wir von Aristoteles' Haltung in dieser Hinsicht wissen, ist ziemlich lückenhaft, dennoch scheint er eine erstmalige Entstehung des Lebens abgelehnt und angenommen zu haben, daß dieselben Lebewesen, die durch geschlechtliche Zeugung entstehen, auch 70 auf andere Weise ins Dasein treten könnten.

Über Theophrastos (372–287 v. Chr.), Poseidonios (gest. um 50 v. Ch.), Cicero (106–43 v. Chr.), Seneca (4?–65 n. Ch.) und andere geht es nun schnell in der Richtung des christlichen Mittelalters fort, das uns ebenfalls reichliche Quellen zum Gedanken der 75 Urzeugung liefert. Justinus (100–165 n. Chr.) läßt die ersten Pflanzen und Tiere beim Trockenwerden der Erde entstehen. Arnobius (gest. nach 325) aber zweifelt schon daran, daß Insekten, Frösche, Mäuse und Ratten durch die Wärme der Sonne aus den Elementen hervorgebracht würden. Demgegenüber sagt der 80 hl. Basilius (315–379) aus, Gott habe allerlei Pflanzen, Insekten, Vögel und Fische aus der Erde selbst ohne irgendwelchen Beistand erstehen lassen. Laut Plotinus schuf Gott außer der anorganischen Welt auch noch die organische, worin allerlei geheime

54 **lauten** to state
54 **gemäß** according to
56 **bedenken** to consider
58 **beurteilen** to evaluate
60 **bezeichnen** to designate
63 **aussprechen** to state
68 **erstmalig** original
69 **ablehnen** to deny
74 **Richtung** direction
75 **ebenfalls** likewise
78 **zweifeln** to doubt
80 **hervorbringen** to produce
80 **demgegenüber** in contrast to that
82 **Beistand** assistance
83 **laut** according to

Keimkräfte enthalten seien, welche nur günstige Bedingungen 85
bedürfen, um ins Leben zu springen; d.h. Gott habe allen diesen
Dingen ursprünglich Keime gegeben, die alle Entwicklungs-
gesetze schon in sich tragen. Man sieht also, wie die Fragestellung
nach dem Geheimnis des Lebens sich mit dem Erscheinen des
Christengottes an diesen heftet; mit anderen Worten, wie der 90
christlich religiöse Gedanke sich in die sonst freie aber noch in
ihren Anfängen stehende Wissenschaft einschiebt und diese beeinflußt. So wird es auch bis zum Erscheinen des rational einge-
stellten Intellekts des 18. Jahrhunderts bleiben. Zunächst aber
ist es lehrreich, wenn wir einen kurzen Einblick in das Mittelalter 95
tun, das ja ohnehin so reich an philosophischen und religiösen
Gedanken ist.

Daß die Schriften der Alten erst in späterer Zeit wieder in ihren
Originalen bekannt werden, ist geschichtliche Tatsache; sogar
ihre Übersetzungen geben zu allerhand Miszverständnissen, 100
Irrtümern und Übertreibungen Anlaß. Dies ist besonders von
den Schriften Aristoteles wahr, und noch Hrabanus Maurus
(776–856), aus der Fuldaer Schule, erwähnt in seiner Enzyklopädie De Universo, daß allerhand Pflanzen und Tiere aus dem
Fäulnisvorgang aller Art hervorgehen, was auch in dem berühmten 105
Salernitanischen Codex (1160–1170) sein Echo findet, wenn
wir lesen, daß Würmer aus dem Blut oder verdorbenen Säften
entstehen. Bartholomaeus Anglicus (um 1230) geht in dieser
Beziehung sogar bis auf das Wunder Moses' zurück, als er vor
Pharao, von dem die Bibel berichtet, Stäbe in Schlangen ver- 110
wandelt. Nur sagt er, jenes Wunder sei nur eine Beschleunigung
des sonst natürlichen Vorgangs gewesen, wonach faulendes Holz
sich langsam in Würmer und Schlangen verwandelt. Solch eine
Beschleunigung sei nun übernatürlichen Wesen wie Teufeln und
Dämonen möglich, ein Echo der christlichen Einstellung aller 115
Wissenschaft gegenüber, demzufolge die fragende Wissenschaft
mit den schwarzen Künsten identisch ist. Auch Albertus Magnus
(1193–1280), der einer der größten Geister des deutschen Mittelal-

85 **günstig** favorable
86 **bedürfen** to need
87 **ursprünglich** original
90 **heften** to fasten
93 **einstellen** to orient
95 **Einblick** insight
98 **Schrift** writing
100 **Übersetzung** translation
103 **erwähnen** to mention
110 **berichten** to report
111 **Beschleunigung** acceleration
116 **demzufolge** according to which

ters war, ist davon überzeugt, daß Pilze, Schwämme, allerhand Kräuter und sogar Bäume unter dem Einfluß von Wärme und Gestirne aus den Dünsten der Erde und Wasser hervorgehen. Er bezieht sich in dieser Hinsicht auf die Erscheinung, daß verwesende Eichen und andere Bäume oft andersartige Pflanzen aus ihren Stämmen wachsen lassen. Auch Tomas von Aquino (1205–1274) folgt in seinem großen Werk, der Summa Theologiae, welches ja sein Hauptwerk ist, den Anschauungen des Albertus Magnus. Die spätere Scholastik hat dieselbe Einstellung, daß Vorgänge wie Fäulnis, Verwesung und Gärung für die Entstehung gewisser Lebensformen verantwortlich sind. Von besonderem Interesse ist hier die Sage vom Homunculus, wonach ein Embryo, also ein fertiger Mensch, aus dem passiven weiblichen und dem aktiven männlichen Element entstehe, was ganz analog der Entstehung des Steines der Weisen ist. Der Gedanke des schon fertigen Wesens findet auch späterhin weitere Annahme, wie z.B. bei Harvey (1578–1657), der uns zwar den berühmten Satz omne virum ex ovo gegeben hat aber dennoch Jünger der sog. Präformationstheorie war. Der erste, große deutsche Arzt, Parazelsus (1493–1541), bringt schon einigen Zweifel in den ganzen Problemkreis, worin er seine Vorstellung des Makrokosmus, und des Mikrokosmos, widergespiegelt findet. Ist der erstere ganz belebt, so ist er es auch in seinen kleinsten Teilen, also auch im letzteren. Was aber das Tierreich anbelangt, so können aus dem Sperma der vier Elemente alle Lebewesen hervorgehen, und zwar entweder durch die Kraft der Sonne, Fäulnis, Gärung oder einer sog. „vulkanischen Digestion“. Die „Väter der Botanik“, der Züricher Naturforscher Gesner (1516–1565), ja sogar die schöne Literatur der damaligen und auch späteren Zeit, halten noch an diesem Glauben fest. Und es ist deshalb auch nicht überraschend, wenn wir unter diesen Anhängern Männer wie Descartes (1596–1650) — siehe seine Œuvres philosophiques — und Galilei (1564–1642) finden, welch letzterer aber nicht versucht, diese Frage zu beantworten. Im allgemeinen aber kann man sagen, daß die scharfsinnigen und rationalen Franzosen schon

123 **andersartig** of different kinds
129 **verantwortlich** responsible
134 **Annahme** acceptance
135 **zwar** to be sure
147 **damalig** at that time
149 **Anhänger** follower
153 **scharfsinnig** keen

eine klare Spaltung in ihrer Einstellung zu diesem Problem schaffen. Réaumur (1683–1757) lehnt den Gedanken der Urzeu- 155 gung entschieden ab; dagegen glaubt Montesquieu (1689–1755), einer der scharfsinnigsten Philosophen des französischen Rationalismus', daß wenigstens Pflanzen durch die generatio aequivoca entstehen. Und Buffon (1707–1788) rationalisiert die Frage fort, indem er die überall vorhandenen Lebenseinheiten — die 160 Monaden Leibniz' — eine physische Eigenschaft der Materie nennt. Auch in England macht sich die obengenannte Spaltung bemerkbar. Priestley (1732–1804) wurde dadurch geehrt, indem nach ihm die grüne Algenschicht, welche sich unter dem Einfluß der Sonnenwärme auf der Oberfläche des Wassers bildet, genannt 165 wurde. Er war ein Anhänger der Urzeugungstheorie. In Schweden fand sie zuerst ihren Anhänger und Verfechter in von Linné, der sie aber später aufgab. Dasselbe Schicksal erfuhr dieser Gedanke auch in Deutschland. Man sieht also, wie er im Laufe der Zeit und dem Wachstum der Beobachtungsgabe zwei ganz 170 entgegengesetzte Schulen hervorruft, die ihre Vertreter unter den Naturforschern sowie Philosophen haben. In Deutschland werden besonders zwei Schulen sichtbar: eine, die sich an den französischen Vitalismus lehnt und die andere, die sich unter den Schutz der immer stärker werdenden Naturphilosophie stellt. Für Kant 175 (1724–1804) ist Urzeugung ganz außerhalb der Vernunft, gibt aber die theoretische Möglichkeit zu, daß der Geist des Menschen Vieles nicht wissen kann. Die drei großen deutschen Philosophen Fichte (1762–1814), Hegel (1770–1831) und Schelling (1775–1854) haben sich scheinbar wenig mit diesem Problem befaßt, und, um 180 ihn weiter in die Neuzeit hinein zu verfolgen, müßten wir nun zu den älteren deutschen Naturforschern und Medizinern übergehen. Damit aber begeben wir uns in das Gebiet der modernen Wissenschaft, welche so weitläufig in allen ihren Zweigen ist, daß wir uns größerer Organisation bedienen müßten, als es uns hier 185 möglich ist. Kurz zusammenfassend aber können wir sagen, daß die besprochene Anschauungsweise ganz von jedweder grundle-

155 **schaffen** to create
160 **vorhanden** present
160 **Einheit** unit
162 **obengenannt** above-mentioned
164 **Schicht** layer
168 **erfahren** to experience
170 **Gabe** gift
171 **entgegengesetzt** opposite
171 **hervorrufen** to bring about
176 **Vernunft** reason
176 **zugeben** to admit
184 **weitläufig** extensive

genden und maßgebenden Philosophie abhängig ist; daß sie sich im Laufe der Jahrhunderte darauf hin und her bewegt hat und erst wohl in ganz neuer Zeit als endgültig gelöst betrachtet werden darf. 190

188 **maßgebend** determining 190 **endgültig** final

CHAPTER 6

THE PARTICIPIAL MODIFIER

The participial modifier, or extended adjective construction or boxed construction, as it is also known, is a variant of the relative clause which appears in the position of an attributive adjective. A type of construction which is very common in German, especially in technical German, it must be thoroughly mastered. Though there are both simple and compound participial modifiers in German, nevertheless the latter is based upon the former. Thus it may be said that, if the student masters the nature and translation pattern of one construction, he has a fair grasp of them all. Since a number of variants occur, they will be treated at the appropriate place.

A. The Simple Participial Modifier

Wir besprechen nun die in dieser Hinsicht darin waltenden Verhältnisse und beobachten das folgende.

We shall now discuss the conditions existing in it in this respect, and observe the following.

An examination of the above sentence reveals several striking features. (1) The noun construction (doubly underlined) is split up in such a manner that its limiting word (**die**) remains in its customary place and the noun itself (**Verhältnisse**) is far removed from it. (2) The intervening space is taken up by a more or less lengthy construction called the participial modifier (underlined once). (3) The remainder of the sentence is in regular order. An examination of the intervening construction, the participial modifier, reveals two features. It contains a participle at the end (either present or past, or sometimes an adjective); the participle is located directly in front of the noun. Thus the participial modifier, being dependent in nature, results in this procedure: (1) Begin as usual. (2) Restore the split-noun construction. (3) Translate the participial modifier as though it were a relative clause, making the participle its verb in a suitable tense form. (4) Conclude as usual. Thus the translation of the example given above will be as follows: (1) *We are discussing now* (2) *the conditions* (3) *which exist in this respect in it* (4) *and observe the following.*

Applied to the noun construction and its participial modifier, we may draw a translation diagram in which **N** is the noun construction and **P** the participle.

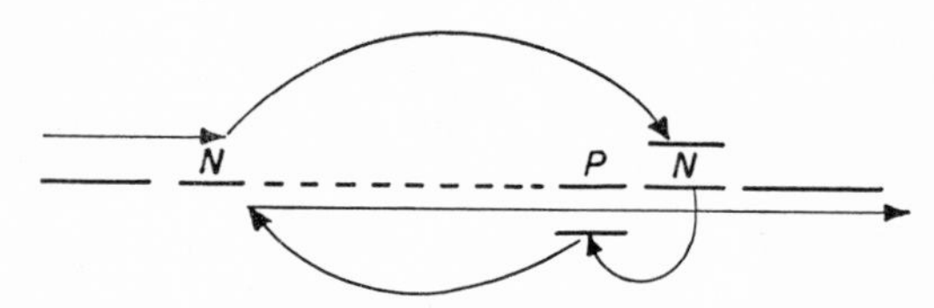

B. The Compound Participial Modifier

Allerdings handelt es sich dabei zumeist um mit Chemikalien behandelte und dadurch veränderte Stoffe.

To be sure, it is mostly a question of substances which are treated with chemicals and thereby changed.

Such a construction usually contains a series of two participial modifiers within the split-noun construction. Obviously, the natural procedure is to translate the participles in the order of their occurrence. Since **behandelte** signifies the end of the first and **veränderte** that of the second participial modifier, we shall translate the passage thus: *To be sure, it is for the most part a question of substances which are treated with chemicals and (which are) thereby changed.* Series consisting of more than two participial modifiers are rare.

The student should be conscious of the fact, however, that since a participial modifier modifies a noun, nouns in any grammatical function may be characterized by such a modifier.

Nominative

Allerdings gehen mit deren Bildung auch andere für das niedere Pflanzenleben unvorteilhafte Wirkungen Hand in Hand.

Genitive

Genaue Kenntnis des bisher noch nicht völlig verstandenen Vorgangs war dazu unbedingt notwendig.

Dative

Er schrieb das dem bisher noch nicht völlig verstandenen Vorgang zu.

Accusative

Er berechnete die für das Experiment nötige Kalkkarbonatkonzentration.

C. Variants

Although the pattern of the participial modifier as illustrated under (A) is basic in every respect, there are several variations of form which warrant attention.

1. *Substitution of an Adjective for the Participle.* The present or past participle may be replaced by an adjective. In this case the translation requires the insertion of the proper form of *to be*. E.g., **die der modernen Forschung zugänglichen Probleme** *the problems which are accessible to modern research.*

2. *The Use of a Series of Modifiers before the Noun.* When the noun which is separated from its limiting word is preceded by a series of modifiers, all modifiers except the first belong to the noun and must be translated with it. Modifier Number 1 becomes the relative clause verb. E.g., **Ein sich durch günstige Verhältnisse selbst erhaltender, ertragreicher, durchlufteter Boden.** *A productive, aerated soil which maintains itself through favorable conditions.*

3. *The Split Series of Modifiers.* A series of several modifiers may be split in such manner that one or more may occur directly after the limiting word. In such a case, translation should proceed beyond the limiting word and should include the directly following modifiers before the split-noun construction is restored. E.g., **Ein ertragreicher, sich durch günstige Verhältnisse selbst erhaltender durchlufteter Boden** *a bearing, aerated soil which . . . etc.* Note that in such cases a comma that separates the displaced modifier(s) from the remaining intervening construction is usually present.

4. *A Participial Modifier within Another.* This construction is rarely met with. Translation proceeds by resolving the larger construction (the frame construction) first, and then translating the inner construction in its appropriate place. E.g., **Ein aus zwei in Bezug auf die Elektronenaffinität verschiedenen Atomen A und B aufgebautes Molekül kann bei Umsetzung in Lösung von Kryptoionen reagieren.** *A molecule constructed of two atoms* A *and* B *and different in reference to their electron affinity can react in a solution of crypto ions.*

Concluding Remarks. Two points should be observed. First, if the participial modifier is not very long, it may be translated straight. E.g., **ein lang anhaltender Regen** *a long-lasting rain.* Second, practice will obviate the continued use of *which is*, *which were*, and similar expressions as an introduction to the relative clause. A translation may then run as follows: **ein sich durch günstige Verhältnisse selbst erhaltender Boden** *a soil maintaining itself . . . etc.*

D. Translation Exercise

1. Der noch heute vertretene Standpunkt ist mit dieser neuen Kenntnis nicht immer vereinbar. 2. Diese aus seinem Laboratorium hervorgegangene Entdeckung war auf lange Zeit maßgebend. 3. Das durch diese Entdeckung hervorgerufene Aufsehen war sehr groß. 4. So hatte wieder einmal die reine um ihrer selbst willen betriebene Wissenschaft zu großen Erfolgen geführt. 5. Trotz mancher noch zu überwindenden Schwierigkeit wurden von nun an die Erfolge immer größer. 6. Wir werden zuerst beleuchten, wie seine für uns so wichtigen Entdeckungen von seinen Mitarbeitern aufgenommen wurden. 7. Die von der Natur in Unendlichkeit hervorgebrachten Formen lassen gewisse Gesetzmäßigkeiten erkennen. 8. Alle von alters her für ursprünglich gehaltenen Lebensformen konnten jetzt genau klassifiziert werden. 9. Dieses von Newton der Erfahrung entnommene Gesetz kann in wenigen Worten formuliert werden. 10. Das dieser Aufgabe zugrunde liegende Problem war weder neu noch unbearbeitet.

The following examples were taken directly from German technical works. Translate them.

1. (One Modifier within the Other) Da die Walze aber nur eine beschränkte Tiefenwirkung hat, empfiehlt es sich, in solchen Fällen die sogenannten Krumenpacker zu verwenden, eine aus einzelnen in größerem Abstand voneinander angebrachten Ringen bestehende Walze, die nicht oberflächlich eindrückt, sondern tiefer in den Boden einschneidet und den „Schluß" des Bodens fördert.[a] 2. (One Modifier within Another) Ganz allgemein gesprochen: ein aus zwei in Bezug auf die Elektronenaffinität verschiedenen Atomen oder Atomgruppen *A* und *B* aufgebautes Molekül *AB* kann bei Umsetzung in Lösung von Kryptoionen reagieren, ...[b] 3. (Compound Modifier) Die Wachstendenzen der Blätter und Blüten der Amsupka-Reihe scheinen im Vergleich zu den übrigen Volldüngerreihen darauf hinzuweisen, daß die durch die Ballaststoffe dieses Düngemittels und möglicherweise auch die durch seine saure Reaktion bei geringer Pufferung des vorliegenden Bodens ausgelösten Wirkungen entwicklungshemmender gewirkt haben, als die mit diesem Düngemittel verabfolgten höheren Konzentrationen.[c] 4. (One Modifier within Another) Unter den Lebensbedingungen der Bakterien nimmt selbstredend eine passende Nahrung den ersten Platz ein, hat ja doch die Assimilation der Nahrung einen doppelten Zweck, 1. Baumaterial für das Wachstum und die Vermehrung der Zellen herbeizuschaffen und 2. die für diese Prozesse sowie für andere direkt oder indirekt in Verbindung mit dem Erhalten des Lebens stehende Funktionen notwendige Energie zu erzeugen.[d] 5. (One Modifier within Another) Die unter Benutzung des von Kellner angegebenen Verdauungswertes für organische Masse errechneten Werte für verdauliche und unverdauliche organische Masse stimmen nicht mit der Summe der verdaulichen bzw. unverdaulichen Nährstoffe überein. 6. (Successive Modifiers) Die Hälfte des zur Oxydation der salpetrigen Säure zu Salpetersäure nötigen Sauerstoffs wird aus dem bei der Reduktion des dreiwertigen Kobalts entstandenen Sauerstoff gedeckt.[e] 7. (Compound

Modifier) Es gelang auch, mit Cholesterin- bzw. Lecithinantiserum eine passive Anaphylaxie herbeizuführen; sie war aber wegen der in vitro-Bindung der Antikörper mit dem normalerweise im Blut vorhandenen Cholesterin bzw. Lethicin relativ schwach.[f]

REFERENCES

a. Heuser, Otto: Grundzüge der praktischen Bodenbearbeitung. Berlin 1928, Verlag Paul Parey. S. 133.
b. Müller, Eugen: Neuere Anschauungen der organischen Chemie. Berlin 1940, Verlag Julius Springer. S. 63, 64.
c. Vogel, F., Biermann C., Schneble K.: Zur Topfpflanzendüngung mit wasserlöslichen Volldüngemitteln. Aus: Die Gartenbauwissenschaft. 14. Bd. Berlin 1940, Verlag Julius Springer. S. 498.
d. Schmidt, J. und Weis, F.: Die Bakterien. Jena 1902, Verlag Gustav Fischer. S. 102.
e. Gedroiz, K. K.: Chemische Bodenanalyse. Berlin 1926, Verlag Gebrüder Bornträger. S. 79.
f. Kunze, Rudolf, Dr. phil.: Lethicin. Aus: Arzneimittelforschungen, 1. Bd. Berlin NW 40; 1941 Verlag Rosenmeier und Dr. Saenger, K. G. S. 115.

E. Practical Review Questions

1. What is the origin of the participial modifier? 2. What other names has it? 3. Where does it appear in a sentence or clause in relation to the noun? 4. What is its basic construction? 5. What variations of it are you familiar with? 6. To what extent do these differ in construction from a basic participial modifier pattern? 7. What is the translation pattern of a basic participial modifier construction? 8. Can you diagram it? 9. Can you diagram a compound participial modifier? 10. Can you explain a construction that contains one modifier within another? 11. What would you do in translating such a construction if the participle in question were an adjective?

F. Die Traumpsychologie und Sigmund Freud

Unter den schon im Abschnitt über das allgemeine Wesen der Psychologie erwähnten modernen Zweigen derselben ist der der Tiefenpsychologie zu ganz besonderer Bedeutung herangewachsen. Was Sigmund Freud durch seine Studien über das Wesen der Verdrängung seelischer Elemente ins Unbewußte begründet hat, 5

5 **Verdrängung** displacement 5 **Unbewußte** unconscious

ist von einer immer wachsenden Anzahl Wissenschaftler zu einem ganzen System ausgebaut worden. Heutzutage hat es schon den Anschein einer selbstständigen Wissenschaft und hat in vielen Kulturgebieten seine praktische Anwendung gefunden.

Was ist ein Traum? Der Große Brockhaus gibt uns eine Antwort auf diese Frage, indem er sagt, „Der Traum sind die im Schlaf auftretenden eigenartigen seelischen Erlebnisse, von deren Vorhandensein wir im Wachzustande nur durch Erinnerungen wissen.“ Daß aber diese sonst nur im Schlaf vorkommenden Erscheinungen auch im Wachzustande Tatsache sind, weiß jeder, der sich schon einmal dem sog. Tagträumen übergeben hat. Wir wollen nun kurz untersuchen, was die Eigenart des Traumes ist, wie er entsteht und inwiefern er auf einen verborgenen Sinn hindeuten kann. 10 15

Genaue Kenntnisse über das Wesen des Traumes hat man erst in verhältnismäßig neuer Zeit erlangt. Schon lange aber hat der Mensch vor dem Geheimnis dieser Erscheinung dagestanden. Die Literatur der verschiedenen Kulturvölker, besonders die der Ägypter, Griechen und Juden ist voll von diesbezüglichen Angaben. Man erinnere sich nur an die Bibel und die zahlreichen darin verzeichneten Träume sowie deren Deutungen. Der bekannteste darunter ist ohne Zweifel der Traum Pharaos und seine Deutung durch Joseph. Aber erst mit dem Ausbau moderner Untersuchungsmethoden hat man sich an die Erforschung der Geisteswelt in allen ihren Seiten herangewagt. Die Wurzeln der wissenschaftlichen Methoden sind natürlich in den mathematischen Wissenschaften, der Physik und der Mathematik selbst zu suchen. Sich auch auf dem Gebiete der allgemeinen Psychologie bewährend, wurden sie nun von Tiefenpsychologen wie Hacker und Köhler auch auf die Traumerscheinung angewandt. Erste dazu nötige Aufgabe war natürlich, das Gebiet des Traumes durch bestimmte Tatsachen zu bereichern und befestigen. Man ging also daran, den Unterschied zwischen Traum und Wachsein 20 25 30 35

8 **Anschein** appearance
11 **Traum** dream
12 **auftreten** to occur
13 **Vorhandensein** presence
14 **sonst** otherwise
17 **Eigenart** characteristic
18 **inwiefern** in how far
21 **erlangen** to obtain
24 **diesbezüglich** such
26 **Deutung** interpretation
28 **Ausbau** development
30 **Geisteswelt** psychic world
30 **Wurzel** root
38 **Wachsein** being awake

festzustellen und fand, daß dieser darin bestand, daß höhere dem Wachsein charakteristische Vorgänge wie Denken, Willensausübung usw. im Traum unterdrückt werden, und sogenannte niedere Erscheinungen in den Vordergrund treten. Mit dem Versinken des Willens und des mit ihm im Wachzustande verbundenen Disziplinselements ist es dann möglich, daß sich allerlei Unregelmäßigkeiten beim Traumvorgang zeigen. So wird z.B. das Selbstbewußtsein großen Änderungen unterworfen, und bewußte moralische Werte werden so verzerrt, daß sie den im wachsamen Zustand vorhandenen Werten gar nicht mehr entsprechen. Man stellte ferner fest, daß gewisse Fähigkeiten in verstärktem Maße ins Traumbewußtsein treten, so die Vorstellungskraft, das Gedächtnis und das Gefühlsleben. Die Frage nach dem Entstehen des Traumes kann auch von mehreren Seiten her beantwortet werden. Die physische und besonders die leiblich physische Welt liefert genügend Material für einen Traum. Physische Eindrücke auf den Schläfer selbst sind oft Ursachen dazu, so u.a. zu hohe oder niedere Temperatur des Schlafortes, zu großer oder leichter Druck der Schlafdecken, manche Geräusche, die vom Schlafenden unbewußt vernommen werden, usw. Unter die Leibesreize werden gewöhnlich Hunger, Durst, Sexualbedürfnisse, usw. gezählt. All diese Reize erfahren beim Traumvorgang Änderung je nach der Tiefe des Schlafes, Erregsamkeit des Geistes, Gesundheitszustand des Schlafenden und anderen Einwirkungen. An dieser Stelle greift nun Sigmund Freud mit seinen Untersuchungen ein und baut allmählich sein so berühmt gewordenes System auf. Aber davon später. Eine andere aber ebenso ergiebige Quelle für den Inhalt eines Traumes sind die Ereignisse des vorhergegangenen Tages. Je eindrucksvoller solche Begebenheiten waren, desto leichter ist es ihnen, sich im Traumbewußtsein in ihrer Identität zu behaupten, andere weniger starke Vorgänge zu unterdrücken und dem Schläfer die Traumvorstellung zu

41 **unterdrücken** to suppress
42 **Vordergrund** foreground
45 **Unregelmäßigkeit** irregularity
47 **verzerren** to distort
56 **u.a.** and others
57 **Druck** pressure
58 **vernehmen** to perceive
59 **gewöhnlich** usually
60 **Reiz** stimulus
61 **Tiefe** depth
61 **Erregsamkeit** excitability
62 **Einwirkung** effect
63 **eingreifen** to start
66 **ergiebig** rich
67 **eindrucksvoll** impressive
67 **Begebenheit** event
68 **sich behaupten** to assert oneself
70 **Vorstellung** idea

geben, er setze die Tagestätigkeit in ihrer natürlichen Entwicklung fort. Auch hier macht sich die schon erwähnte Schlaftiefe bemerkbar, indem sie mehr oder weniger im Stande ist, den Tatsachenbestand zu ändern. Ebenso muß man hierzu starke aber sonst unterdrückte Gefühlszustände rechnen wie Hoffnung, Ent- 75 täuschung, Angst oder Schrecken.

Ein schon seit alters her geahnter aber auf seine wirkliche Bedeutung noch nie erforschter Sinn soll einigen Forschern nach im Gewebe des Traumes verborgen sein. Objektiv betrachtet, sagen andere, enthält ein Traum kaum mehr als zusammenhang- 80 loses Spiel von vorstellungshaften Bildern und vergangenen Begebenheiten. Im allgemeinen aber hat man sich neuerdings dieser Erscheinung auch mit wissenschaftlichen Werkzeugen genähert und sie auf ihre Bestandteile hin analysiert und gedeutet. Vor allem ist es Freud gewesen, der sich darin hervorgetan hat. 85

Der am 6. Mai 1856 in Freiberg, Mähren, geborene und sich 1885 in Wien habilitierende Nervenarzt Sigmund Freud kann als Bahnbrecher und Begründer der neuen Wissenschaft der Psychoanalyse angesehen werden, denn er hat nicht nur als erster Moderner der Traumdeutung feste Wirklichkeit verleiht, er hat auch deren 90 praktische Anwendung auf vielen Gebieten des Lebens entwickelt. Während seiner ersten Periode befaßte er sich mit dem Problem der Hirnsprachstudien und Kinderlähmung. Von 1885 bis 1886 studierte er unter dem durch seine Forschungen über die Hysterie bekannten Franzosen Charcot in Paris. Im Jahre 1895 begann er 95 in Verbindung mit dem Wiener Nervenarzt J. Breuer seine Studien über die Enstehung von hysterischen Symptomen. Auf Grund der von ihnen erlangten Ergebnisse errichtete Freud sein System psychokathartischer Behandlung und näherte sich damit seiner späteren bekannten Psychoanalyse. Diese entwickelte er 100 aus der Praxis. In den meisten Fällen wurde seine Aufmerksamkeit nämlich darauf gerichtet, daß bei dem Patienten jegliche krankhafte Erinnerung an vergangene Begebenheiten fehlte.

71 **Tätigkeit** activity
73 **Tatsachenbestand** state of affairs
74 **ebenso** likewise
79 **Gewebe** tissue
80 **zusammenhanglos** disconnected
82 **sich nähern** to approach
85 **sich hervortun** to excel
87 **Arzt** physician
87 **Bahnbrecher** pioneer
96 **Verbindung** connection
102 **richten** to direct
102 **jegliche** any
103 **krankhaft** pathological
103 **fehlen** to be lacking

Er erklärte dies, indem er annahm, solche Erinnerungen würden von einer stärkeren seelischen Kraft verdrängt. Um aber Heilung zu verschaffen, müßten diese krankheiterregenden Erinnerungen aus dem Unbewußten des Patienten entfernt werden. Sie müßten also erst wieder ins Bewußtsein gehoben werden, indem man die Kraft bricht, die sich in der Verdrängung kund gibt. Diese Erkenntnis lieferte die Grundlage der Psychoanalyse; die Anwendung selbst wird heute Psychiatrie genannt. Und, obwohl Freud mit seinem neuen Fund ungemein große Gegensätze in der wissenschaftlichen Welt hervorbrachte, haben sich eine immer größer wachsende Anzahl von Gelehrten in aller Herren Länder so ernstlich damit befaßt, daß man heutzutage von der Psychoanalyse als von einem neuen Lehrgebäude sprechen kann. 105 110 115

Unter den von Freud geschriebenen Werken über seine Arbeit sind besonders drei hervorzuheben: die berühmte Traumdeutung aus dem Jahre 1900, die Psychopathologie des Alltagslebens, 1901 und Drei Abhandlungen zur Sexualtheorie aus dem Jahre 1905. Das bekannteste darunter ist ohne Zweifel die Traumdeutung, ein Werk, das gewiß zu den umstrittensten der Neuzeit zu zählen ist. Wie Freud dazu kam, es zu schreiben, ist oben schon erwähnt worden. Noch zu erwähnen ist aber die Tatsache, daß ein großer Teil desselben stark autobiographisch ist; d.h. der Verfasser gibt seine eigenen Traumerlebnisse wieder, und zwar tut er das so offen und analytisch, daß dieses Werk einen ungemein wertvollen Beitrag zur Bekenntnisliteratur darstellt. Man hat mit Recht gesagt, dieses Buch ist ein ganz bemerkenswertes Werk. Manches darin Enthaltene ist ausführlich dargestellt, manches nur angedeutet oder unvollkommen ausgearbeitet. Freud selbst fügte späteren Ausgaben Material zu, das ihm von seinen vielfach ergebenen Schülern zur Verfügung gestellt wurde. Also ist es in dieser Hinsicht nicht mehr autobiographisch. Es verliert dadurch auch an Wert für den interessierten Leser. Wenn dieser sich ernstlich den Freud- 120 125 130 135

106 **Krankheit** disease
112 **Gegensatz** contrast
114 **Gelehrte** scientist, savant
116 **Lehrgebäude** science
117 **Werk** work
118 **hervorheben** to emphasize
122 **Zweifel** doubt
126 **Verfasser** author
128 **wertvoll** valuable
131 **ausführlich** in detail
132 **Ausgabe** edition
133 **vielfach** often

schen Quellen der Traumliteratur zuwenden will, so muß er deshalb oft zu den Schriften seiner Schüler greifen. Ganz besonders wichtig ist hier das von Steckel geschriebene Werk *Die Sprache des Traumes.* 140

Fragen wir uns endlich, was denn ein Traum eigentlich im Sinne Freuds ist, so erhalten wir als Antwort, daß er nicht das vom Schläfer ungewollt hervorgebrachte Traumgewebe darstellt, sondern etwas ganz Anderes. Er ist als Maske dessen zu betrachten, was der Träumer verbergen will. Eine Deutung kann 145 sich also nicht mit den tatsächlich erschienenen Bildgeweben befassen, sondern muß sich der tieferen Wahrheit des zu Verbergenden zuwenden. Einmal erschlossen hat der Traum für den Schläfer auch seine bestimmte Bedeutung. Meistens weist sie auf unterdrückte Wünsche, auf Verbotenes oder Gefühle der Liebe 150 oder des Hasses hin. Das gesamte niedere Empfindungsleben, welches den Menschen zum Verbrecher, Mörder oder sonstigen Übeltäter macht, bricht hervor. Dieses Emporbrechen ist die Widerspiegelung des niederen Selbst, ja, man sagt, des wahren Selbst. Die Deutung aber ist nicht immer leicht, denn die Traum- 155 bilder stellen oft die verzerrte Wahrheit dessen dar, was der Träumer verbergen will. Das ist eine seelische Schutzmaßnahme, die der Träumer unbewußt trifft, um sich gegen die Selbsterkenntnis, Scham und Schuldgefühl zu schützen. Die Verzerrung enthebt ihn des Verantwortungsgefühls in seinen eigenen Augen 160 und gibt ihm das Gefühl der Schuldlosigkeit, das er im Zustande des Wachens haben muß. Lastet das in seinem tiefsten Wesen schlummernde Schuldbewußtsein zu schwer auf ihm, oder wird es durch irgendwelche Begebenheiten verstärkt, so kann es sich zu einem seelischen Krankheitsbild entwickeln, das nur klinisch 165 zu deuten und behandeln ist.

Was Freud durch seine Forschungen erreicht hat, ist heute noch schwer zu sagen. Die Tatsache, daß die durch ihn gemachten Entdeckungen solch ungemein praktische Anwendung gefunden haben, läßt auf ausgesprochene soziale Werte hinweisen; die 170 Tatsache, daß so Vieles in seiner Lehre noch so stark umstritten ist, zeigt aber auch, daß die mit modernen experimentellen Mitteln

154 **Widerspiegelung** reflection
157 **Schutz** protection
160 **entheben** to relieve
164 **irgendwelche** some sort of

erforschte, tiefere seelische Welt des Menschen noch manches in sich birgt, was genauer zugänglich gemacht werden muß. Daß Psychoanalyse auch Übergang zu anderen noch tieferen geistigen 175 und seelischen Problemen sein kann, haben Forschungen auf anderen Gebieten der Psychologie schon zur Genüge bewiesen.

175 **Übergang** transition

CHAPTER 7

THE INFINITIVE

The student should be familiar with several kinds of infinitive constructions. Usually these may be divided into two larger groups — the infinitive without **zu** and that with **zu.** The former is less troublesome than the latter.

A. Infinitives without *zu*

1. The infinitive in the future tense is characterized by the fact that its finite verb is a present tense form of **werden.** The translation procedure which applies here is that of the main clause or simple statement. A common mistake, however, is that of translating a present passive construction as a future. The student should remember that the future tense contains an infinitive, whereas the passive construction contains a past participle.

Das werden wir im folgenden untersuchen.
We shall examine that in the following.

Das wird gegenwärtig von ihm untersucht.
That is being examined by him at present.

Moreover, the passive may change the respective form of **werden** to one of **wurde** in the past tense. The future uses **werden** only in the present tense.

2. When an infinitive is used with a modal auxiliary, it forms a compound tense and always occurs at or near the end of the clause, as does the future infinitive.

Das müssen wir noch einmal untersuchen.
We must examine that again.

3. The reflexive verb **sich lassen,** when used with an infinitive, is translated by *can be* and a past participle.

Das läßt sich dadurch gut bestimmen.
That can be well determined by this method.

The two most frequently used tense forms of this construction are set out below.

Present Tense: **Es läßt sich dadurch gut bestimmen.**
Past Tense: **Es ließ sich dadurch gut bestimmen.**

The persons most frequently used are the third singular and plural.

3rd Singular: **Es läßt sich dadurch gut bestimmen.**
3rd Plural: **Sie lassen sich dadurch gut bestimmen.**

B. Infinitives with *zu*

1. An infinitive used with **(an)statt** *instead of* or **ohne** *without* is translated into English by means of the . . .*ing* form.

Anstatt es sofort zu untersuchen, verschob er es bis auf den folgenden Tag.
Instead of examining it at once, he postponed it until the following day.

Ohne es noch einmal zu untersuchen, kam er zu demselben Schluß.
Without examining it again, he came to the same conclusion.

2. An infinitive used with **um** results in the so-called **um . . . zu** construction.

Um es noch einmal zu untersuchen, hieß er ihn, den Apparat aufstellen.
In order to examine it again, he asked him to set up the apparatus.

Several features of this construction should be noted. First, **um** may be omitted. E.g., **Es noch einmal zu untersuchen, ...** This gives constructions that are parallel to *in order to* and *to.* E.g., *in order to examine; to examine.* Second, the fact that **um** is often followed by a noun should not mislead the student into construing it as a preposition. Rather, he should determine the translation on the basis of the presence or absence of the **zu**-infinitive at the end of the construction. Infinitives given under (1) and (2) above are separated from the main clause by a comma.

3. The **zu**-infinitive that is dependent upon a preceding adjective.

Es ist noch nicht möglich, es endgültig zu bestimmen.
It is not yet possible to determine it definitely.

This infinitive will also usually be found separated from its main clause by a comma, except when **zu** and its infinitive are the only words in the construction.

Es ist nicht möglich zu arbeiten.
It is not possible to work.

The student should remember that since infinitives are by nature dependent, translation must begin with the infinitive at the end. E.g., *It is not yet possible to determine. . . .*

4. The construction that includes tense forms of **sein** plus the **zu**-infinitive may occur in either a main or a dependent clause. It may be translated in two ways.

is to be . . . (past participle)
must be . . . (past participle)

Das ist noch einmal zu untersuchen.
That is to be examined again.
That must be examined again.

The two tense forms of this construction that are most frequently used are the present and the past.

Present: **Es ist noch einmal zu untersuchen.**
Past: **Es war noch einmal zu untersuchen.**

The persons that are most frequently used in this construction are the third singular and the third plural.

3rd Singular: **Es ist noch einmal zu untersuchen.**
3rd Plural: **Sie sind noch einmal zu untersuchen.**

C. Translation Exercise

1. Wir wollen das allgemeine Wesen der Psychologie noch einmal besprechen. 2. Das allgemeine Wesen der Psychologie wird morgen noch einmal wiederholt. 3. Es wurde gestern besprochen. 4. Dazu muß man ganz genaue Kenntnisse haben. 5. Es war ihm nie ein leichtes, sich von dem Standpunkt der fortschrittlichen Wissenschaft zu trennen. 6. Alle diese Daten sind noch einmal zu prüfen. 7. Vieles ist noch in der Traumpsychologie zu untersuchen. 8. Ein Traum läßt sich nicht immer leicht deuten. 9. Oft ließen sich dieselben Schlüsse ziehen. 10. Alle Daten waren noch einmal zu durchlaufen.

D. Practical Review Questions

1. How can you differentiate a future tense from a present tense passive? 2. Can you usually translate a form of **wurde** in the passive as *became?* 3. In translation, what are the points of similarity between a future and a modal auxiliary construction that contains a complementary infinitive in the present tense? 4. What is the translation procedure for an **anstatt**-infinitive? For an **ohne**-infinitive? 5. What is the translation procedure for an **um zu**-infinitive? 6. In translating, why must you begin with the infinitive? 7. What are the two ways of translating a **sein**-infinitive? A **sich lassen**-infinitive? 8. Is it possible to translate the latter by: *It lets itself be . . .* ? 9. What two tense forms of the **sein**-infinitive and the **sich lassen**-infinitive are most frequently met with? 10. What persons are most commonly employed in these two constructions?

E. Seelenheilkunde im Kriege

Es ist augenblicklich noch nicht möglich, ein genaues Bild der Anwendung und Ergebnisse der Seelenheilkunde während des vergangenen Krieges zu geben. Einerseits sind alle maßgebenden Eindrücke noch zu frisch im Gemüt der Beteiligten, und anderseits sind diesbezügliche Daten noch unvollständig gesammelt und 5 deshalb ungenügend gedeutet. Da wir aber ein ziemlich zufriedenstellendes Bild in dieser Hinsicht vom ersten Weltkrieg besitzen, können wir dennoch eine vergleichende Studie unternehmen und so zu einigen Schlüssen kommen. Um zu diesem Punkt zu gelangen, wäre es dienstlich und wesentlich, beide 10 Kriege auf ihre allgemeinen Eigenschaften hin zu vergleichen.

Sofort fallen uns dabei gewisse Eigenschaften auf. Verglichen mit dem ersten Weltkrieg, welcher noch ziemlich lokalisiert war, wurde der zweite auf weit größeren geographischen Weiten ausgefochten. Ebenso ist zu beachten, daß Methoden und Instru- 15 mente der Kriegsführung sich radikal geändert haben. Folge davon ist, daß die unmittelbaren Ergebnisse sich ebenfalls von denen des ersten Weltkrieges unterscheiden. Das Element der

2 **Kunde** knowledge, science
4 **Beteiligte** participant
12 **auffallen** to come to one's attention

Zerstörung wurde quantitativ und qualitativ hervorgehoben. Dazu läßt sich hinzufügen, daß das Zeitelement eine unmittelbar weit wichtigere Bedeutung erlangt hat. Schlachten werden heutzutage schneller und intensiver ausgeführt. Tank, Geschoß, Flugzeug und Unterseeboot bewegen sich schneller. Früher war die Front im Schützengraben, heutzutage ist sie weit hinter ihnen und sogar bis in die Städte und unter die Zivilbevölkerung des Hinterlandes vorgedrungen. Folglich betrifft die Nervenanregung nicht mehr den einzelnen Soldaten auf dem Kampfplatz sondern die gesamte Bevölkerung. Anregungen haben sich also quantitativ vermehrt. Das statische Wesen der Kriegführung ist dynamisch geworden, was besonders gut durch die Art des Blitzkrieges veranschaulicht werden kann. Heutzutage ist niemand mehr sicher; das ist eine Tatsache, deren sich der Soldat sowie die Zivilperson bewußt geworden ist. Rückschlag dieses Bewußtseins hat bestimmte seelische Folgen gehabt: der Mensch lebt unter ständiger innerer Spannung, denn er fühlt sich bedroht; er lebt in Erwartung dessen, was kommen könnte; er lebt in Furcht.

Trotz dieser allgemeinen Aussagen aber hat es sich feststellen lassen, daß die Zivilbevölkerung weit besser unter dem Kriegsdruck ausgehalten hat als der Kampfsoldat. Der Grund dafür liegt zweifelsohne darin, daß die Zivilperson, der Bauer, Fabrikarbeiter und Angestellte keinen Zufluchtsort hatte, denn das ganze Hinterland war gleich schwer gefährdet. Resignation in die herrschende Lage führte wohl zu einer gewissen seelischen Entspannung, die der Kampfsoldat nicht kannte. Der Sinn des Aggressiven wurde ferner durch das Bewußtsein unterstrichen, daß das gesamte völkische Schicksal mit dem Ergebnis militärischer Aktion eng verknüpft war. Furcht vor Versklavung, der Wille, die Freiheit des Lebens zu erhalten und das Bewußtsein der Zusammengehörigkeit waren ohne Zweifel starke Anregungskräfte dafür.

Angesichts dieses Befundes wollen wir uns nun an die im Militär herrschenden Zustände wenden und versuchen, die Etiologie,

22 **ausführen** to carry out
26 **vordringen** to advance
31 **veranschaulichen** to illustrate
33 **Rückschlag** reaction
35 **ständig** steady
41 **zweifelsohne** without doubt
46 **unterstreichen** to emphasize
49 **erhalten** to preserve
52 **angesichts** in the face of
52 **Befund** finding

d.h. den Ursachenbestand zu verfolgen. Es wird zwar allgemein von Fachleuten zugegeben, daß Auswahlmaßnahmen während der ärztlichen Untersuchungen, welche beim Militäreintritt abgelegt werden müssen, weit erfolgreicher waren als beim ersten Weltkrieg; dennoch aber waren die auf seelischen Ursachen beruhenden Verlustlisten viel zu lang, um als über die Schulter betrachtet zu werden. Man hat daran gedacht, die Ursachen in einer Verweichlichung der Jugend u. dgl. zu suchen; aber vieles spricht dagegen. Trennung von der Familie und der dem Einzelnen vertrauten Umgebung, die straffe Militärzucht, der Mangel an Freiheit im Militärleben und die Furcht vor dem Unbekannten und dem Schrecken der modernen Kriegsführung stellen sich immer klarer als Gründe einer übergroßen Nervenspannung ein, die sich später unter tatsächlichen Kampfbedingungen in einer Nervenerschütterung auslöste. Das heißt mit anderen Worten, daß eine ursprüngliche Neigung zu Nervenkrankheit schon bestanden haben muß, ehe der Soldat eingezogen wurde. Das ist eine Aussage, welche natürlich in ihrer ganzen Tragweite nicht zu prüfen ist. Jedenfalls muß man dabei auch vor Augen halten, daß sogar ein sonst ganz normaler Mensch unter genug Druck ebenso zusammenbricht wie ein Soldat unter modernen Kampfzuständen. Es ist nur eine Frage, wieviel der menschliche Organismus aushalten kann. Man hat aber festgestellt, daß der Prozentsatz der durch eine Familienetiologie gekennzeichneten Nervenkranken größer war als der derjenigen, die keine familiengeschichtlichen Faktoren besaßen.

Wie macht die Kriegsnervenerschütterung sich nun bemerkbar? Was sind die Symptome und wie werden solche Fälle behandelt? Um die erste Frage beantworten zu können, müssen wir analytisch verfahren. So hat man feststellen können, daß im britischen Heer fast ein Drittel aller psychosomatischen Fälle auf Herzstörungen zurückzuführen waren. Während des ersten Weltkrieges waren es besonders Magen- und Darmkrankheiten, welche

54 **Bestand** condition
55 **Fachleute** experts
59 **Verlust** loss
62 **Trennung** separation
63 **Umgebung** environment
67 **tatsächlich** actual
68 **auslösen** to result in
69 **Neigung** inclination
71 **Tragweite** significance
76 **aushalten** to endure
76 **Prozentsatz** percentage
83 **verfahren** to proceed
85 **zurückführen** to trace back

die Aufmerksamkeit der Ärzte erregten. Darnach kamen die Zuckerkrankheit und der Kropf. Der zweite Weltkrieg brachte keine neuen Symptome, es sei denn, wir erwähnen die Psychorrhexis, bösartige Angstzustände, die sich besonders während des 90
spanischen Bürgerkriegs zeigte. Anstatt aber den Soldaten zu befallen, heftete sich diese Krankheit an den Zivilisten. Um diese Krankheit zu beschreiben, müssen wir uns einen Patienten vorstellen, wie er von Angstzuständen befallen wird, die sich zu völliger Ratlosigkeit entwickeln. Er besitzt wenig spontane 95
Handlungsfähigkeit, der Puls schlägt ständig höher als 120 Schläge pro Minute, der Druck der Rückgratsflüssigkeit vermehrt sich, ebenso die Körpertemperatur. Nach einer Woche wird der Patient unruhig, seine Bewegungen werden immer mehr automatisch und nach einigen weiteren Tagen endlich stirbt er. Die 100
während des zweiten Weltkrieges am zahlreichsten auftretenden seelischen Störungen im Heer waren Angstzustände. Klinische Anzeichen lassen es als wahrscheinlich erscheinen, daß diese eine viel größere seelische Tiefe offenbarten, als es früher der Fall war. Deshalb auch die größere Schwere der Erkrankung. Ohne auf 105
die seelische Verwickelung zu achten, glaubte man früher, derartige Nervenerschütterungen waren auf Gehirnverletzungen zurückzuführen; heute aber wissen wir, daß solche Ursachen in den wenigsten Fällen bestehen, und daß Nervenerschütterungen zumeist auf eine überempfindliche Natur, zu große Strapazen und 110
körperliche Erschöpfung zurückzuführen sind. Dazu kommt noch der tiefsitzende Wunsch nach Geborgenheit und Entfernung aus Gefahrslagen.

An diesem Punkt angelangt, werden wir auch die Behandlungsweisen berühren können. Aus dem Gesagten läßt sich folgern, 115
daß diese dementsprechend komplizierterer Art sind als während des ersten Weltkrieges, denn sie müssen verhältnismäßig tiefer in das menschliche Seelenleben greifen. Neue Methoden hat man zwar nicht erfunden, statt dessen sind die alten besser ausgebaut

87 **erregen** to stir up
92 **befallen** to attack
93 **beschreiben** to describe
93 **sich vorstellen** to imagine
103 **Anzeichen** sign, symptom
103 **wahrscheinlich** probable
104 **offenbaren** to reveal
106 **Verwicklung** complexity
106 **derartig** such
110 **zumeist** mostly
114 **anlangen** to arrive
115 **berühren** to touch
115 **folgern** to conclude
116 **dementsprechend** corresponding

worden. Während des ersten Weltkrieges pflegte man den Kranken aus der Gefahrszone zu entfernen. Ruhe, gutes Essen, Medikamente, sympathische Behandlung waren die Regel. Man beschäftigte den Patienten mit einfachen Arbeiten, die seinen Geist von der Krankheit ablenkten, indem man ihn im Krankenhaus oder draußen in der freien Luft anstellte. Wiedererziehung zu normaler Lebensweise war das Stichwort. Dasselbe kann aber auch gegenwärtig gesagt werden. Überredung soll Beruhigung verschaffen. Der Hypnotismus wird angewendet, um dem Patienten durch das Wiedererleben, die Katharsis, die Gelegenheit zu geben, seinen Geist und sein Nervensystem zu reinigen. Körperliche Übungen, künstliches Sonnenlicht und Gesellschaftsspiele werden demjenigen verschrieben, der unter physischer Erschöpfung leidet. Insulin wird angewendet, wenn es sich um Gewichtsverlust, eines der ersten Krankheitsanzeichen, handelt. Unter den verschiedenen feststellbaren Symptomen, welche das Herannahen oder auch das Bestehen der Krankheit melden, ist besonders das Tagträumen oder das Vorhandensein abstrakter Momente zu nennen. Dies ist an sich ein kritisches Moment und muß dementsprechend bekämpft werden. Es ist deshalb ratsam, den Patienten so schnell wie möglich vom Zustand des tiefen Schlafes durch die Übergangsperiode in den vollen Wachzustand zu bringen. Schlafstörungen werden durch Medikamente bekämpft, um dem Patienten so die Möglichkeiten zu nehmen, wiederholt die Schreckerlebnisse durchlaufen zu müssen. Demzufolge soll die Tagesbeschäftigung auch so eingerichtet sein, daß Arbeit mit Ruheperioden abwechseln, daß diese Ruheperiode aber zu keiner Schweigezeit wird, denn sie könnte zu Träumereien führen. Gemeinschaftssingen, Filmvorführungen, Lesen und Radioprogramme sollen solche Ruheperioden ausfüllen.

Einer der bemerkenswertesten Unterschiede in der angewandten Seelenheilkunde, so wie sie im ersten und zweiten Weltkrieg gepflegt wurde, ist die Einführung der Psychiatrie in die Kriegs-

120 **pflegen** to be accustomed to
124 **ablenken** to derive, to divert
125 **anstellen** to occupy
130 **Gelegenheit** opportunity
131 **Übung** exercise
131 **künstlich** artificial
132 **verschreiben** to prescribe
140 **ratsam** advisable
144 **wiederholen** to repeat
145 **einrichten** to arrange
153 **Einführung** introduction

führung. Sie ist zu einem besonderen Zweig der medizinischen Wissenschaft im Militärwesen gemacht und dementsprechend 155 organisiert worden. Ferner sind die Ergebnisse der Erfahrung und Theorie dazu gebraucht worden, daß man sie zur Grundlage dieser modernen aber dennoch so nötigen Behandlungsweise gemacht hat. Seelenkunde und Seelenheilkunde sind heute unumgänglich notwendige Instrumente der Kriegsführung ge- 160 worden.

Um aber dem Irrtum vorzubeugen, daß Seelenheilkunde im Krieg nur den Soldaten betrifft, wollen wir uns noch einmal vor Augen halten, daß der Zivilist derselben Gefahr ausgesetzt ist. Furcht vor materiellem Verlust, vor körperlicher Schädigung und 165 Tot sind ihm ebenso gegenwärtig wie dem Soldaten an und hinter der Front. Die Unterschiede, die der erste Weltkrieg zwischen dem Soldaten und der Zivilperson kannte, sind nicht mehr festzustellen. Zudem ist diese einem verstärkten sozialen Druck ausgesetzt, wie er früher nicht dagewesen ist. Dieser soziale Druck 170 ist ein neues Element, welches der Analyse unterzogen werden muß, ehe man zur Behandlung eines Zivilfalles vorschreiten kann. Es ergeben sich also wieder neue Ursachen, und es fragt sich, ob man deshalb auch neue Behandlungsmethoden wird erfinden und entwickeln müssen. Im Großen und Ganzen ist zu sagen, daß 175 die moderne Kriegsführung dazu beigetragen hat, ein neues Krankheitsbild zu schaffen oder, wenn nicht, dann doch ein schon bestehendes in verstärktem Maße ans Licht zu bringen. Unter dem Druck der modernen Lebensweise ist uns eine neue Gefahr erwachsen. 180

154 **besonder** special
157 **brauchen** to use
160 **unumgänglich** absolute
160 **notwendig** necessary
162 **vorbeugen** to prevent
169 **zudem** moreover
170 **dasein** to be present
171 **unterziehen** to subject to
172 **vorschreiten** to progress

CHAPTER 8

CERTAIN FEATURES OF VERBS

A. General Remarks about Tenses, Persons, and Numbers

The student will immediately discover that in all technical language, German included, more use is made of certain tenses than of others. Those most often employed are the present and the past. This is due to the fact that technical speech largely concerns itself with the description of conditions and procedures existing at the time of observation. The past is often used as an instrument of comparison between present and past statements of achievements, e.g., relating to historical aspects of scientific work. Likewise, because of the objective nature of scientific work and the description of it, the persons most often used are the third singular and the third plural. The student is urged to examine an excerpt from a German scientific article or treatise and so assure himself of these facts.

Many mistakes are made regarding the number of the nouns used, i.e., regarding the singular or plural of the noun. In this regard, correct observation of verbal endings will eliminate many errors. The student should remember that accuracy in the use of tenses and the number of nouns is a basic requisite for the effective reading of scientific German.

B. Separable Verbs

During his first year of German the student learned that the so-called separable verbs are actually separable in only the present and past tenses when these occur in a simple statement or main clause. This knowledge may now be turned to good use because the presence of a separable particle at the end of a simple statement or main clause reminds one that the meaning of the finite verb will have to be changed; i.e., the separable particle will have to be attached to the finite verb before the latter can be either translated or looked up in the dictionary. Otherwise the translation procedure is similar to that having to do with the compound verb in a simple statement or main clause.

Es {kommt / kam} nur unter besonderen Bedingungen {vor. / vor.}

It {occurs / occurred} only under certain conditions.

There are instances, however, when the student will find verbal adjuncts removed from their final position and brought nearer the finite verb. Occasionally, verbal adjuncts, especially prepositions, infinitives, and past participles, occur directly after the finite verb. This is likely to lead the student to believe that the German word order is identical with that of the English.

Das sieht aus wie eine neue Art.
That looks like a new species.

Das Ergebnis wurde erzielt under besonderen Bedingungen.
The result was obtained under special conditions.

C. Verbs Followed by Certain Prepositions

Ordinarily a verb may be followed by any prepositional phrase, the choice of the latter depending only upon the need of expression. There are certain verbs, however, which must be followed by certain prepositions if they are to express the correct meaning. Compare, for example, English *to think about* and *to think of*. The same may be said about certain German verbs. For example: **abhängen von** *to depend upon*, **anwenden an** *to apply to*, **sich interessieren für** *to interest oneself in*, and many others.

Das hängt von dem Druck und der Temperatur ab.
That depends upon the pressure and temperature.

The important point for the student to keep in mind is that he must not translate the prepositions of such verbs literally, but rather choose the correct English preposition.

D. Imperatives

Usually, imperatives are not met with in technical German except for the following forms:

1. **Es sei(en)** . . . (past participle).

    Es seien nur drei Arten davon genannt.
    Let us mention only three species of them.

2. The third person singular of the present tense subjunctive.

    Man bedenke, daß es sich nicht darum handelt.
    One should realize that it is not a question of that.

3. The inverted first person plural of the present tense.

    Untersuchen wir zuerst die Wirkung der Temperatur.
    Let us first examine the effect of temperature.

In translating the last-mentioned form of the imperative, the student will often find a source of error by translating such a construction by *If*. . . . The difference is, however, easily recognized. The imperative form occurs only in a simple statement or a main clause, whereas the *if* . . . form appears in a dependent clause and is followed by a **so**-clause.

Untersuchen wir dies zuerst.
Let us examine this first.

Untersuchen wir dies zuerst, so finden wir, daß . . .
If we examine this first, we find that . . .

E. Translation Exercise

1. Man stelle sich die ganze Sache anders vor. 2. Er bereitete sich durch jahrelange Arbeit auf seinen Beruf vor. 3. Die Annahme wurde bewiesen durch zahlreiche Versuche. 4. Er war nur darauf bedacht, seine Arbeit gut auszuführen. 5. Wir befassen uns nun mit der Einwirkung des Druckes und der Temperatur auf diese Flüssigkeit. 6. Das beruht auf einer ganz anderen Annahme. 7. Seine Studien gestalteten sich zu einem großen Werk. 8. Es sei noch einmal erwähnt, daß wir mit einer Annahme arbeiten. 9. Man stelle sich vor, daß dies die Wirkung der Temperature ist. 10. Schreiten wir nun zur

Untersuchung der Bodenzusammensetzung vor. 11. Schreiten wir nun zu dieser Aufgabe vor, so fällt uns auf, daß wir mit einer allgemeinen Annahme arbeiten.

F. Practical Review Questions

1. What tenses are most often used in technical German? 2. What persons are most often used? 3. What does the presence of a so-called *dangling* particle at the end of a simple statement or main clause indicate? 4. How do you solve this problem in translation? 5. Will such or other verbal adjuncts always be found at the end of the clause? 6. How do you proceed when translating certain verbs which must be followed by certain prepositions? 7. What are the three imperative forms which may occur in technical German? 8. How do you translate each?

G. Ursachen und Verhütung des Verbrechens

Das Gebiet der Kriminologie stellt ein verhältnismäßig großes und in gewisser Beziehung nicht gut definierbares Arbeitsfeld dar, denn es befaßt sich mit der Natur des Menschen, welche an und für sich ein großer und verzweigter Fragenkomplex ist, sowie des Menschen Umgebung. Diese muß ebenfalls in ihrer ganzen 5 Verwickeltheit und in Beziehung zu den biologischen, physiologischen und seelischen Seiten des Menschen betrachtet werden. Schlechthin gesagt ist die Kriminologie die Lehre vom Verbrechen, von der wissenschaftlichen Erforschung des Verbrechens in seinen inneren Ursachen und äußeren Erscheinungen. Das Wort Kri- 10 minologie ist der Inbegriff aller kriminalistischen Sondergebiete. Es seien nur einige davon genannt: die Kriminalanthropologie, die Kriminalbiologie, die Kriminalpsychopathologie, die Kriminalpsychologie, die Kriminalsoziologie, u.a.m.

Untersuchen wir einiges über die Geschichte der Kriminologie, 15 ehe wir uns der Studie der Ursachen und Verhütung zuwenden. Die Kriminologie an sich ist noch ziemlich jung. Sie reicht mit ihren modernen Anfängen nur bis ins 18. Jahrhundert zurück und machte sich damals in Italien fühlbar, später auch in Deutsch-

11 **Inbegriff** epitome
16 **Verhütung** prevention
19 **fühlbar** felt

land, wo sie zuerst von Feuerbach verlangt und von Hans Groß gefördert wurde. Es seien die wichtigsten Schulen und Theorien kurz erwähnt. Die erste geschichtliche Schule, wenn man sie so nennen kann, befaßte sich mit dem Gedanken, daß der Verbrecher zum Verbrechen geboren sei. Dieser Gedanke beruht auf darwinistischer Grundlage und gab Anstoß zu einem Sondergebiet der Kriminologie, nämlich der Kriminalanthropologie. Der Hauptvertreter dieser Schule ist Cesare Lombroso, der die Ansicht vertrat, daß gewisse Menschen als Rückschläge oder auf primitiver sogar tierischer Stufe Zurückgebliebene zu betrachten sind. Man könne dies an gewissen Körpereigenschaften, den sog. Verbrechermerkmalen (stark fliehende Stirn, stark hervorspringende Backenknochen, Unregelmäßigkeiten an den Schädelknochen, usw.) erkennen. Natürlich werden derartige biologische Ursachen von neuzeitlichen Kriminologen abgelehnt. Eine noch frühere Schule, die ohne Zweifel bis ins Mittelalter zurückzuführen ist, vertrat den Standpunkt, daß es das vererbte Sündliche im Menschen sei, welches ihn zum Verbrecher werden läßt. Ein radikaler Bruch mit allen veralteten Anschauungen kam aber erst mit Lombroso, der zum erstenmal in seinem Werk L'uomo delinquente (1876) die Notwendigkeit aussprach, daß man in der Erforschung des Verbrechens nicht nur den Verbrecher sondern auch die in ihm liegende Persönlichkeit studieren müsse. Einige seiner Anhänger gingen sogar so weit zu behaupten, es gäbe auch besondere von Geburt gekennzeichnete Arten von Verbrechern. Die Arbeiten Gorings aber lehnten derartige Annahmen entschieden ab. Goring, ein Engländer, war Dr. Griffith, einem Gefängnisleiter, als Nachfolger gefolgt und setzte dessen Forschungen über die Frage fort, ob es denn wirklich ausgesprochene Kriminaltypen gebe oder nicht. Der einzige positive Befund Gorings war, daß Verbrecher im allgemeinen vier bis fünf cm kleiner und drei bis sieben Pf. leichter als andere Menschen waren. Auch vermutete er stark, daß sie geistig minderwertig waren, konnte es aber nicht beweisen, da man damals moderne psychologische Verfahren noch nicht zur Verfügung hatte. Nichtsdestoweniger

21 **fördern** to further
27 **Ansicht** opinion
28 **Rückschlag** reversion
29 **Stufe** level
34 **neuzeitlich** modern
38 **Bruch** fraction, break
38 **veralten** to become obsolete
52 **minderwertig** below normal
54 **nichtsdestoweniger** nevertheless

war es erfreulich, daß die Meinungsverschiedenheiten, die sich aus den sogenannten italienischen und englischen Schulen ergaben, zur Annahme der Theorie führten, die Ursachen des Verbrechens seien in einer Vielheit von Umständen und Lagen zu suchen. 55

Diese Vielheitstheorie kann in einigen ihrer Bestandteile erforscht werden. Wenden wir uns diesen zu. Vier Gesichtspunkte werden darin betrachtet: der biologische, primär soziale, sekundär soziale und der Persönlichkeitsfaktor. Der erste Faktor wird heutzutage in der Kriminalbiologie vertreten und hat sich als solcher aus der Kriminalanthropologie, Kriminalpsychologie und der Biologie entwickelt. Man kann sagen, er stellt ein Sondergebiet der Biologie dar und befaßt sich mit dem Wesen und der Entwicklung der Verbrecherpersönlichkeit, greift also entschieden in den vierten Gesichtspunkt über. Ja, in der deutschen Auffassung dieses Begriffs sind beide Faktoren zusammen enthalten, während hier in Amerika beide getrennt voneinander betrachtet werden. Der deutschen Auffassung nach verwertet die Kriminalbiologie das ganze physische und seelische Leben des Verbrechers zur Erkenntnis seiner Persönlichkeit. Diese wird wieder als Gesamtbild aller ererbten und erworbenen Eigenschaften angesehen. Klarer umrissen stellt sie dar die Zusammenfassung aller schon gegebenen Tatsachen bezüglich obengenannter Eigenschaften und orientiert sie in der Richtung einer wirkungsvollen Behandlung. Sie zergliedert die Einstellung des Täters zur Tat und nimmt in Betracht nicht nur Beweggründe und sonstige seelische Erscheinungen, sondern auch die Gesellschaftsordnung und die Art und Wirkungsweise der im Lande waltenden Gesetze. Mit anderen Worten, sie ist in ihrem Wesen ein breites Gebiet und umfaßt, was wir hier in Amerika auch mit Kriminalpsychologie und Kriminalsoziologie bezeichnen. Hier hat man das Problem der Kriminalbiologie lösen wollen, indem man die Sterilisation anwendet. Diese scheint man als das wirksamste Mittel anzuerkennen, das Verbrechen im Zaume zu halten; es sei denn, man berücksichtigt die Aussonderung geistig minderwertiger Verbrecher und deren Überweisung an Heil- und Irrenanstalten. 60 65 70 75 80 85

58 **Vielheit** multiplicity
58 **Umstand** circumstance
67 **übergreifen** to reach over
75 **Zusammenfassung** summary
77 **orientieren** to orient
77 **wirkungsvoll** effective
78 **zergliedern** to analyze
79 **Beweggrund** motive
80 **Gesellschaft** society
81 **walten** to prevail

Vom biologischen Standpunkt gesehen vertritt Patrizi den Gedanken, kriminelle Neigungen seien oft auf emotionelle Verwirrungen zurückzuführen, die ihren Ursprung wiederum in einem zu stark entwickelten Egoismus haben. Auch gibt man den Ansichten der Psychoanalytiker angemessene Berücksichtigung, die sich darauf stützen, daß geistige Konflikte, deren Wurzeln im Sexualen zu suchen sind, kriminelle Neigungen begünstigen. Hier spielt folglicherweise das Persönlichkeitsproblem hinein. Schenken wir nun den Faktoren der primären sozialen Gestaltungskraft unsere Aufmerksamkeit, so erkennen wir sofort, daß in Deutschland ungefähr dieselben Elemente als verbrechensbegünstigend angesehen werden wie hier in Amerika: die Familie, Gesellschaftskreise, physische Umgebung, Lebensweise, usw., während die sekundären Erscheinungen mit dem Geschäftsleben und seinen darin enthaltenen Bräuchen, dem Gesetzsystem und seinem damit verbundenen Strafverfahren, usw. zu tun haben. Das letztere enthält dann auch das Wesen der Polizei- und Gerichtsbestechlichkeit. Überblicken wir aber noch einmal die verschiedenen Ursachen, von denen noch lange nicht alle aufgeführt worden sind, so können wir eine ziemlich klare Zweiteilung vornehmen: Ursachen, die im Täter selbst wurzeln und solche, die sich aus der Situation heraus entwickeln. Das heißt, unsere neuzeitliche Auffassung ist einfach eine Kombination der Kriminalanthropologie Lombrosos und der gegen Ende des 19. Jahrhunderts waltenden Anschauung, Verbrechen seien gänzlich auf die Umwelt zurückzuführen.

Es seien nun einige Methoden genannt, welche augenblicklich in unserem Kriminalwesen Anwendung gefunden haben. Die am breitesten gebrauchte ist wohl die ins Einzelne gehende Buchführung; d.h. man hat die Weisheit der Italiener anerkannt, die schon vor mehreren Jahrzehnten die Forderung erhoben, man solle alle Tatsachen sammeln, welche auf den Verbrecher und das Verbrechen Bezug haben. Und heutzutage befaßt man sich demgemäß mit solchen Tatsachen wie der Einwirkung des Wetters, den Beziehungen zwischen Festnahmen und Verurteilungen, den

91 **Neigung** inclination, tendency
94 **Berücksichtigung** consideration
96 **begünstigen** to favor
102 **Lebensweise** standard of living
107 **überblicken** to survey
108 **aufführen** to cite
110 **wurzeln** to root
120 **Forderung** demand

Einwirkungen ökonomischer Elemente auf den Menschen, und 125
einer Unmasse anderer Tatsachen, welche alle zusammen ein
umfangreiches Bild geben sollen. Eine natürliche Folge davon
ist, daß sich allmählich die Methode des Studiums des Einzelfalles
herausgearbeitet hat. Zwar ist diese wirkungsvoll, da sie oft, und
besonders im Falle jugendlicher Verbrecher, bis in die Familie 130
hineinreicht; es spricht aber dagegen, daß sie langsam sein muß
und infolge der wenigen zur Verfügung stehenden Facharbeiter
nur eine verhältnismäßig kleine Anzahl von Einzelfällen berühren
kann. Man hat also auch zu anderen Behandlungsmethoden
greifen müssen. So hat man von Reform, Wiedererziehung, 135
handwerklicher Ausbildung von Strafgefangenen und anderen
Mitteln Gebrauch gemacht. Am wirksamsten aber hat sich die
Verhütung des Verbrechens vor der Tat erwiesen. Man bedenke,
daß ein Verbrecher, der aus einer ungünstigen Umgebung kommt
und wieder nach seiner Strafentlassung in dieselbe hineinversetzt 140
wird, mit allen denjenigen Faktoren zu kämpfen hat, welche aus
ihm anfänglich einen Verbrecher gemacht haben. Die Möglichkeit besteht stark, daß er sich zum Gewohnheitsverbrecher entwickelt. Man hat in dieser Beziehung zwei große Anhaltspunkte
gefunden: soziale Arbeit unter der delinquenten Jugend und den 145
Umbau sozialer Elendsquartiere. Ferri, welcher der italienischen
Schule angehört, schlägt auch noch einen anderen vor, nämlich
die Eliminierung derjenigen Faktoren, welche allgemein sozial
verbrechenbegünstigend sind, wie Herabsetzung des Alkoholver-
brauchs, Verminderung der täglichen Arbeitsstunden, die Fort- 150
schaffung des Metallgeldes, niederen Zinsfuß auf Geldanleihen,
usw. Diese und ähnliche will er durch Förderung solcher Faktoren
ersetzt sehen wie Freihandel, Gebrauch von Papiergeld, bessere
Beleuchtung von Häusern, öffentlichen Plätzen und Straßen,
politische Lokalreform und viele andere Neuerungen. Soziale 155
Arbeit unter der Jugend scheint umso leichter, als man sie in
Verbindung mit Schulverwaltungen ausführen kann, und auch,

126 **Unmasse** great mass of
131 **hineinreichen** to reach into
142 **anfänglich** at the beginning
144 **Anhaltspunkt** point of attack
146 **Umbau** reconstruction
146 **Elendsquartier** slum
149 **Herabsetzung** decrease
150 **Fortschaffung** elimination
153 **ersetzen** to replace
154 **öffentlich** public
155 **Neuerung** reform
157 **Verwaltung** administration

als man sich bewußt ist, daß die moralischen Veranlagungen des jugendlichen Verbrechers noch in plastischer Ausbildung begriffen sind. Neuerdings ist man auch dazu vorgeschritten, durch öffentliche und kirchliche Zensur das Kino zu reformieren. Demgegenüber ist der Umbau sozialer Elendsquartiere oft auf großen Widerstand gestoßen, denn viele schon bestehende Geschäftsinteressen sehen sich in ihrem Lebensunterhalt gefährdet und versuchen oft, den Umbau zu verhindern. Um diese Situation zu umgehen, ist man oft gesetzlich vorgegangen und hat auch gute Erfolge erzielt. 160 165

Im Großen und Ganzen muß man sich aber vor Augen behalten, daß Methoden der Verhütung in enger Verbindung stehen mit den Ursachen des Verbrechens und daß beide praktisch angegriffen werden können; Ursachen kann man durch soziale oder biologische Maßnahmen beseitigen, sodaß eine erwünschte Besserung im Laufe der Zeit erzielt werden kann. Vieles wird heutzutage in dieser Beziehung getan und auch erzielt. Der Fortschritt von den ersten Anfängen der Kriminologie, so wie sie uns Lombroso gegeben hat, bis in die Gegenwart hinein, wo wir mit allerhand wissenschaftlichen Mitteln und Methoden vorgehen, ist dennoch ein vielversprechender. 170 175

158 **Veranlagung** disposition

173 **erzielen** to achieve

CHAPTER 9

THE SUBJUNCTIVE

The subjunctive appears in technical German only in particular instances. These may be divided into two groups: (1) certain phrases and (2) certain situations.

1. Except for the last phrase in the following list, these should be known from Chapter 8.

(a) **Es sei(en) . . .** (past participle)
(b) **Man bedenke, daß . . .**
(c) **Untersuchen wir . . .** (wir-imperative)
(d) **Es sei denn, daß . . .** *unless*

2. The following subjunctive constructions, which are frequently met with in technical German, should be recognized immediately.

(a) Translation of indirect discourse subjunctives should cause the student little trouble, since English usually uses the indicative.

Er berichtete, daß der Mageninhalt nur Pflanzenreste gewesen wären.
He reported that the stomach content had been only plant remains.

(b) The present contrary-to-fact construction occurs in all its variations of form but is a source of trouble only when the first conditional appears in its modified form, i.e., the simple past subjunctive.

Conditional

Wenn es sich so verhielte, (so) würde man nichts davon bemerken können.
If this were the case, one would not be able to notice anything about it.

Simple Past Subjunctive

Wenn es sich so verhielte, könnte man nichts davon bemerken.

If the simple statement or main clause contains a simple past subjunctive, translate by *would* . . . (*infinitive*). The example above would be translated thus: *If this . . . , one would not be able to. . . .* Similarly, if the simple statement or dependent clause contains a past perfect subjunctive, translate by *would have* . . . (*past participle*). Accordingly, the example above would be translated in the past time thus: *If this had been the case, one would not have been able to. . . .*

A. Translation Exercise

1. Es sei daran erinnert, daß es noch andere Fälle dieser Art gibt. 2. Man verfahre immer in derselben Art und Weise. 3. Wenden wir uns zuerst der Hand des Menschen zu. 4. Der Mageninhalt besteht fast ausschließlich aus Pflanzenresten, es sei denn, daß Sauerstoffmangel die Pflanzen zum Absterben brachte. 5. Diese Angaben besagten, daß die Zahlenwerte viel zu hoch gewesen wären. 6. Man würde sie besser untersuchen, wenn man bessere Instrumente hätte. 7. Man verwechsele die Kolonien nicht mit den Kratzern, die in dem Glase oft benutzter Platten sind. 8. Man bekäme ganz andere Ergebnisse, wenn man die bekratzten Platten zum Experiment benützte. 9. Wenn man die bekratzten Platten zum Experiment benützte, würde man ganz andere Ergebnisse bekommen. 10. Wenn man die Brucellus Kolonien eher zum Absterben gebracht hätte, so würde man nicht die eigenartigen Ränder derselben haben beobachten können. 11. Man hätte alles besser beobachten können.

B. Practical Review Questions

1. What are the four subjunctive phrases which are most likely to occur in technical German? 2. Analyze each for its characteristic features so that you will recognize them when you see them. 3. Under what circumstances can you expect indirect discourse to appear in technical readings? 4. How do you handle it when translating? 5. What is the most complicated subjunctive form that is to be found in technical readings?

6. Analyse a complete contrary-to-fact expression in the present. In the past. 7. In translating, how do you treat each when the conditional has been replaced by the subjunctive?

C. Der Fingerabdruck, Geschichte und Anwendung

Aus den Versuchen der menschlichen Gesellschaft, das Verbrechen zu bekämpfen und so weit wie möglich zu verhüten, haben sich verschiedene Maßnahmen ergeben, die man im Laufe der Zeit angewandt hat. Das wirksamste ist immer das gewesen, welches mit der Erkennung und Wiedererkennung der einzelnen 5 Verbrecher zu tun hat. Dies ist der Fingerabdruck. Machen wir zuerst einige allgemeine Bemerkungen über den Tatsachenbestand, ehe wir uns seiner Geschichte zuwenden. Das Wort Fingerabdruck wird auch in seiner griechischen Form Daktyloskopie gebraucht und bedeutet die Wissenschaft vom Haut- 10 relief der Finger einschl. der Hand und im Grunde genommen auch der Fußballen. Man berichtet, diese Erkenntnis wäre zuerst von der Anthropologie angewandt worden, die sie zum Festlegen gewisser Tatsachen und Daten verwendet hätte. Wie dem auch sei, man erkannte bald, daß sie sich auch vorzüglich in 15 der Kriminologie gebrauchen ließe. Folglicherweise begann man, mit ihr zu arbeiten, und heute hat sie sich universalen Ruf erworben. Es wäre für unsere Betrachtungen vorteilhaft, wenn wir etwas über die Physiologie der Hauteigenschaften der Finger sagten. Wie bekannt, haben sich bei den Affen und Menschen 20 an den Sohlen, Händen und Fingerspitzen sogenannte Tastlinien ausgebildet. Das sind bestimmte Linien, welche sich aus vielen Tausenden von mikroskopisch kleinen Mündungen der Schweißporen formen. Und untersuchen wir sie näher, so finden wir, daß diese Linien sich zu ganz bestimmten Mustern, zu Schleifen, 25 Wirbeln, Spiralen und Triaden (Dreistrahlen) zusammentun. Man wende sich z.B. der Daumenspitze, der Kleinfingerballen und anderen gewissen Stellen an der Hand zu und man wird sie dort besonders zahlreich vertreten finden. Daß diese Linien sich nicht während der Lebensdauer des Menschen bilden, daß sie 30

2 **verhüten** to prevent
7 **Tatsachenbestand** state of affairs
11 **einschl.** inclusive of
17 **Ruf** reputation
18 **vorteilhaft** advantageous
22 **Linie** line
23 **Mündung** opening
25 **Muster** pattern
27 **Spitze** tip
28 **Stelle** place

sich während dieser ganzen Zeit nicht verändern, ist bekannte Tatsache. Ja, es wird uns berichtet, sie seien schon beim Embryo vorhanden und blieben dann nach Zahl und Gestalt konstant. Bestimmte Forschungen haben auch ergeben, daß die verschiedenen Muster sich zu gewissen Gruppen klassifizieren lassen. 35 Demnach wäre es möglich, bestimmte Muster oder deren Kombinationen mit bestimmten Menschen zu assoziieren. Die Kombinationsmöglichkeiten sind natürlich äußerst groß; so erfahren wir aus betreffenden Quellen, daß diese bei den Triaden allein sich auf viele Millionen belaufen. 40

Während, wie schon oben gesagt wurde, solche Finger- Hand- und Fußlinien früher allein von den Anthropologen angewandt wurden, um darin ganz bestimmte Merkmale zu erkennen, die für ihre Arbeit von Wichtigkeit waren, ist die wirksamste Anwendung heutzutage im Polizeiwesen zu suchen. Da hat die 45 Wissenschaft der Fingerabdrücke das sogenannte früher allgemein gebrauchte System Bertillon verdrängt. Es seien die bedeutsamsten Tatsachen dieses so berühmten Systems erwähnt. Alphonse Bertillon wurde 1853 in Paris geboren; er starb 1914, nachdem er sich jahrelang ethnographischen und anthropologischen 50 Studien gewidmet hatte. 1880 wurde er Chef der Pariser Polizeipräfektur und während er im Polizeidienst stand, entwickelte er das nach ihm genannte Erkennungssystem. Er selbst berichtet in seinen Werken, von denen das wichtigste wohl die Identification anthropométrique. Instructions signalétiques aus 55 dem Jahre 1893 ist, daß sein System aus einer großen Anzahl von Körpermessungen bestünde. Dazu kämen noch genaue Beschreibungen des Gesichts und aller sonstigen körperlichen Eigentümlichkeiten. Das System beruhe auf der Erkenntnis, daß das ganze Längenverhältnis aller Knochen eines Menschen vom 20. Lebens- 60 jahr an konstant ist. Es ist für je zwei Menschen nie das gleiche. Bertillon berichtet ferner, daß die Anwendung seines Systems genaue Messungen von Körperlänge, Sitzhöhe, Kopflänge und -breite, Jochbogenbreite, Länge des linken Ohres und des linken Fußes, des linken Mittelfingers, kleinen Fingers sowie des linken 65

32 **berichten** to report
38 **äußerst** extremely
39 **sich belaufen auf** to amount to
47 **verdrängen** to replace
50 **jahrelang** for years
50 **sich widmen** to devote oneself to
58 **sonstig** other
58 **Eigentümlichkeit** peculiarity

Vorderarms verlange. Über all diese Daten werde genau Buch geführt. Es wäre zu eingehend, wenn wir uns den Einzelheiten einer solchen Buchführung zuwendeten. Es sei nur erwähnt, daß Bertillons System seit 1890 bei allen größeren Kriminalämtern eingeführt worden war, aber, wie schon gesagt, neuerdings fast 70 ganz durch das schnellere und sogar noch genauere System des Fingerabdruckes ersetzt worden ist.

Wenden wir uns nun der Geschichte des Fingerabdruckes zu, so werden wir dadurch erstaunt, daß sich nur verhältnismäßig wenig Material daraus ergibt. Was man aber auch findet, scheint 75 auf die große Möglichkeit hinzudeuten, daß er schon in grauer Vorzeit als äußerst wichtig erkannt worden war. Man würde es für kaum glaublich halten, daß sich Anzeichen des frühen Gebrauches des Fingerdruckes hier in Amerika schon unter den Eingeborenen vorgefunden haben sollen. Dem ist aber so, denn in 80 Nova Scotia befindet sich ein Handabdruck an einer Felsenseite. Dieser zeigt recht sichtbar nicht nur die Umrisse der Hand sondern auch parallel gelegene Linien auf der Handoberfläche, die anscheinend die sogenannten Tastlinien vorstellen. Daneben sieht man auch unregelmäßige Linien, ohne Zweifel die schon erwähnten 85 Spiralen vorstellend. Auf dem Daumenballen ist eine solche Spirale ganz besonders klar eingeritzt, andere sind auf drei anderen Fingern wenigstens angegeben. Anthropologen bestätigen, daß diese Abdrücke bis in die Zeit vor der Ankunft des weißen Mannes hineinreichen, daß sie also bis auf die Ureinwohner zurückgeführt 90 werden müssen. Auch in China hat man aus Lehm angefertigte Siegel gefunden, die im zweiten Jahrhundert v. Chr. gemacht sein müssen. Eines dieser Siegel befindet sich gegenwärtig im Field Museum in Chicago. Es wird berichtet, dieses Siegel besitze vollkommen scharfe Umrisse und zeige die Linien der Hand tief in 95 den Lehm hineingedrückt. Man ist also berechtigt anzunehmen, daß dieser Abdruck in Absicht gewisser Zwecke gemacht worden sei, daß es sich also kaum um zufällig Hervorgebrachtes handeln

66 **verlangen** to demand
67 **eingehend** detailed
67 **Einzelheit** detail
70 **einführen** to introduce
76 **hindeuten** to point to
78 **Anzeichen** sign
82 **Umriß** outline
83 **Oberfläche** surface
84 **vorstellen** to represent
84 **daneben** besides this
88 **angeben** to indicate
88 **bestätigen** to confirm
91 **anfertigen** to make
96 **berechtigt** reasonable
98 **zufällig** accidental

könne. Aber nicht nur auf Siegeln hat man Fingerabdrücke gefunden, auch alte Dokumente tragen sie. So entdeckte z.B. Sir Aurel Stein, der englische Forscher, eine ganze Anzahl derselben in unter Sand begrabenen Städten im östlichen Turkestan. Darunter hat man Kontrakte entdeckt, bei denen es sich um Geldanleihen handelt. Sie datieren aus dem Jahr 782 n.Chr. und besagen ausdrücklich, daß Leiher und Leihender ihre Fingerabdrücke zum Zeichen ihrer kontraktuellen Verbindlichkeit gemacht hätten. Eines der drei in Frage kommenden Dokumente besagt ferner, daß es auch die Fingerabdrücke der Frau und Tochter des Leihers trage, was uns übrigens einen klaren Einblick in die schon damals übliche gerichtliche Verbindlichkeit gibt. In die neuere Zeit kommend wissen wir ferner, daß ein Landverkaufskontrakt aus dem Jahre 1839 ebenfalls einen solchen bindenden Fingerabdruck trägt. Man bedenke, der Gebrauch des Fingerabdruckes unter anderen Völkern ist schon wenigstens über zweitausend Jahre alt! Wie dem auch sei, der erste Europäer, der sich mit dem Liniensystem auf der menschlichen Hand beschäftigt hat, war Nehemia Grew, ein Arzt, welcher 1684 zum erstenmal eine Vorlesung darüber gab. Zwei Jahre darnach gab der bekannte Marcello Malpighi, der bekannte Professor der Anatomie an der Universität Bologna, eine ähnliche Beschreibung der Hand- und Fingerlinien, so wie er sie unter dem Mikroskop gesehen und beobachtet hatte. Von diesem Datum bis zum nächsten, das uns weitere Angaben liefert, sind es über achtzig Jahre. Um 1770 fertigt Thomas Bewick, ein englischer Verfasser und Holzschnitzer, seine eigenen Holzschnitte an, die seine eigenen Fingerabdrücke zwecks Handelszeichen tragen. Von nun an vermehren sich Verfertigungen und Anwendungen verschiedener Arten dieses Erkennungszeichen. Tatsächliche Verwendung aber ist Dr. Henry Faulds, einem schottischen Arzt in Tokio, Japan, zuzuschreiben. Er schrieb die erste wissenschaftliche Abhandlung über die Identifizierung von Verbrechern, welche am 28. Oktober 1880 in der englischen Zeitschrift „Nature" veröffentlicht

105 **ausdrücklich** positively, expressly
108 **besagen** to state
109 **übrigens** by the way
110 **üblich** customary
118 **Vorlesung** lecture
123 **weiter** additional
126 **zwecks** for the purpose of
130 **Abhandlung** treatise
132 **veröffentlichen** to publish

wurde. Darin stellt er die Behauptung auf, daß keine zwei Fingerabdrücke gleich wären und daß sie folglicherweise nie miteinander verwechselt werden könnten. Die gesamte polizeiliche Anwendung heutzutage geht auf folgenden Satz zurück, daß, wenn blutige Fingerzeichen oder Abdrücke sich auf Glas, Lehm, und anderen glatten oder plastischen Oberflächen befinden, sie zur wissenschaftlichen Identifizierung von Verbrechern gebraucht werden können. 135 140

Schon zwanzig Jahre früher hatte ein anderer Engländer, Sir William Herschel, ein höherer Verwaltungsbeamter in Indien, Fingerabdrücke zwecks Identifizierung von Gefangenen in Gefängnissen gebraucht. Vom Fangen einzelner Verbrecher aber war bei ihm keine Frage. Dieser Vorschlag ist das Verdienst Faulds'. Klassifizierung der verschiedenen Linien kam aber erst später mit der Arbeit wieder eines anderen Briten, Sir Francis Galton, der 1892 eine Schrift veröffentlichte, worin sich die Wiedergabe einer durch einen Fingerabdruck beglaubigten Geldübertragung befindet. Die betreffende Summe war mit Tinte in den Fingerabdruck hineingeschrieben. Wir werden ferner unterrichtet, daß es der bekannte Samuel L. Clemens (Mark Twain) gewesen sei, welcher das Fingerabdrucksysstem von England nach den Vereinigten Staaten übertrug. In seinem berühmten Roman Puddinhead Wilson vertritt er dann auch öffentlich die Meinung, das System sei wissenschaftlich zuverlässig und könne in Gerichtsfällen gebraucht werden. Die erste tatsächliche Anwendung in den Vereinigten Staaten aber wurde erst im Jahre 1903, und zwar in den Gefängnissen des Staates New York, gemacht. Ein Jahr später wurde es dann in dem Gefängnis zu Leavenworth, Kansas, angewandt. Es sei noch erwähnt, daß die Sammlung von Fingerabdrücken, die man unter dem Bertillon System gemacht hatte und die inzwischen nach Washington, D.C. gebracht worden war, mit derjenigen in Leavenworth zu einer einzigen verschmolzen wurde, sodaß sich dadurch eine schon gut ausgebaute Grundlage für unser heutiges landesweites System ergab. Man stelle sich nur vor, was in dieser Beziehung unter der Leitung John Edgar 145 150 155 160 165

133 **Behauptung** assertion
135 **verwechseln** to mistake
145 **Vorschlag** suggestion
145 **Verdienst** merit
149 **Wiedergabe** reproduction
149 **beglaubigen** to confirm
156 **zuverlässig** dependable
161 **Sammlung** collection
163 **inzwischen** in the meantime
164 **verschmelzen** to combine

Hoovers in neuester Zeit geleistet wurde. Unser amerikanisches System, das übrigens nicht nur zur Wiedererkennung von Verbrechern dient, sondern schlechthin zur Erkennung der weitesten 170 Kreise der Zivilbevölkerung gebraucht wird, umfaßt augenblicklich viele Millionen von Fingerdruckeinträgen.

Wollten wir uns mit diesen wenigen Angaben einer uns so vertraut gewordenen Einrichtung begnügen, so könnten wir an diesem Punkt Schluß machen. Statt dessen wenden wir uns aber 175 noch kurz der Art und Weise zu, wie ein Fingerabdruck zustande kommt.

Man braucht dazu entweder Druckerschwärze oder Stempelkissentinte sowie reines weißes Papier. Die Hand, der Fuß oder die Finger, es hängt davon ab, welchen der drei genannten Kör- 180 perteile man abdrucken will, wird mit dem Farbmaterial geschwärzt und dann sorgsam auf das Papier gedrückt. Falls man Fingerabdrücke machen will, muß man die Finger langsam von einer Seite zur anderen rollen, um dergestalt einen möglichst vollständigen Abdruck zu erhalten. Wenn man die Lage des 185 einzelnen Fingers auch noch so wenig änderte, so würde sich das Bild verwischen und man müßte noch einmal vorgehen. Es ist heutzutage üblich, daß alle zehn Finger in dieser Art und Weise verzeichnet werden. Jeder Abdruck wird dann nach Washington D.C. geschickt, um dort der großen nationalen Sammlung ein- 190 verleibt zu werden. Man kann aber auch unsichtbare Fingerabdrücke, die etwa an Türklinken, auf Glasoberflächen oder sonstigen glatten Oberflächen haften, abheben, indem man die betreffende Stelle zuerst mit einem dazu vorbereiteten Staub bedeckt, diesen vorsichtig abbläst und dann an Hand des noch 195 anhaftenden Staubes die Merkmale des Abdruckes abliest. Diese Anwendung hat viele Verbrechen einer schnellen Lösung nahegebracht. Wie schon erwähnt, bietet das System Bertillon die Möglichkeit zu Verwechselungen, denn es könnte sein, daß Messungen sich manchmal im einzelnen decken oder einander doch 200 nahe kommen. Beim Fingerabdruck aber ist so etwas ausgeschlossen. Es lag also in der Natur der Sache, daß das System des letzteren nach und nach allgemeine Anerkennung finden mußte.

171 **augenblicklich** at the moment
182 **sorgsam** careful
190 **einverleiben** to embody
193 **haften** to be attached to
193 **abheben** to lift off
194 **vorbereiten** to prepare
201 **ausgeschlossen** impossible

CHAPTER 10

ORIENTATION FOR TRANSLATION

A. What Is Orientation?

Orientation is the orderly procedure of exploring the manner in which a complex sentence is put together for the purpose of translating it into clear and effective English. It is accomplished on the basis of the various sentence units (clauses) and the manner in which they are worded. Thus an effective orientation can be a valuable tool for the solution of the most complicated translation problems. As such it is of special value to the student whose accomplishments do not as yet enable him to complete his work with reasonable speed and accuracy. The more talented student will also find, however, that observance of the principles of orientation will speed him along on his path of accomplishment more rapidly than he would normally progress.

B. The Mechanical Aspects of Orientation

Of course the full value of orientation is obtained only with fairly complicated sentences. Those of shorter length may be scanned almost instantaneously. If we have a sentence before us, however, which is three or more lines long and which is broken up by a number of punctuation marks such as commas, semicolons, and colons, we are definitely faced with a problem, namely, how to render such a seemingly formidable construction into acceptable English. In such a case we can arrive at a satisfactory solution by proceeding in an orderly fashion and by following four separate steps. These are set out below.

1. *To determine the length of the entire sentence.* It may be one or two or more lines in length. Be sure to mark the end of the

sentence in such a way as to make it readily noticeable. Use light pencil marks of your own choosing.

2. *To determine the number of clauses or clause-like constructions in the sentence.* This step is more difficult to follow than Step 1 because we must now be able to recognize quickly not only main and dependent clauses but also relative clauses which may have been placed within a main or adverbial clause, or a so-called absolute participial construction, or a dependent infinitive. In this connection it is worth while for the student to know by heart the most frequently used subordinating conjunctions.

3. *To determine the type of clauses and clause-like constructions in the sentence.* This step is a most logical procedure after determining the number of clauses and other parts of the sentence. To know that the sentence contains one main and two dependent clauses, for example, is in itself an approach to the effective solution of the entire problem of translation. At this point another factor of great value may be added, namely, that of being conscious of the psychological frame which is characteristic of the sentence before one. Let us say the sentence contains three clauses or clause-like constructions: an introductory dependent infinitive, a following main clause, and an *although*-clause. The formula for the frame of such a sentence would be this: *In order to do something, it is necessary . . . , although. . . .* Each complex sentence contains such a frame, and one's awareness of this may be a decided asset in the mastery of the problem at hand. In addition, when the student looks at each individual clause he should note such constructions within it as appositives, enumerations, or participial modifiers. To be aware of their presence and location is an advantage.

4. *To determine the unknown words.* This is best done by means of light pencil marks. All unknown words in the sentence should be ascertained together and not separately. They should also be looked up in the dictionary for their meanings before translation is begun.

C. The Procedure in Translating

Once having determined all unknowns in the sentence, as outlined above, the student may then begin to translate by applying to each clause or clause-like construction that pattern of movement (syntax) which is characteristic of each and which he has studied and previously mastered.

D. Remarks Concerning Orientation

It is recommended that until he has achieved the required mastery, the student regularly select a brief passage containing fairly difficult sentences for the purpose of practicing orientation. In the course of a short time he will find that certain steps may be quickly and easily accomplished so that the time spent in orientation will be appreciably reduced. In the end it will require only a few seconds and it will be so accurate in results that the process of translation itself will be merely a matter of finishing the orientation. The aim of all training in the skills of technical German, as it should also be in the case of French and other languages, is, of course, fluent reading rather than translating. Such reading skills are the next step after the mastery of making accurate translations. The observance of the steps outlined above will aid the ambitious student in his progress towards actual reading.

E. Orientation Exercise

Prepare the translation of the following sentences: 1. Die Beobachtung, daß sich Cellulose und Cellulosederivate in den meisten Lösungsmitteln kolloid lösen, war zu dieser Zeit mit den unter (a) angeführten Beobachtungen vereinbar; denn viele nieder molekulare Stoffe, wie Seifen und manche Farbstoffe, lösen sich in gewissen Lösungsmitteln kolloid auf, in anderen dagegen niedermolekulardispers.[a] 2. Wenn man die Ergebnisse dieser Versuche zusammen faßt, so hat es sich gezeigt, daß man das Holz durch siedende wasserhaltige Essigsäure bei 106–107° allein nicht aufschließen kann, während dies mit Chloressigsäure oder den Chlorhydrinen bei etwa gleichen Temperaturen in wenigen Stunden möglich ist.[b] 3. Die berühmten Versuche von Moissan wurden lange und werden vielleicht auch heute noch als eine, wenn auch nur in bescheidenem Umfang geglückte und damit prinzipiell gelungene Synthese von Diamant angesehen.[c]

REFERENCES

a. „Über den micellaren, makromolekularen und übermolekularen Bau der Cellulose" von H. Staudinger. *Cellulosechemie,* Januar/Februar 1942, S. 1. Verlagsgesellschaft Otto Elsner, Berlin, Wien, Leipzig.
b. „Holzaufschluß mit Salzsäure oder Chloriden als Katalysator in essigsaurer Lösung" von Franz Schütz und Wilhelm Knackstedt, Stettin. Ebd. S. 15.
c. „Untersuchungen zum Diamantproblem" von Paul L. Günther, Paul Geselle und Wolfgang Rebentisch. Zeitschrift für Anorganische und Allgemeine Chemie, 12. Februar 1943. Johann Ambrosius Barth Verlag, Leipzig. S. 357.

F. Practical Review Questions

1. What are the two major steps to be taken when translating a complicated technical German sentence? 2. What are the steps of orientation? 3. What is meant by procedure? 4. If you do not consider the steps outlined above sufficient for your purpose, have you a definite method of your own? 5. What is it? Outline it in very concise statements and show its effectiveness.

G. Die Bevölkerung und die Einwanderung

Wer die Weltgeschichte studiert, wird die großen Bewegungen der Menschheit sicher als auffällige Erscheinungen erkennen. Diese Bewegungen oder Wanderungen, deren Ursprung übrigens nicht festzustellen ist, begegnen uns überall in der überlieferten Geschichte. Man kann sogar verschiedene Arten solcher Massen- 5
wanderungen erkennen, ebenso wie es möglich ist, verschiedene Motive dahinter sowie verschiedene Arten der Ausführung selbst festzustellen. Rein äußerlich betrachtet können es Militärunternehmen sein oder auch Wanderungen, die von der Zivilbevölkerung gemacht werden. Dahinter kann Hungersnot, Militär- 10
zwang oder vielleicht auch irgend eine Art von Naturkatastrophe

1 **Bewegung** movement 2 **auffällig** conspicuous

stecken. Endlich können sich große Massen Volkes auf einmal auf die Wanderung begeben, oder dieselbe kann sich auf mehrere Jahrzehnte, ja sogar Jahrhunderte erstrecken. Betrachtet man sie vom Standpunkt der Zurückgebliebenen, so spricht man von Auswanderung; von der sie empfangenden Bevölkerung werden solche Wanderer als Einwanderer bezeichnet. Die verschiedenen Einflüsse, welche sie in ihrer alten und neuen Heimat ausüben, sind aber keineswegs unwichtig für unsere Betrachtungen. Beide müssen zusammen ein ganzes Bild ergeben.

Schon äußerlich sind solche Wanderungen durch ihre geographischen Bestimmungen sowie ihren Umfang gekennzeichnet. So hat es Wanderungen gegeben — und es gibt auch noch heute solche — die sich von einem Weltteil zum andern erstrecken, die sich von einem Kontinent zum andern ziehen. Allen bekannt ist der Ursprung der drei Arten von Ureinwohnern, die man auf dem nordamerikanischen Kontinent vorfand: der Mayas, Azteken und der Indianer. Allen dreien spricht man eine asiatische Herkunft zu, und man vermutet stark, daß sie über die Beringstraße von Asien nach Alaska gewandert seien, um sich dann im Laufe der Jahrhunderte langsam nach dem Süden zu verschieben. Neuerdings wird diese Theorie in Frage gestellt. Weiterhin benutzten die Indonesier die sogenannte indonesische Inselbrücke, als sie sich aus ihrer nördlichen Heimat nach ihren neuen Sitzplätzen im Südpazifischen Ozean begaben. Die indische Mythologie spricht von einer Massenauswanderung der Urbevölkerung Indiens nach dem Süden zur Zeit, als sich die himalayasche Gebirgskette erhob. Allgemein bekannt sind ferner die Wanderungen der Israeliten von Nordostafrika nach Südwestkleinasien, d.h. nach Palästina. Ebenso dürfen wir nicht die Araberzüge vergessen, die bis nach Spanien reichten. Eng verknüpft mit unserer eigenen Geschichte sind endlich die Wanderungen der germanischen Stämme, besonders die der Vandalen, welche ja bekanntlich in Nordafrika ein großes Reich gründeten. Am wichtigsten für unsere Betrachtungen sind aber die großen europäischen Auswanderungswellen nach dem amerikanischen Konti-

16 **empfangen** to receive
22 **Umfang** extent
24 **sich erstrecken** to extend
26 **Ur . . .** original
27 **vorfinden** to find
29 **Herkunft** origin
30 **sich verschieben** to move
32 **weiterhin** furthermore
41 **reichen** to reach, to extend

nent, besonders dem nordamerikanischen und hier wieder den Vereinigten Staaten. Wir wollen später noch ausführlicher darauf zu sprechen kommen. Anthropologen und Historiker wollen sogar bestimmte Völkerwanderungsstraßen erkennen. 50

Eine zweite Art von Wanderungen ist die, welche sich innerhalb eines Kontinents abspielt. Auch hierfür gibt es eine ganze Anzahl von Beispielen. Genghis Khan durchzog große Strecken Asiens, ehe er das erste Mongolenreich gründete. Wer kennt nicht die Hunnenzüge aus Asien nach Europa, die Normannenzüge ins 55 südlichere Europa, die geschichtliche Völkerwanderung der germanischen Stämme aus Skandinavien nach Mittel- und Westeuropa? Wir müssen endlich auch noch einmal der Azteken und Mayas gedenken, die sich von Nordamerika über die mittelamerikanische Festlandbrücke nach Südamerika resp. Mittel- 60 amerika und Mexiko begaben.

Weit wichtiger aber als die ebengenannten Wanderungen sind für uns hier diejenigen, welche innerhalb eines Landes selbst stattgefunden haben; denn sie berühren oft in sehr weitgehendem Maße die innere Stabilität und das Wohlergehen eines Volkes. 65 Erwähnen wir hier nur einige derselben: In den Vereinigten Staaten erfuhr man im vorigen Jahrhundert die Ausbreitung der Bevölkerung über die Alleghany Berge und die Zentralebenen nach dem Westen. Weiterhin kam mit dem industriellen Aufschwung des Nordens die Nordwärtswanderung des Negers und die große 70 Bewegung der Landbevölkerung nach den Städten, eine Bewegung, die auch jetzt noch nicht ins Stocken gekommen ist. Verschiedene Anforderungen des Krieges und die damit verbundenen höheren Löhne in den Fabriken sind mächtige Lockmittel für die sonst weniger gut bezahlten Landarbeiter. 75

Einer der mächtigsten Antriebe zur Auswanderung liegt in dem geschichtlich immer wiederkehrenden Sichübervölkern eines Landes. Aus dieser Erscheinung wächst innerer Druck sozialer und ökonomischer Art. Landgesetze unter der einheimischen

48 **ausführlich** in detail
51 **sich abspielen** to develop
60 **resp.** respectively, or
62 **ebengenannt** just mentioned
64 **berühren** to touch
64 **weitgehend** extensive
67 **Ausbreitung** expansion
69 **Aufschwung** advance
73 **Anforderung** requirement
76 **Antrieb** urge
77 **wiederkehren** to repeat

Bevölkerung, möglicherweise auch Erbgesetze, veranlassen viele, 80
sich anderswo günstigere Lebensverhältnisse zu verschaffen.
Neuerdings hat auch der Druck der Militärpflicht zur Auswanderung gezwungen. Man denke nur an die Auswanderung der
Mennoniten während der letzten Jahrzehnte des vorigen Jahrhunderts aus Rußland nach den Vereinigten Staaten. Wird es be- 85
kannt, daß es irgendwo weniger dicht bewohnte Landstrecken
gibt, die sonst günstig zu sein scheinen, so ergießt sich der Strom
der Auswanderer in diesen Hohlraum. Daß solch ein Vorgang
nicht immer friedlich und reibungslos verläuft, beweist die Geschichte zur Genüge. Früher, als die verschiedenen Völker- 90
gruppen sich noch nicht zu hochentwickelten nationalen Einheiten
ausgebildet hatten, so wie es z.B. heute der Fall ist, war das
Massenwandern ein verhältnismäßig einfacher Vorgang. Friedlicher Durchzug wurde verlangt und oft gewährt. Heutzutage
aber, da die Menschheit zu einer Bevölkerung von über zwei 95
Milliarden herangewachsen ist, und fast alle bewohnbaren Landmassen besiedelt sind, ist das eine andere Geschichte. Und man
hat versucht, die Auswanderung durch nationale Gesetze zu
regeln. Ein vollkommen freies und dynamisches Handeln ist
nach und nach ins Stocken gekommen und hat die schwersten 100
Folgen gehabt.

Mit Ausnahme gewisser Gegenden in Australien sind es heute
die Vereinigten Staaten und ihre einheimische Bevölkerung,
welche den ganzen Vorgang der Aus- und Einwanderung aufs
Klarste beleuchten. Es ist deshalb zweckmäßig, daß wir uns ihnen 105
zuwenden. Ein kurzer geschichtlicher Rückblick bringt uns am
ehesten zum Ziel. Er hebt eine Anzahl ganz besonders starker
Einwanderungswellen hervor. So kann man wohl sagen, daß die
erste Welle, obwohl sie nicht besonders groß war, schon im Jahr
1710 stattfand. In den nächsten hundert Jahren, genauer gesagt, 110
bis 1820, kamen die meisten Einwanderer hauptsächlich aus
England, daneben auch aus Frankreich, Schweden, Holland und
Deutschland. Franzosen siedelten sich in Süd Carolina an,

80 **möglicherweise** possibly
80 **veranlassen** to cause
81 **sich verschaffen** to procure
87 **sich ergießen** to pour
96 **bewohnbar** habitable
97 **besiedeln** to settle
103 **einheimisch** native
105 **beleuchten** to illuminate, to make clear
106 **Rückblick** review
108 **Welle** wave

Schweden in Delaware, und die Deutschen zerstreuten sich ziemlich gleichmäßig über die Oststaaten. Holländer fanden New York und New Jersey besonders für ihre Zwecke geeignet. Die erste große massenhaft Einwanderer bringende Welle aber fand erst in den späten 40ern des vorigen Jahrhunderts statt. So zwangen im Jahre 1846 die Korngesetze Englands und die große irische Kartoffelhungersnot viele Tausende von Iren, sich anderswo — in den Vereinigten Staaten — ihr Fortkommen zu suchen. Ebenso veranlaßte das Fehlschlagen der 48er Revolution in Europa viele, besonders Deutsche, der politischen Verfolgung zu entgehen. Sie wandten sich nach den Vereinigten Staaten. Mit dieser Einwanderungswelle beginnt das Zeitalter der modernen Auswanderung aus Europa. Bis um 1880 verstärkt sich dieser Strom, der sich zumeist aus Einwanderern germanischer Herkunft zusammensetzt. Und da diese Ankömmlinge der eingesessenen Bevölkerung im Denken, Verhalten und allgemeiner Lebensweise sehr nahe waren, paßten sie sich dem neuen Land und seinen Verhältnissen sehr gut an. Während der 80er Jahre verschwächte sich diese mittel- und nordeuropäische Welle, weil neugewonnene Kolonialreiche viele Auswanderungslustige von Amerika ablenkten. Dafür aber verstärkte sich der Zudrang aus dem Südosten Europas, wo wir eine Bevölkerung vorfinden, die der amerikanischen unähnlich ist. Und es ist gerade die Unähnlichkeit der Ideale und allgemeinen Lebensweise innerhalb einer sonst homogenen Bevölkerung, welche scharfgezogene Probleme mit sich bringt. Daß solche immer klarer werdenden Verhältnisse die Aufmerksamkeit der Landesverwaltung auf sich ziehen, ist natürlich. Das Einwanderungsproblem verschärfte sich noch dadurch, daß nun Einwanderer auch aus allen anderen Ländern besonders den orientalischen kamen. Dadurch wurde das innere Gleichgewicht der einheimischen Bevölkerung in den Vereinigten Staaten derart gestört, daß man ernstlich daran ging, die Einwanderung gesetzlich zu regeln. Diese neuen Gesetze erlauben es uns auch, die weitere Geschichte des Einwanderungsproblems zu verfolgen. Wenden wir uns ihnen deshalb zu.

114 **sich zerstreuen** to scatter
115 **gleichmäßig** uniformly
120 **anderswo** elsewhere
122 **Fehlschlagen** failure
124 **sich wenden** to turn
126 **sich verstärken** to grow strong
132 **sich verschwächen** to grow weak
134 **ablenken** to divert
141 **sich verschärfen** to become acute

Die ersten gesetzlichen Einschränkungen stammen aus den Jahren 1875 und 1882. Die ersteren verboten Verbrechern und unmoralischen Frauen den Eintritt in die Vereinigten Staaten; das letztere ist ein Gesetz, welches sich gegen die damals massenhaft stattfindende Einwanderung der Chinesen richtete. Es waren nämlich viele Tausende nach den Vereinigten Staaten gekommen, um am Bau der großen Überlandbahnen lohnende Beschäftigung zu finden. Und da sie für weit geringere Löhne als die einheimischen Arbeiter angeworben werden konnten, stellten sie einen gefährlichen Wettbewerb auf dem Arbeitsmarkt dar. Man verbot ihnen folglicherweise, hierher zu kommen. Um 1910 wurde solch ein Gesetz auch für die Japaner nötig. An der Westküste hatten sich so viele festgesetzt, daß die einheimische Bevölkerung in Unruhe geriet. Es wurde somit ein sogenanntes „Gentlemen's Agreement" mit Japan abgeschlossen, wonach die japanische Regierung selbst den Japanern die Ausreise nach den Vereinigten Staaten verbot. Im Jahre 1924 wurde dann noch ein weiteres wichtiges Gesetz erlassen, wonach die Einwanderer von nun an von der amerikanischen Regierung selbst ausgewählt werden sollten. Die Auswirkung dieses Gesetzes kann am besten gesehen werden, wenn wir uns die Zahl der Einwanderer vergegenwärtigen, die von 1921 bis 1938 nach Amerika kamen. Im Jahr 1921 waren es 805 228, im Jahr 1922 waren es 309 556; im Jahr 1925 sank die Zahl auf 294 314 herab, im Jahr 1930 noch weiter auf 241 700. Im Jahr 1933 waren es nur noch 23 068 und im Jahr 1938 67 895.

Das hebt ein neues Prinzip hervor, nämlich die Auswahl solcher, welche am besten von der einheimischen Bevölkerung assimiliert werden können. Ein weiteres Gesetz, welches im Jahr 1917 erlassen wurde, verlangte dann auch von den Einwandernden, daß sie lesen und schreiben konnten. Und seit dem Jahre 1921 schränkte man die Zahl der Einwanderer weiter durch sogenannte Quoten ein; d.h. auf Grund der Volkszusammensetzung von 1880 gestattete man nur 2 Prozent der jeweiligen Nationalitäten den Eintritt. Das letzte wichtige Gesetz von 1929 setzte endlich die Gesamtzahl der Einwanderer auf 153 714 fest. Und zwar sollte diese Zahl so verteilt werden, daß sie die im Jahr 1920 vorhandenen

149 **Einschränkung** limitation
151 **Eintritt** entrance
155 **lohnend** profitable
156 **gering** small
181 **gestatten** to permit
181 **jeweilig** respective

Nationalitäten jeweils quotenmäßig betraf. Man wollte nämlich die Stabilität und soziale Zusammensetzung des Volkes so bewahrt wissen, wie sie sich in jenem Jahr befand. 185

Man könnte sich nun fragen, warum die Einwanderungsgesetze sich seit 1921 so sehr verändert haben. Eine Antwort darauf ist nicht schwer zu finden. Ohne Zweifel haben die beiden letzten Weltkriege so katastrophal auf das Gleichgewicht der Bevölkerung aller Länder gewirkt, daß sie ganz und gar aus ihrer gewohnten Lebensweise gerissen wurde. Amerika als Land der unbegrenzten Möglichkeiten war noch als einziges Land in seiner inneren Sicherheit verschont geblieben. Nun lockte es Millionen an. Man mußte zu Maßregeln greifen, um es vor ähnlichen Verhältnissen zu verschonen. So wurde man wählerisch: man öffnete Tausenden die Pforte des Landes und wies Millionen zurück. 190 195

Wir können das Bild der Einwanderung nicht abrunden, ohne einige der inneren Probleme zu erwähnen, die sich naturgemäß aus einer Verschmelzung der einheimischen mit der neueingewanderten Bevölkerung ergeben. So kann man als nicht wünschenswert bezeichnen, daß massenhafte Einwanderung die Tendenz hat, die Lebenshaltung der Einheimischen herabzusetzen. In den meisten Fällen kommen Einwanderer aus weit niederen Lebens- und Löhnungsverhältnissen, als sie für Eingeborene bestehen. Und da es natürlich das Bestreben der Arbeitsgeber ist, möglichst billige Arbeitskräfte anzuwerben, wenden sie sich oft an die Neuankommenden. Diese sind oft geneigt, für niedere Löhne zu arbeiten. Dadurch kommt es zu schweren Klagen der einheimischen Arbeiter; manchmal sogar zu Reibereien. Eine ebenso wenig wünschenswerte Erscheinung liegt in dem Bestreben der Neuankommenden, sich in den Großstädten bei ihresgleichen anzusammeln und dort mit ihnen ihre frühere Lebensweise fortzusetzen, ohne den Wunsch zu haben, diese zu dem Niveau der Eingeborenen zu heben. So entstehen verarmte und verschmutzte Stadtviertel. Die Verschmutzung der Städte ist eins der größten Probleme unserer Zeit, das nur durch ungeheure Geldausgaben und Kraftanstrengungen gelöst werden kann. Man denke in dieser Hinsicht nur an New York. Unmittelbar aus solchen 200 205 210 215 220

194 **unbegrenzt** unlimited
199 **abrunden** to round out
200 **naturgemäß** naturally
204 **herabsetzen** to lower
219 **Kraftanstrengungen** expenditure of energy

Lagen erhebt sich das Problem des Verbrechens, dem eigentlich ein besonderes Kapitel gewidmet worden ist. Daß Anhäufungen von nicht assimilierten und nicht assimilierbaren Bevölkerungsschichten in allerhand unangenehme politische Erscheinungen ausarten, ist leicht möglich und vielleicht auch beweisbar; daß sie besondere Erziehungsprobleme aufwerfen, hat man längst erkannt. Auch hat es sich herausgestellt, daß manche der Neuangekommenen wenig Gebrauch von den konstruktiven Vorzügen machen, welche ihre neue Heimat ihnen bietet. Das hat man auch zahlenmäßig zeigen können. 225 230

Anderseits kann aber auch klar bewiesen werden, daß die Einwanderung, besonders wenn sie verständig gehandhabt wird, ihre guten Seiten hat. Zuerst sollte man erwähnen, daß ja die meisten Amerikaner die Abkömmlinge von Einwanderern sind. Ebenso, daß eine ganze Anzahl bedeutender Männer aus ihren Reihen gekommen sind und viel zum Wohl ihres neuen Vaterlandes beigetragen haben. Es seien nur Namen wie Carl Schurz, Jacob Riis und Joseph Pulitzer genannt. Viele andere könnten diesen hinzugefügt werden. Es waren zumeist Einwanderer, die über das Allegheny Gebirge nach dem Westen drangen und die unendlichen Weiten der Wälder und Ebenen der Kultur zugängig gemacht haben. Auch heute noch wird ein großer Prozentsatz der amerikanischen Farmbevölkerung von Neuangekommenen oder deren Kinder gebildet. Im allgemeinen erfüllen sie ihre Pflichten als Bürger ihrer neuen Heimat und sind in ihrer Arbeit produktiv. Man sieht also, das Volksproblem, durch die Perspektive der Aus- und Einwanderung gesehen, ist ein breites und vielseitiges. Manches haben wir im Laufe unserer Besprechung gar nicht einmal berührt. Ob es eine Lösung dafür gibt, wissen wir nicht. Vielleicht wird es die Zeit mit sich bringen, daß irgendeine zufriedenstellende Lösung herbeigeführt wird. Jedenfalls sind die Zeiten einer freien und uneingeschränkten Einwanderung in die Vereinigten Staaten vorüber. Ist dies wirklich der Fall, dann haben wir vielleicht ein weiteres Zeichen vor uns dafür, daß die Vereinigten Staaten als einheitliches Staatsgebilde reifen und sich mit dieser Frage an die Stellungsnahme anderer Völker in einer bestimmten Aus- und Einwanderungspolitik anschließen. 235 240 245 250 255

222 **Anhäufung** piling up
225 **ausarten** to degenerate
226 **aufwerfen** to present
257 **sich anschließen** to join

PART II

Besides continuing his vocabulary studies in Part II, the student is asked to concentrate on the following:

1. The accumulation and mastery of certain expressions which are frequently found in technical German. These appear at the bottom of the page below the various reading selections.

2. The study and mastery of certain points of grammar. These are listed, according to reading selections, in a separate section at the end of Part II.

CHAPTER 11

DIE ENTSTEHUNG DES ERDGERÜSTES *

Ein Blick auf eine Landkarte der Erde oder auf einen Globus lehrt uns, daß sich die Oberflächenverhältnisse von Festland zu Wasser der Menge nach [1] sehr zu Gunsten des letzteren verhalten. Ebenso kann man in demselben Bilde sofort an eine allgemeine Zweiteilung der Erdoberfläche denken: einen Kontinentalblock sowie ein Tiefseebecken. Der erstere wird geologisch auch als Lithosphäre und das letztere als Hydrosphäre bezeichnet. Wo diese sich dem dem Auge sichtbaren Festland nähert, überlagert sie sich der sogenannten Kontinentaltafel. Deren [2] äußerer Teil wird als Schelf bezeichnet und grenzt seinerseits wieder an den Kontinentalrand, welcher in den Kontinentalabhang übergeht und sich schließlich in der Tiefseetafel verliert. Es ist uns ein erstes, die Höhenunterschiede zwischen beiden großen Massen, dem Festlande und den Wassermassen festzustellen; und, wenn wir den Gaurisankar in den Himalajas in Nordindien einerseits und vielleicht die größte Meerestiefe, den bekannten Philippinengraben, andererseits als den höchsten resp. tiefsten Punkt annehmen, so haben wir eine Differenz von 18 628 Metern vor uns. Die mittlere Höhe der Landmasse über dem Meeresspiegel wird [3] auf ungefähr 820 Meter, die des Meeres auf ungefähr 3 700 Metern berechnet. Verteilte man aber spekulativ die gesamte Landmasse gleichmäßig über den ganzen Erdball, so läge alles Land noch ziemlich tief unter Wasser.

Dem Auge nach kann man die verschiedenen Landmassen in sechs Kontinente, Eurasien, Afrika, Nordamerika, Südamerika, Australien und die Antarktis, und in drei Weltmeere, den Pazifik,

3 **zu Gunsten der** in favor of
12 **es ist uns ein erstes, zu** the first thing for us to do is to
15 **einerseits, andererseits** on the one hand, on the other
24 **(dem Auge) nach** according to (the eye)

* The reference numbers that appear in Part II pertain to the points that are set out in the section that begins on page 201.

den Atlantik und den Indik, einteilen. Dabei darf man wieder nicht aus dem Auge verlieren, daß die Landmassen sich zumeist auf der nördlichen Halbkugel der Erde ansammeln. Auch reichen sie verhältnismäzig weiter nördlich als die Erdmassen auf der 30 südlichen Halbkugel südlich. Ferner unterscheiden wir zwei Hauptreliefzonen der Erde: den mediterranen und den pazifischen Gürtel. Sie enthalten die hauptsächlichsten Gebirgszüge der Erde sowie die tiefsten submarinen Gräben und zeichnen sich auch dadurch aus, daß sie die beiden mächtigsten Aufwölbungen, 35 die Geantiklinalen, besitzen. Vom Gesichtspunkt der geologischen Geschichte aus betrachtet stellen diese beiden großen Zonen die jüngsten und zugleich beweglichsten Teile der Erde dar. Fast alle großen Erdbeben und magmatischen Erschütterungen haben da ihren Ursprung; demzufolge sind die wichtigsten tätigen 40 Vulkane auch an ihren Rändern gelegen. Die tektonische Entwicklung, d.h. die geologisch-geschichtliche Entwicklung der Erdkruste, wird mit dem Namen Tektonik bezeichnet. Sehen wir uns die Ränder der beiden Hauptreliefzonen noch ein wenig näher an, so erkennen wir sofort, daß die Umreißung der Küstenlinien 45 oft durch die Antiklinalen und die Richtung, in der die großen Gebirgszüge verlaufen, gekennzeichnet wird. Man sehe [4] sich nur u.a. die Westküsten von den beiden amerikanischen Kontinenten an. Ein weiteres Verfolgen dieser Eigenschaft rund um die pazifischen Reliefränder zeigt, daß dies hier viel auffallender ist als 50 beim atlantischen Hauptrelief, wo wir öfters gewaltige Tiefländer an den Ozean herantreten sehen, wie es z.B. an der Ostküste Südamerikas, der Westküste Afrikas, sowie bei den Tiefländern Indiens der Fall ist. Die Bildung dieses Küstentypus' muß also selbstständiger, d.h. stabiler, vor sich gegangen sein als beim 55 pazifischen. Es ist auch darauf hingewiesen worden, daß die submarinen Gräben sich auffallend regelmäßig an den Küsten der Kontinente oder doch an denen von kontinentalen Inselreihen entlangziehen. Es ist deshalb nicht nur von allgemeinem Interesse

27 **dabei darf man aber nicht aus dem Auge verlieren, daß** but one must not lose sight of the fact that

33 **sie zeichnen sich dadurch aus, daß** they are characterized by the fact that

36 **vom Gesichtspunkt aus** from the point of view

43 **sehen wir sie uns noch ein wenig näher an** so if we look at them a little more closely

47 **man sehe sich nur . . . an** look at

56 **es ist auch darauf hingewiesen, daß** it must also be pointed out that

sondern auch von wissenschaftlicher Wichtigkeit, daß wir uns den verschiedenen Theorien zuwenden, die man im Laufe der Zeit betreffs der möglichen Entstehung der Kontinente entwickelt hat. 60

Die erste Theorie, die sich auf die Schwerkraftsuntersuchungen von Hayford stützt, besagt, daß sich ein Schwerkrafts- und Dichteausgleich in den Erdschichten in einer Tiefe von rund 120 km ereignet hat. Unterhalb der Kontinente hat sich infolge des Druckes der Erdmassen ein sog. Massenüberschuß gebildet, der sich in einer Massenauflockerung ringsherum kundgab. Das Umgekehrte ist dann in den Schichten unter dem Meeresboden der Fall: das entstandene Massendefizit zeigte sich in einer respektiven Massenverdichtung. Diese beiden geologischen Vorgänge haben also allmählich als grundlegend bildende Kräfte an der Formierung der Erdoberfläche teilgenommen. Hierbei ist zu beachten, daß man gewöhnlich die dichteren Schichtenmassen unter den Ozeanen und die weniger dichten in den kontinentalen Massen findet. Darnach ist es möglich, einzelne Tiefengürtel ihrer Dichtigkeit, mit anderen Worten ihrer Schwere nach, zu unterscheiden: einen äußeren, leichteren, der bis in eine Tiefe von rund 1 200 km reicht, einen mittleren, der ungefähr 1 700 km dick ist und einen inneren, den eigentlichen Kern der Erde, welcher rund 7 000 km im Durchmesser hat. Man kann also sagen, die leichteren Schichten schwimmen sozusagen auf den dichteren und schwereren. Der äußere Mantel hat eine mittlere Dichte von 3,4, der zweite eine von 6,0 und der eigentliche Erdkern eine von 9,2. Untersucht man ferner die Zusammensetzung der einzelnen Gesteinsmassen, so wie sie einen jeden Mantel kennzeichnen, so kommt man ohne Zweifel zu dem Schluß, daß die Schichtung in drei Teile aus stofflichen Verschiedenheiten und nicht aus Gründen des Druckes hervorgegangen ist. 65 70 75 80 85 90

Eine zweite und ebenso plausible Theorie von Trabert ist die sich auf die Wärmeverteilung stützende Betrachtung, welche bei der Abkühlung der Erde verschiedenartig vor sich gegangen

69 **das Umgekehrte ist der Fall** the converse is the case

74 **hierbei ist zu beachten, daß** here we must observe that

77 **darnach ist es möglich, zu** according to this it is possible to

82 **man kann also sagen, daß** so it can be said that

87 **so kommt man ohne Zweifel zu dem Schluß, daß** so, no doubt, one can conclude that

sein soll. Demnach entspricht die Temperatur, welche auf dem Meeresboden herrscht, Null Grad, während die, welche sich auf dem gleichen Niveau unter der Landmasse befindet, 140 Grad ist. Dieser Temperaturunterschied hat demnach eine Dichteungleichheit, d.h. eine Schwereungleichheit bewirkt. Die Schichten unter dem Meer haben sich schneller abgekühlt und sind einem schnelleren Zusammenziehungsvorgang unterzogen worden. Ist dies wahr, so könnte man folgern, daß die allgemeine Gestaltung der Erdoberfläche in ihrer großen Zweiteilung kein geschichtlich junger Vorgang gewesen ist, sondern, daß sie ihre Anfänge in den geologisch vorgeschichtlichen Zeitaltern der Erdabkühlung hat. Erdmassen seien also immer Erdmassen und Wassermassen immer Wassermassen gewesen.

Eine andere Theorie ist die, wonach die verschiedenen Kontinentalmassen sich allmählich horizontal verschoben haben. Auch diese Betrachtung stützt sich anfänglich auf die Dichteverschiedenheit der leichten und schweren Gesteinsmäntel. Sie nimmt an, man habe es ursprünglich mit einer die gesamte Erdoberfläche darstellende und aus leichten Gesteinen bestehende Deckschicht zu tun gehabt. Diese sei nach und nach zerrissen und verschoben worden. Durch Abkühlung habe sie sich stark zusammengezogen. In Einzelfällen sei sie den isostatischen Gesetzen folgend in die darunterliegenden schwereren Schichten untergetaucht und durch Druck in verschiedenen Richtungen verschoben worden. Wiederauftauchend stellen sie heute die Kontinentalblöcke dar.

Dies sind natürlich nicht alle Theorien, die mit in das Feld der Geophysik und besonders in das Werden unseres Erdballes hineinspielen. So könnte man z.B. noch die sogenannte Tetraederhypothese anführen, wonach ein sich abkühlender Himmelskörper in seinen schweren Gesteinsmassen die Form eines Tetraeders annehmen soll, denn diese Figur besitzt bekanntlich den kleinsten und die Kugel den größten Rauminhalt. Alle inneren den Erdkern bildenden Massen sammeln sich folglich in der Form eines Tetraeders an, dessen Umreißungen man in der geographischen Lage der kontinentalen Massen und ihrer Gebirgszüge erkennen will. Zuletzt soll auch die Hypothese nicht vergessen

101 **man kann folgern, daß** one can reason that

111 **man hat es zu tun mit** one deals with

werden, welche besagt, daß sich der Mond aus den ehemals in den Ozeanen vorhandenen Erdmassen gebildet haben solle. Dies wäre besonders aus dem Massendefizit, das im Pazifik herrscht, der Fall. Die Mondablösung habe dann auch dazu beigetragen, das Hauptzonenrelief des Pazifik zu bilden. 135

CHAPTER 12

ERDBEBEN

Erdbeben sind für den Menschen immer große und oft schreckenerregende Naturbegebenheiten gewesen, und doch geschehen sie nach ganz bestimmten Naturgesetzen, welche man teilweise schon wirksam erforscht hat. Als Teilgebiet der Geophysik beschäftigt sich die Erdbebenkunde mit zwei im allgemeinen zu unterscheidenden großen Arten von Erdbeben: denjenigen, welche man körperlich wahrnehmen kann und die man als makroseismische Beben bezeichnet, und solchen, welche man körperlich nicht wahrnehmen statt dessen aber mit feingebauten Instrumenten, den Seismographen, aufzeichnen kann. Die letztere Sorte wird auch die mikroseismische genannt. Zusammengefaßt bietet das Studium beider Arten ein weitgehendes Feld. Also wollen wir uns deswegen mit den uns interessanteren Beben, den makroseismischen, beschäftigen. Wir wollen kurz die makroseismischen Komponente eines Bebens erwähnen und woraus sie bestehen; ferner wollen wir etwas über die Häufigkeit, Verbreitung und Ursachen der Beben aussagen, um endlich mit dem Erwähnen zweier besonders wichtiger Beben zum Schluß zu kommen.

Der klaren Übersicht halber wollen wir vorweg die Eigenschaften des makroseismischen Erdbebens aufzählen. Diese[1] sind: Intensität, die Lage der sog. Zentren, nämlich des Epizentrums und des Hypozentrums, die Isoseisten und Homoseisten, sowie die weniger erlebten Seebeben und Flutwellen, welche oft im Zusammenhange damit angetroffen werden. Intensität eines Erdbebens ist die Stärke, mit welcher eine Erderschütterung in ihrem sog. Schüttergebiet auftritt. Man hat natürlich versucht, die Intensität in verschiedene Stufen einzuteilen und hat sich folglich auf

18 **zum Schluß kommen** to come to a conclusion

19 **der klaren Übersicht halber** for the sake of a clear survey

26 **man hat natürlich versucht, zu** of course, one tried to

die Rossi-Forel-Mercalliskala geeinigt. Grundlage dieser Skala, sowie auch anderer ebenso angewandter Skalen, ist die besonders typische Wirkung auf Menschen, Häuser, Tiere, Hausgeräte und Landschaft, usw., welche ein Beben zeitigt. Die Mercallische Skala, welche vielleicht am meisten für Erdbebeneinschätzungen gebraucht wird, ist in zehn Grade eingeteilt, von denen wir hier einige anführen wollen. Der erste Grad auf dieser Skala ist so gering, daß er von den Menschen nicht gemerkt wird sondern nur vom Seismographen verzeichnet werden kann. Der dritte Grad wird als leicht gekennzeichnet. Solch ein Beben wird von einzelnen Menschen physisch vernommen, von den meisten aber gar nicht empfunden. Der fünfte Grad ist schon ziemlich stark, wird allgemein in den Häusern bemerkt, Schlafende wachen auf, Türen werden aufgerissen, Uhren bleiben stehen und aufgehangene Gegenstände schwingen hin und her. Der siebente Grad wird als sehr stark bezeichnet. Die Menschen werden von allgemeinem Schrecken ergriffen, sie fliehen aus den Häusern, Schornsteine stürzen um, Gebäude werden beschädigt, wenn auch [2] noch leicht. Der schärfste und letzte Grad, der zehnte, ist außerordentlich verheerend, viele Gebäude werden zerstört, viele Menschen kommen ums Leben, im Erdboden bilden sich Risse und Sprünge, und in Gebirgen finden Massenabstürze von Gesteinen und Erde statt. Natürlich ist die Anwendung einer solchen Skala immer nur als relativ aufzufassen. Um [3] zu absoluten Werten zu gelangen, bedient man sich mathematisch festgelegter Größen.

Nehmen wir nun an, ein Erdbeben habe stattgefunden, und wir wollen nun alle diejenigen Örter mit Linien auf der Landkarte verbinden, welche alle denselben Grad von Intensität aufgewiesen haben. Die dazu gezogenen Linien werden als Isoseisten bezeichnet. Nehmen wir ferner an, daß der zweite Intensitätsgrad mit derjenigen Grenze übereinstimmt, bei welcher der Mensch ein Erdbeben körperlich wahrnimmt, so ist es einfach, alle Beben vom zweiten Grade aufwärts als makroseismisch und alle diejenigen, welche unterhalb und innerhalb des ersten Grades liegen, als mikroseismisch aufzufassen. Nehmen wir nun auch noch an, daß die Isoseisten des stärksten Grades sich um ein verhältnismäßig kleines Landschaftsgebiet, vielleicht sogar um einen fast

53 **nehmen wir nun an, daß** let us now assume that 59 **es ist einfach, zu** it is simple to

punktartigen Platz, ziehen, und daß die anderen Isoseisten sich mehr oder minder regelmäßig von da ausbreiten. Wir sprechen in Bezug auf diejenige Stelle, welche den stärksten Grad aufweist, als das Epizentrum; das ganze Gebiet, falls es sich um eine größere Fläche handelt, wird als Epizentralgebiet bezeichnet. Die Tiefe aber, in welcher der eigentliche Erdbebenstoß stattfindet, ist als das sog. Hypozentrum bekannt. Wiederholte und nun schon auch oft bestätigte Untersuchungen haben aber ergeben, daß die betreffende Tiefe sehr gering sein aber auch bis zu 25 km tief liegen kann. Es ist besonders das Verdienst R. v. Koevesligethys und J. v. Jánosis, die Grundlagen der Tiefenbestimmung eines sogenannten Erdbebenherdes auf der Mercalli-Cancanischen Intensitätsskala gesucht zu haben. Für das deutsche Erdbeben vom 16. Januar 1911 ergab sich eine Herdtiefe von 9,5 km; für das verheerende Messina Erdbeben wurde eine Tiefe von 5 km gefunden und für das bekannte Erdbeben von San Francisco von 1906 ist das Hypozentrum in einer Tiefe von ungefähr 20 km gefunden worden. Im Verhältnis zum gesamten Erddurchmesser sind das nur sehr geringe Tiefen, und es kann wohl behauptet werden, daß die meisten Erdbeben in einer ziemlich geringen Tiefe ihren Ursprung haben. Endlich ist auch noch zu beachten, daß Verschiedenheiten in der Struktur der einzelnen Erdschichten, welche eine Erdbebenwelle durchläuft, d.h. Verschiedenheiten in Bezug auf Dichte, Härte oder chemische Zusammensetzung der Gesteine, der gleichmäßig schnellen Ausbreitung der Welle bestimmte Hindernisse entgegensetzen werden, sodaß sie an verschieden entfernt gelegenen Orten zu gleicher Zeit wahrgenommen wird. Verbindet man nun solche Orte wiederum durch Linien, Zeitlinien, so haben wir endlich die schon oben erwähnten Homoseisten vor uns. Diese fallen natürlich mit den Isoseisten nicht zusammen.

Manchmal kommt es vor, daß ein Erdbeben an der Küste eines Landes vorkommt, wie das z.B. bei dem San Francisco Erdbeben

66 **wir sprechen in Bezug auf** we speak in reference to
68 **es handelt sich um** it is a question of
82 **im Verhältnis zu** in relation to
83 **es kann wohl behauptet werden, daß** no doubt it can be asserted that
85 **endlich ist auch noch zu beachten, daß** finally, we must pay attention to the fact that
96 **manchmal kommt es vor, daß** sometimes it happens that

der Fall war. Und wenn die Epi- und Hypozentren dann ebenfalls noch dicht an der Küste liegen, so pflanzen sich die einzelnen Stoßwellen nicht nur in der Richtung des Landes sondern auch seewärts fort. Im ebengenannten Falle hat man berechnet, daß das kontinentale Schüttergebiet fast eine halbe Million Kilometer im Geviert einnahm. Das gesamte Schüttergebiet wäre dann also auf nahezu eine Million Quadratkilometer zu berechnen. Liegt das Epizentrum, und vielleicht sogar auch das Hypozentrum, nun irgendwo unter dem Meeresgrund, so haben wir es mit einem Seebeben zu tun. Diese sind in einzelnen Fällen von sich auf hoher See befindlichen Schiffen bemerkt worden, und es erhebt sich also [4] die interessante Frage, wie die einzelnen Intensitätsgrade eines solchen Seebebens mit denen eines Landbebens zu vergleichen wären. Es war E. Rudolph, der die Seebeben zum erstenmal einer Skaleneinreihung unterworfen hat; und, obwohl er damit rechnen mußte, daß der unmittelbare Meeresboden ganz andere Durchgangsmedien darstellte als die obersten Erdschichten auf dem Lande, stellte er dennoch fest, daß der unterste Grad eines Seebebens schon dem dritten Grad in der Rossi-Forelliskala entsprach. Natürlich ist es mit weit größeren Schwierigkeiten verbunden, Seebeben zu studieren und ähnliche Daten zu sammeln, als man es bei Erdbeben tun kann. Die verhältnismäßige Häufigkeit und Verbreitung aller Beben kann natürlich nur mit Hilfe von mikroseismischen Beobachtungen, und dann nur im Laufe einer langen Zeitspanne, kennen gelernt werden. Endlich sei noch die so oft mit einem Seebeben verbundene Flutwelle genannt, welche manchmal erstaunliche Höhe und Verheerungskraft besitzt. Bei der Gelegenheit des Krakataua-Ausbruches im Jahre 1883 pflanzte sich die durch submarine Beben hervorgerufene Flutwelle über fast alle Ozeane bis an die entferntesten Küsten fort und erreichte eine nicht unerhebliche Höhe. Man konnte sie sogar an den Westküsten Europas deutlich messen und spüren. Das an der Westküste von Südamerika entstandene Erdbeben von Iquique (1877) vermochte man ebenfalls an den westlichen Rändern des Stillen Ozeans wahrnehmen. Ist man aber auf hoher See während eines Seebebens, das eine starke Flutwelle auszulösen imstande ist, so ist es aber kaum möglich,

108 **es erhebt sich nun die Frage, wie** the problem now arises as to how

115 **er stellte fest, daß** he determined that

dieselbe durch ihre Stoßkraft zu empfinden, denn oft belaufen sich 135
die Abstände von „Berg“ zu „Berg“ oder „Tal“ zu „Tal“ bis auf
mehrere hundert km.

Was die Häufigkeit und Verbreitung der Erdbeben anbetrifft,
so kann man sagen, daß sie weit öfter stattfinden, als man gewöhnlich annimmt. F. de Montessus de Ballore hat die Anzahl 140
der in einem Jahre stattfindenden Erd- und Seebeben auf rd.
80 000 geschätzt, und zwar sind in dieser Zahl nur solche ein-
begriffen, die vom Menschen physisch wahrgenommen werden
können. Das wären über 200 täglich. Rechnet man aber noch
alle mikroseismischen Beben hinzu, so beläuft sich die jährliche 145
Gesamtzahl weit höher. Aufzeichnungen, die sich mit der Häufigkeit des Auftretens der Erd- und Seebeben befassen, sind wiederholt und besonders in erdbebenreichen Ländern, wie z.B. Japan
oder Italien, gemacht worden. Selbst in sonst erdbebenarmen
Ländern, wie Deutschland und England, sind sie viel häufiger, als 150
man annimmt. Um die den Erdbeben verschieden unterworfenen
Gegenden der Erde seismologisch zu klassifizieren, hat man sie in
seismische, d.h. erdbebenreiche, peneseismische, d.h. manchmal
heimgesuchte, und aseismische, d.h. erdbebenarme Gegenden
eingeteilt. Zu der ersten Sorte gehören die Kalifornische Spalte 155
sowie auch das Gebiet um Japan und Formosa; zur zweiten zählt
man Südwestdeutschland, Großbritannien und Ungarn und zur
dritten die Tiefländer Frankreichs, Deutschlands und Englands.

Den Ursachen nach spricht man von tektonischen und vulkanischen Erdbeben. Auch hier ist die Trennungsgrenze nicht ganz 160
scharf zu ziehen, denn bei einem Erdbebenausbruch können
mehrere Ursachen mit hineinspielen. Ein tektonisches Erdbeben
ist ein solches, das auf der Bewegung und Verschiebung von Erdschichten an oder unter der Erdoberfläche beruht. Das war z.B.
bei dem großen San Francisco Erdbeben der Fall. Während eines 165
solchen Erdbebenvorganges können sich die betreffenden Erdschollen bis auf mehrere Meter lateral und bis zu einem halben
Meter vertikal verschieben. Die Linie, an welcher zwei sich
bewegende Schollen begegnen, heißt die Dislokationslinie oder
auch die Bruchlinie. Diese kann verschieden lang sein, hat aber, 170
wie man beim San Francisco Erdbeben festzustellen vermochte,
manchmal eine Länge von mehreren hundert km. Eines der inter-

138 **was . . . anbetrifft** as to

essantesten Erdbeben ist dasjenige, welches auf der sog. Denudation und Sedimentation beruht. Das heißt, im Laufe der Zeit werden ungeheure Mengen von Erdmassen von der Oberfläche der Hügel und besonders Gebirge in die niedriger gelegenen Fußlandschaften befördert. Dadurch findet eine im Laufe der Zeit immer schwerer ins Gewicht fallende Massenverschiebung statt, sodaß endlich, wenn der Druck auf die unter den niederen Landstrecken sich befindenden Erdschollen zu groß wird, die Spannung sich in einem Erdbeben auslöst. 175 180

Die zweite Art von Erdbeben ist die sogenannte vulkanische, welche auch oft die magmatische genannt wird, denn sie beruht darauf, daß sie durch die unter den festen Erdschollen sich befindlichen flüssigen Massen, das Magma, verursacht wird. Am deutlichsten kommt das bei den vulkanischen Ausbrüchen zum Vorschein. Das können wir besonders gut an den vesuvianischen Ausbrüchen und den damit verbundenen Erderschütterungen sehen. Das gleiche kann auch in Bezug des Strombolis und Aetnas gesagt werden. Es ist aber völlig im Bereiche der Wahrscheinlichkeit, daß durch die Bewegungen des Magma sowie der darin vorkommenden Geschehnisse zugleich tektonische Begleiterscheinungen hervorgerufen werden. Man kann in einem solchen Falle also kaum von einem rein magmatischen Erdbeben sprechen. Endlich könnte man noch von sog. Einsturzbeben sprechen, die dadurch zustande kommen, daß große Hohlräume im Inneren der Erde zusammenstürzen, und die daran beteiligten gewaltigen Erdmassen die Stabilität der getroffenen Schollen stören. In diesem Falle wäre das Hypozentrum also sehr flach gelegen. Erdbeben solcher Art sind aus den dalmatischen Küstengebieten und den Salzlagergegenden von Leopoldshall und Staßfurt gut bekannt. 185 190 195 200

Laßt uns zum Schluß noch kurz zwei Erdbeben besprechen, von denen das erste ein ausgesprochen tektonisches und das zweite ohne Zweifel gemischter Art war. Wir haben hier erstens Bezug auf das schon mehrere Male erwähnte Erdbeben von San Fran- 205

177 **im Laufe der Zeit** in the course of time

185 **am deutlichsten kommt das zum Vorschein bei** it is most clearly expressed in the case of

189 **das gleiche kann gesagt werden in Bezug** one can say the same about

196 **es kommt dadurch zustande, daß** it comes about by the fact that

205 **wir haben hier erstens Bezug auf** we refer here firstly to

cisco, das am 18. April 1906 stattfand. Wie schon besprochen, hatte dieses ein Schüttergebiet von fast 1 000 000 Quadratkilometern und lehnte sich eng an das bekannte System der San Andreas Spalte an. Diese erstreckt sich in einer Länge von ungefähr 210 450 km an der Küste entlang. Die interessante Begebenheit während des Bebens aber lag in der Tatsache, daß sich während desselben eine neue Spalte bildete. Das hypozentrale Gebiet lag in einer Tiefe von ungefähr 20 km zwischen Olema und dem Südende der Tomalesbucht. Das Epizentrum befand sich unge- 215 fähr 45 km NNW von San Francisco. Die Intensitätsverteilung ist auf Grund der Rossi-Forelliskala berechnet worden und zeigte, trotzdem sie ziemlich genau den ihr zugrunde liegenden Gesetzen folgte, deutliche lokale Unterschiede. So schwankten die Intensitätsgrade in der Stadt San Francisco selbst innerhalb dreier 220 Grade; weiter von der Stadt entfernt machten sich ebenfalls Gradunterschiede bemerkbar, wenn auch nicht in solch ausgesprochenem Maße. Das San Francisco Erdbeben lehrte aber auch, daß man auf Grund der tektonischen Struktur der betreffenden Schichten mit einem sich im Laufe der Zeit langsam ansam- 225 melnden Spannungssystem rechnen müsse, das sich endlich, wenn das Spannungschöchstmaß erreicht ist, im Erdbebenstoß selbst auslöst. Proportional mit dem Heranwachsen und Nachlassen der Spannung treten dann eine Reihe mehr oder minder großer Entladungsstöße vor und nach dem eigentlichen Erdbeben ein. 230 Das Erdbeben von Messina wird so genannt, weil es an und in der Straße von Messina, gegenüber der Zehenspitze Süditaliens stattfand. Das Datum ist der 28. Dezember 1908. Es erreichte den elften Intensitätsgrad der zwölfteiligen Mercalli-Cancaniskala und umschloß das Gebiet der Straße von Messina sowie die Städte 235 Messina, Reggio und Villa San Giovanni. Das Epizentralgebiet war unterseeisch und erstreckte sich entlang einer nord-südlichen Achse von ungefähr 20 km Länge. Die Ursache ist ohne Zweifel darin zu suchen, daß die Erdschichten, die der Straße von Messina unterliegen, ein geologisch stark disloziertes Gebiet darstellen. 240 Es ist ungewiß, ob an diesem Erdbebenvorgang nur tektonische

217 **auf Grund der** on the basis of the
238 **die Ursache ist ohne Zweifel darin zu suchen, daß** no doubt the cause is to be found in the fact that
241 **est ist ungewiß, ob** it is uncertain whether

oder magmatische Elemente teilgenommen haben. Jedenfalls trat noch die Begleiterscheinung einer heftigen Flutwelle auf, die sich in mehreren „Bergen“ über das Mittelmeer ausbreitete. An der sizilianischen Ostküste erreichte sie eine Höhe von 9½ Metern, 245 bei San Alessio soll sie sogar 11¾ Meter betragen haben. Die Mareographen (Flutmesser) auf der Insel Malta zeigten noch Wellen mit einer Höhe von fast einem Meter.

Die vorgehenden Bemerkungen über Erd- und Seebeben sind natürlich nicht ausführlich. Die Erdbebenkunde stellt ein ganzes 250 Sondergebiet der Geographie und Geologie dar. Heutzutage betrachtet man sie als Teilgebiet der Geophysik, wo man stark mit mathematischen Werten zu rechnen hat.

CHAPTER 13

WASSERFORMEN DES LANDES

Wasser befindet sich[1] nicht nur in Ozeanen, Flüssen oder Seen. Gewaltige Mengen desselben sind dem menschlichen Auge verborgen und befinden sich in und unter der obersten Erdschichte. Wird[2] die Jahreszeit kälter, so ändert sich Regen, eine der Hauptformen des Wassers, zu Schnee und auf dem Erdboden zu Eis. Wir sehen: nicht nur besteht Wasser aus verschiedenen Formen, sondern es erscheint uns in diesen mehrfachen Formen, je nachdem[3] wir uns in warmen, gemäßigten oder kalten Gegenden befinden; d.h. klimatische Kräfte sind bei der Gestaltung der jeweiligen Wasserform oft mitentscheidend. Im allgemeinen unterscheidet man auf dem Lande das Wasser in und unter der Erde von dem auf der Erde; man spricht also von Bodenwasser als in und unter der Erde vorkommend, von Flußwasser als im Regen und Schmelzwasser erscheinend, und endlich von Wasserkörpern als in Flüssen und Seen vorkommend.

Das Vorhandensein des Bodenwassers ist abhängig von der es enthaltenden Erdschichtenstruktur. Es kann also demgemäß in verschiedenen Tiefen vorkommen, es kann sich verschiedentlich zusammensetzen, es kann im Umfang seiner physischen Lage mehr oder minder beschränkt sein. Sind durchlässige und undurchlässige Erdschichten mehrfach übereinandergeschichtet, so kann es vorkommen, daß Wasser sich in mehreren Stockwerken vorfindet. Natürlich steht es oft unter Druck und kann, wenn man an einer passenden Stelle ein Loch in die wassertragenden Schichten gräbt, hoch und dauernd aus dem Erdboden emporschießen. Man spricht dann von einem artesischen Brunnen. Befindet sich ein Wasserlauf auf passendem Untergrunde, sagen wir sehr durchlässigem Kalkstein, so kann es vorkommen, daß Oberflächenwasser wieder in die Tiefe versinkt. Das kann eine

8 **je nachdem** depending on whether

dauernde oder periodische Erscheinung sein. Eines der bekanntesten Beispiele dafür liefert die Donau einige Kilometer östlich von Donau-Eschingen, wo sie eben über solch durchlässige Kalkgesteine fließt und durch welche hindurch sie während Trockenzeiten auf undurchlässige und tieferliegende Schichten versinkt, um nun, auf einem festen Unterbett angelangt, sich teils westwärts unterirdisch in das Abflußgebiet des Rheines zu begeben. Enthält solch durchlässiger Untergrund nun noch Hohlräume, so können unterirdische Seen und Flüsse entstehen, welche mitunter marine Lebewesen enthalten können, wie es z.B. der Fall an einigen Stellen der Sahara in Nordafrika ist. Quellen können verschiedene Eigentümlichkeiten besitzen. Obwohl die Temperatur ihrer Wasser ziemlich konstant zu bleiben trachtet, gibt es dennoch solche, die besonders heiß sind oder solche, deren Wasser besondere chemische Zusammensetzung haben. Das ist besonders der Fall bei Quellen, die sich in vulkanischen Gegenden befinden, wie im Yellowstone Park. Ihre chemische Zusammensetzung ist natürlich durch die von ihnen durchlaufenen Erdschichten bestimmt und kann oft zur Anlegung von Gesundbädern Anlaß geben. Deren gibt es besonders viele und weitbekannte in Europa.

Abfließende Wasser setzen sich aus Regen und Schmelzwasser zusammen. Das erstere läuft noch während seines Falles auf der Erdoberfläche in Form von Rinnsalen ab, besonders wenn die oberste Erdschicht so fein granuliert ist, daß ihre mikroskopischen Hohlräume schon durch den ersten Aufschlag des Regenwassers dicht gemacht worden sind. Unter solchen Umständen richtet es oft großen Schaden in landwirtschaftlicher Beziehung an. Seiner Form nach kann es in Fluten, Bächen, Flüssen, Teichen oder Seen erscheinen. Schmelzwasser kommt entweder in dauernder oder periodischer Form vor. Der ungeheure Druck, der durch Gletscher ausgeübt wird, schmilzt tiefliegendes Eis dauernd und entleert es an geeigneten Stellen in Form der bekannten milchigen Gletscherbäche. Seine periodische Erscheinung knüpft sich an die jeweilige Jahreszeit: auf dem Tiefland läuft es nur durch ein einmaliges Schmelzen im Frühjahr ab. Im Gebirge, besonders im Hochgebirge, findet dann noch eine

44 **das ist besonders der Fall bei** this is especially the case in (with)

49 **Anlaß geben** to give rise

Schmelze zu Sommeranfang statt, nämlich dann, wenn die Sonnenstrahlen kräftig genug geworden sind, um ihre Wirkung auch auf die Schneefelder des Hochgebirges auszuüben. Wir haben es dann mit einem zweiten Schmelzwasserabfluß zu tun. 70 Ein bekanntes Beispiel hierzu ist der Doppelabfluß im Missouribecken. Gewöhnlich werden solche Abflußwasser durch vorbestimmte Kanäle, d.h. Bäche und Flüsse, nach den fernen Meeren geleitet. Die Form des Flusses als Wasserleiter erfordert unsere besondere Aufmerksamkeit, denn sie ist äußerst mannigfaltig. 75 Er kann aus einer einzigen Wasserrinne bestehen, setzt sich aber meistens aus einer großen Anzahl, d.h. einem ganzen System, zusammen. Die Hauptrinne kann sich gabeln wie bei der Spree, manchmal sucht die Hauptrinne sich neue Betten und läßt Fragmente des alten zurück, was besonders beim Mississippi zum 80 Vorschein kommt. Besondere Aufmerksamkeit verdienen die verschiedenen Arten von Flußmündungen, welche wieder mancherlei Formen annehmen können. So spricht man von Trichtermündungen, siehe den Rio de la Plata oder den Amazon, beide in Südamerika, oder solch einer Flußöffnung kann eine 85 Barre vorgelagert sein, in welchem Falle man von einem Haff, wie dem Kurischen in Ostpreußen, spricht. Findet die Verzweigung erst in der Nähe des Ozeans statt, so haben wir ein Delta vor uns. In diesem Falle bildet eine Deltarinne gewöhnlich die Hauptrinne des Flusses, kann sich aber von Zeit zu Zeit um 90 ein beträchtliches verschieben. Als besondere Merkmale eines Flusses können sein Gefälle und die damit verbundene Stromgeschwindigkeit betrachtet werden. Bei manchen Flüssen, so beim Rhein oder Missouri, ist die Strömung eine reißend schnelle, bei anderen eine sehr langsame. Ein weiteres augenscheinliches 95 Merkmal ist die Wasserfarbe, denn sie ändert sich oft von Landschaft zu Landschaft. Führt das Flußwasser beträchtliche Mengen Sand mit sich, so kann die Farbe bis in ein tiefes Gelb hineingehen. Der Missouri z.B. führt so viel Sand mit sich, daß man in jedem Glasvoll einen nicht unbeträchtlichen Nieder- 100 schlag erhält. Die Spree ist wiederum braun, denn sie fließt durch ein sumpfiges Gebiet und enthält demgemäß eine große

67 **dann, wenn** when
80 **zum Vorschein kommen** to appear
90 **von Zeit zu Zeit** from time to time

Anzahl von verschwindend kleinen Lebewesen, die ihre Eigenfarbe dem Wasser mitteilen. Wie schon bemerkt sind Gletscherbäche milchig-weiß bis blau, während Flüsse, die durch 105
Zederngehölze fließen, oft fast ganz schwarzes Wasser mit sich führen. Die Beschaffenheit des Flußwassers ist gewöhnlich „süß", kann aber auch salzig sein, was besonders bei denjenigen Flüssen vorkommt, die durch stark alkalihaltige Trockengebiete fließen, wie es bei gewissen russischen Flüssen erscheint. 110

Ebenso interessant erscheinen uns die Seen in ihren verschiedenen Erscheinungsformen. Natürlich passen sie sich in ihren Umrissen und Tiefengestaltungen den sie umgebenden Bodenarten an. Sie sind nichts anderes als Ansammlungen von Regen- Schmelz- oder Grundwassern in seinen schon be- 115
sprochenen Formen. Man teilt Seen gewöhnlich ihrem Durchschnitt nach in flache und tiefe Seen ein. Die ersteren findet man besonders auf Flachland und besonders in großen Gruppen in subarktischen Regionen. Sie können entweder aus Sickerwasser entstehen oder bekommen ihren Wasserzusatz aus unter 120
ihnen gelegenen Quellen. Die letzteren sind besonders für die in ihnen sich aufhaltende Fischwelt wichtig, denn sie sorgen dafür, daß dem Wasser nicht nur eine bestimmte den Fischen zusagende Temperatur sondern auch ein ihnen notwendiger Sauerstoffgehalt erhalten bleibt. Von besonderem Interesse ist die Tatsache, daß 125
man von Seen, besonders Flachseen als wie von Lebewesen sprechen kann, denn sie werden geboren, durchlaufen ihre Lebensbahn nach ganz bestimmten Gesetzen und sterben dann wieder, indem sie allmählich dem in sie eindringenden Pflanzenwuchs weichen. Tiefe Seen findet man gewöhnlich in Hügelländern, 130
wo sie verhältnismäßig klein sind, denn sie werden stark durch die sie umgebenden Hügel eingeengt. Ihr Wasser ist weit kühler als das der Flachseen und enthält ebenso Quellen wie diese.

Eis entsteht, wenn Wasser gefriert, und das Werden des Eises hängt also vom Klima ab. Man unterscheidet auch bei dieser 135
Wasserform mehrere Arten: so die Eisdecken vom Grundeis und dieses wieder vom Bodeneis. Die erstgenannte Art kommt durch

104 **wie schon bemerkt** as already mentioned
114 **nichts anderes als** only
122 **sie sorgen dafür, daß** they take care of
125 **von besonderem Interesse ist die Tatsache, daß** of special interest is the fact that

das Gefrieren von Wasseroberflächen wie den Flüssen, Seen und Teichen zustande. Nimmt die Temperatur allmählich so stark ab, daß sie unter den Gefrierpunkt fällt und bleibt sie anhaltend 140 unterhalb desselben, so bildet sich eine mehr oder minder starke Eisdecke aus, die gegebenenfalls so stark sein kann, daß ein Mensch darüber hinweg gehen kann. Oft findet man zwischen der Unterseite solch einer Eisdecke und dem Wasserspiegel einen Hohlraum, sodaß man auf einer regelrechten Eisbrücke dahin- 145 schreitet. Von größtem Nutzen ist dieser Hohlraum für die Fische, welche sich während der kalten Jahreszeit daraus ihren Sauerstoffbedarf holen. Von noch größerer Wichtigkeit für die Fisch- wie Pflanzenwelt in einem See ist die Ab- oder Anwesenheit einer auf der Eisdecke liegenden Schneedecke. Es ist ja 150 bekannte Tatsache, daß eine zu dicke Schneedecke die Sonnenstrahlen verhindert, bis in die Tiefen zu gelangen, in denen Fische und Pflanzen sich aufhalten. Die Photosynthese wird durch die Abwesenheit des Sonnenlichtes unmöglich, und die Pflanzenwelt unter dem Wasser leidet großen Schaden. Sie gedeiht nicht 155 mehr, kann ihrerseits nicht mehr Sauerstoff abgeben; und, sollte der Hohlraum zwischen Eisdecke und Wasseroberfläche fehlen, so würden die Fische wiederum an Sauerstoffmangel leiden und können unter Umständen in erheblichen Mengen absterben. Eine eigenartige Eisform ist der Schnee, der seinerseits eine 160 vorübergehende oder dauernde sein kann. In ersterer fällt er in Flockenform und bedeckt den Erdboden entweder wie mit einem Mantel oder er sammelt sich in verschiedener Gebirgshöhe in besonders geschützten Stellen zu mehr oder minder großen Flecken an. Da wird er unter Umständen als sogenannter ewiger 165 Schnee bezeichnet. Sind solche Ansammlungen außerordentlich groß und besitzen sie eine besonders große Tiefe, so ist es möglich, daß er sich unter dem immer mehr steigerndem Druck langsam in eine Art Eis verwandelt. Neuerdings ist man dazu übergegangen, die Niederschläge während der warmen Jahreszeiten 170 vorauszusagen, indem man die Tiefe und Dichtigkeit der sich angesammelten Schneedecken im Gebirge mißt und dadurch vermuten kann, wieviel Wasser sich in die Fußhügel und Tieflän-

142 **gegebenenfalls** in a given case
150 **es ist ja bekannte Tatsache, daß** it is a well-known fact that
159 **unter Umständen** under certain circumstances

der ergießen wird. Man ist durch solche Verfahren zu erstaunlich genauen Ergebnissen gelangt. Wird ein immer größer und 175
dichter werdender Schneefleck jahraus jahrein von zerstörenden Witterungseinflüssen geschützt, so vermag er sich allmählich in einen Gletscher zu verwandeln. Obwohl wir auf die einzelnen Bestandteile des Gletschers nicht näher eingehen wollen, soll nur noch erwähnt werden, daß der alte Glaube, der Gletscher bewege 180
sich nur äußerst langsam vorwärts, sich nicht bis in die Jetztzeit hat erhalten können, denn man hat besonders in den das Nordpoleis umgebenden Gletschern eine viel schnellere Gletscherbewegung feststellen können, als man es früher angenommen hatte. Die Eiskappe, die den Südpol umgibt, enthält eine ganze 185
Anzahl solcher Eisflüsse in ungefähr derselben Art und Weise, wie es Ströme in den verschiedenen Ozeanen gibt. Daß Gletscher aber nicht nur an weitab vom Äquator gelegenen günstigen Stellen zu finden sind, beweist die Gegenwart einer ewigen Eiskappe auf dem Kilimandjaro unter dem Äquator im Tangan- 190
yikagebiet in Afrika.

186 **Art und Weise** the manner

CHAPTER 14

DIE PFLANZE IN DER LANDSCHAFT

Eines der wichtigen Teilgebiete der Landschaftskunde beschäftigt sich mit der Pflanze und der Art und Weise, wie sie in der Landschaft erscheint; d.h. es ist hier keine Frage der botanischen Seite der Pflanze, denn die ist ja zum großen Teil analytisch zu bewerten; auch handelt es sich hier nicht um die Einzelpflanze sondern um diese als[1] Vertreter ihrer Art und Familie und der Weise, wie sie sich zu anderen Arten, usf. im Landschaftsbilde verhält. Es[2] kann sich also nur um eine beschreibende Behandlung handeln. Natürlich werden unter Umständen, nämlich wenn das ursprüngliche Landschaftsbild es verlangt, die Einzelpflanzen in Betracht gezogen müssen; mit anderen Worten, wir werden die Pflanzenwelt in der Landschaft von dem doppelten Standpunkt der Einzelpflanze sowie des sog. Pflanzenvereins aus[3] sehen.

Wenden wir uns zuerst den Formen der Einzelpflanze zu, d.h. ihren Erscheinungs- oder Lebensformen, so unterscheiden wir sofort eine ganze Anzahl derselben. So sprechen wir wissenschaftlich von Gehölzpflanzen, Halbsträuchern, Stauden, Kräutern, Gräsern, Moosen, Flechten und so weiter. Natürlich ist es im Angesicht der normalen Natureinrichtungen nicht gut möglich, immer eine scharfe Grenze zwischen den Einzelformen zu ziehen, denn überall gibt es Übergangsformen; ebenso kann man Größe allein nicht als Maßstab der Klassifizierung anwenden, denn botanisch betrachtet, gestattet die Wissenschaft es nicht, reine Größe als Unterscheidungsmerkmal anzusehen. Das wird schon ersichtlich, wenn wir uns vor Augen halten, daß die erstgenannten Pflanzen, die Gehölzpflanzen, sich der Größe nach von den riesigen Sequoiabäumen Californiens bis zu den relativ

4 **zum großen Teil** largely
11 **in Betracht ziehen** to consider
20 **im Angesicht der** in the face of the
21 **eine Grenze ziehen** to differentiate

kleinen Heidekräutern erstrecken. Der Zwischenraum wird, wie jedermann weiß, von einer fast unendlichen Anzahl von Übergangsarten ausgefüllt. Diese Übergangsarten kennzeichnen sich durch große Verschiedenheiten im Bau ihrer Stämme, Belaubung, der Art und Weise, wie das einzelne Blatt entweder an seinem Stengel oder dem Stamm angebracht ist, An- oder Abwesenheit von Stacheln, Blütenart und ihrem Sitz und endlich der Art und Anzahl der Früchte. Oft muß die Art der Wurzelbildung noch mit hinein in unseren Betrachtungskreis gezogen werden. Ausführlichkeit der Beschreibung eines jeden angeführten Kennzeichens ist Sache der Botanik; also werden wir uns darum nicht kümmern. Gehölzpflanzen kommen natürlich selten als Einzelbestand in der Landschaft vor sondern meistens im Verein mit anderen, meist niederen Gewächsarten, in welchem Falle wir dann von Stockwerken in der Pflanzendecke sprechen. Solche Stockwerke gibt es auch in anderen Pflanzenverbindungen. Einzelvorkommen ist dennoch gut möglich; man erinnere sich nur an die in gelockerten Ständen der afrikanischen Steppen vorkommenden Akazien; oder, wenn wir uns nicht so weit von zu Hause fortbegeben wollen, an das Einzelvorkommen von gewissen Baumarten auf unseren Feldern, um die der Bauer rundherum pflügt. Holzstauden sind uns auch in ihrer Form als Halbsträucher bekannt, Stauden und Kräuter in Form von Kakteen oder denjenigen Einzelpflanzen, welche sich nur durch ganz [4] tiefe Wurzelbildung in wasserarmen Gegenden erhalten können, so z.B. das Sage-Gebüsch des amerikanischen Südwestens. Eine besondere Art von Stauden sind die verschiedenen Gräser, von denen man wieder zwei allgemeine Sorten, die sog. süßen und sauren, unterscheidet. Die ersteren kommen auf verhältnismäßig trockenem die letzteren auf nassem Boden vor. Stehen sie vereinzelt, so ist der Erdboden zwischen den Einzelbüschen sichtbar; bilden sie zusammenhängend eine Rasenfläche, so verfilzen sich ihre Wurzeln so, daß diese ein ganzes System für sich bilden können. Moose, Flechten, usw. sollen als Einzelindividuen hier nicht betrachtet werden, da sie im allgemeinen nur in zusammenhängenden oder massenhaft auftretenden Systemen erscheinen. Hiermit wenden wir uns aber auch solchen

41 **im Verein mit** together with   45 **man erinnere sich nur an** one should recall

Systemen zu, die, wie schon oben bemerkt, mit dem Namen Pflanzenvereinen bezeichnet werden.

Die hauptsächlichsten Pflanzenvereine sind Gehölze, Halbstrauchvereine, Gras- und Kräuterfluren und solche, die sich aus den niederen Pflanzen zusammensetzen. Auch spricht man von 70 offenen und geschlossenen Pflanzenvereinen. Auch hier muß gesagt werden, daß man einen solchen Verein nicht immer in reiner Form und Zusammensetzung vorfindet sondern oft mit anderen Vereinsarten gemischt, sodaß sich oft die schon erwähnten Stockwerke ergeben. Diese Stockwerke sind besonders vom forst- 75 wirtschaftlichen Standpunkte aus wichtig, denn sie bedeuten, daß in solch einem Mischwald ein größerer wirtschaftlicher Nutzen steckt als in einem sogenannten Reinwald. Während alles, was wir schon oben über Gehölzpflanzen gesagt haben, auch hier zutrifft, wollen wir nur noch hinzufügen, daß Gehölze eine 80 laterale Ausbreitung besitzen, die sich in demselben Maße und denselben Proportionen zu seiner vertikalen Ausbreitung verhält. Das heißt, in ihrer geographischen Höhenausbreitung kommen ungefähr dieselben Arten in demselben Mengenverhältnis und Formerscheinungen vor, wie man sie von Äquator aus nach Süden 85 und Norden zu sieht. Im allgemeinen sagt man in der Sprache und den Werten des Forstmannes, daß es Hochholz gibt, das sich bis zu einer Höhe zwischen 30 und 40 Metern erstreckt; daß es einen Niederwald gibt, bei dem dieselben Werte unter 10 Metern angewendet werden können. Und haben wir es mit 90 Höhen zwischen 10 und 20 Metern zu tun, so sprechen wir von einem Mittelwald. Der Art der Bäume nach, aus denen sich ein Wald zusammensetzt, unterscheidet man Laub- und Nadelwald oder auch eine dritte Sorte, den Mischwald. Nehmen wir wiederum den Standort des Waldes in Betracht, so sagen wir, 95 es gibt Sumpfwald, wenn er auf einer wasserreichen Erdschicht wächst oder Uferwald, wenn er sich an den Ufern der Flüsse entlang, so besonders in heißen, trockenen Landstrichen, hinzieht, oder Auenwald, wenn er Tiefland bewächst, das mitunter überschwemmt wird oder letztens Bergwald, wenn er sich die 100 Bergabhänge hinauf bis zu gewissen Höhen hin erstreckt. Der Kälte, des Wasserreichtums, Windes und Wetters wegen ändern sich die verschiedenen Formen eines Bergwaldes, sodaß man

83 **das heißt** i.e. 86 **im allgemeinen** generally

ihn schließlich in beträchtlicher Höhe nur in zerfetzten und zerschlissenen Ständen oder gar Einzelbäumen vorfindet. In 105 jenen Gebirgshöhen sind dann auch oft verkrüppelte Formen oder auch Zwergformen ständig, wie z.B. die Zwergföhren auf dem Rücken der Sudetenketten oder den Felsengebirgen Amerikas.

Fluren dagegen setzen sich aus Kräutern, Stauden und Gräsern 110 zusammen. Die beiden ersten sind gewöhnlich gemischt und enthalten dazu noch die Wasserpflanzenvereine von Wasserkörpern. Die letzteren sind neuerdings besonders wichtig geworden dadurch, daß gewisse Formen derselben, wie zum Beispiel der Seetank, u.a.m. Quellen von Nahrungsmitteln und indus- 115 triellen Erzeugnissen geworden sind. Seit die Nahrungsfrage in den letzten Dezennien der Menschheit ein besonders akutes Problem geworden ist, hat man sich in immer größer werdendem Maße und einer immer ernsteren Dringlichkeit den Nahrungsausbeutungsmöglichkeiten der marinen pflanzlichen Quellen zugewandt. 120 Unter den Erscheinungsmöglichkeiten der Fluren sind die Wiesen von primärer Wichtigkeit, denn ihre Anwesenheit hat zu besonderen Kulturerscheinungen der Menschheit Anregung gegeben, so dem Nomadenleben, das so oft mit Viehzucht verbunden ist oder später der Landwirtschaft, indem große Landstrecken 125 unter den Pflug kamen und durch ihre Ertragsfähigkeit ganze neuzeitliche Gesellschaftsformen bedingen. Eine andere interessante Wiesenform besteht in den Schilfsümpfen, welche zwar wenig wirtschaftlichen Wert besitzen, aber dennoch dadurch an Wichtigkeit zunehmen, daß sie fast durchweg Zufluchtsörter für 130 frei und wild lebende Tierarten werden. Ihr wirtschaftlicher Wert ist somit mehr ein indirekter. Diese Erscheinung kann an den Rändern fast aller flachen Seen und ausgedehnten Sümpfe beobachtet werden. Das allerbekannteste Beispiel davon ist ohne Zweifel der Djadsee in nördlichen Zentralafrika. Nähert 135 sich die Trockenzeit, so ziehen sich seine eigentlichen Wassergestade derart zurück, daß er nur noch ein ungeheures Wasserloch darstellt. Die trockengewordenen Ufer dagegen werden zum Sammelpunkt unübersehbarer Wildscharen. Bleibt der Untergrund solcher Sümpfe anhaltend naß, so bilden sich im 140

114 **zum Beispiel** e.g.

126 **unter den Pflug kommen** to be plowed under

Laufe der Zeit Moore, die ihrerseits wieder zu Torfbildungen Anlaß geben. Und wenn diese die menschlichen Wirtschaftsbedürfnisse auf sich ziehen, so können sie zu unmittelbarem ökonomischen Wert anwachsen. Das ist besonders in gewissen Gegenden der nordeutschen Heide in der Umgebung Bremens 145 und anderer Städte der Fall. Interessant sind ferner, wenigstens vom ästhetischen Standpunkte aus betrachtet, die Mischvereine zwischen Wiesen und Gehölzen, die sich oft parkähnlich gestalten. Das Reizvolle solch einer Landschaft hat dann später sogar zur künstlichen Erzeugung solch eines Bildes, besonders in England, 150 Anlaß gegeben in unmittelbarem Gegensatz zu der gekünstelten mathematisch genauen Gartenlandschaft in Frankreich. Anthropologisch wird angenommen, solch eine freie Mischlandschaft sei einer der geschichtlich ersten Wohnsitze der Menschen gewesen, denn sie bot ihm die gemeinsamen Vorzüge des geschlos- 155 senen Waldes und der ganz freien Feldlandschaft. Eine letzte Wiesenform in ursprünglicher Form ist die Steppe, die sich außer in Rußland — der Ursprung des Wortes „Steppe" liegt im Russischen — in anderen Ländern und Erdteilen als Savanne und Prairie wiederfindet. Der Höhe des darin wachsenden Grases 160 entspricht dann auch die Bezeichnung von Hochgras- und Niedergrassteppe. Eigentümlichkeit einer freien Steppenlandschaft ist oft, daß das Gras in bestimmter Höhe gehalten wird und zwar durch die früher massenhaft vorkommenden Wildarten, jetzt aber noch durch mehr oder minder starkes Begrasen. 165 Manchmal werden auch solche Graslandschaften weitläufig dem Pflug unterworfen, und so läßt sich gewissermaßen der Werdegang einer ganzen Zivilisation in der Benutzung nur einer Art von Pflanzendecke beobachten.

Die Vereine der niederen Pflanzen werden als Lagerpflanzen 170 bezeichnet, denn sie lagern sich sozusagen dicht am Erdboden an und bilden dort oft mehr oder minder dicht zusammenhängende Decken. Es werden hier Moose, Flechten, Algen und auch Bakterien in Betracht gezogen. Obwohl wir oft verschiedene Moosarten nur mit der sog. Wetterseite von Bäumen oder Felsen 175 oder vielleicht auch in Form von Moospolstern in feuchten Waldstrichen in Verbindung bringen, so soll man doch nicht aus den

151 **in unmittelbarem Gegensatz zu** in direct contrast to

177 **in Verbindung bringen** to connect

Augen verlieren, daß in den subarktischen Regionen das Moos ausgedehnte Landstriche bedeckt und den dort einheimischen Spaltfüßlern, den Karibu und Rentieren, zur Hauptnahrungs- 180 quelle dient. Natürlich werden sie nicht nur durch die niedere Temperatur bedingt, sondern auch durch die stetige Feuchtigkeit, welche ihre Begründung wohl in der letzten Eiszeit und dem Rückgang der Eismassen hat. Algen werden meistens nur mit Wasser in Verbindung gesetzt und sollen deshalb hier weniger 185 Beachtung finden, es sei denn, wir erwähnen des allgemeinen Interesses halber die Schneealgen, welche dem fallenden Schnee oft bestimmte Farbeigenschaften geben. Letztlich sollen Bakterien nur insofern aufgezählt werden, indem sie dafür verantwortlich sind, daß unter gewissen Umständen manche Sümpfe 190 und andere wasserhaltige Stellen durch sie Eisenoxydhydrat bilden, das sich in besonderen und schleimigen Häuten absondert.

Wir wollen unsere Betrachtungen aber nicht zum Abschluß bringen, ohne den vom Menschen geschaffenen Pflanzenvereinen unsere Aufmerksamkeit zu schenken. Denn der Mensch ist ja 195 notwendigerweise Teil der Landschaft und unter den verschiedenen Wesen, die darin ihr Fortkommen suchen, dasjenige, welches im geschichtlichen Laufe der Zeit die Landschaft wesentlich zu ändern imstande war. So hat er gewissen Landstrichen seine Pflanzendecke radikal fortgenommen, sie dergestalt seinen 200 Bedürfnissen anzupassen gewußt oder sie durch seine eigene manchmal von ihm bewußt entwickelte Pflanzenwelt ersetzt. Natürlich hat er manche Gegenden gar nicht berühren wollen oder auch können; denn was will er z.B. in den weitläufigen Eiswüsten der Arktik und Antarktik? Hat er aber einmal den 205 wirtschaftlichen Wert einer bestimmten Pflanzenart erkannt und erhebt sich ihm die Notwendigkeit einer Ausbeutung derselben, so hat er sich nicht daran hindern lassen, ganze Waldstrecken zu vernichten oder die darin waltenden günstigen klimatischen Verhältnissen anderen von ihm bevorzugten Pflan- 210 zenarten anzupassen. Man denke hier nur an die ausgedehnten

185 **in Verbindung setzen** to connect
186 **Beachtung finden** to be considered
186 **es sei denn, daß** unless
189 **sie sind dafür verantwortlich, daß** they are responsible for the fact that
193 **zum Abschluß bringen** to conclude

Kautschuk- oder Bananenplantagen. Die nach und nach entwickelte Forstwirtschaft soll dem Menschen bessere Ausbeutung der Gehölzer sichern. Neueste Errungenschaft in dieser Hinsicht ist das vor erst wenigen Jahren in Deutschland gegründete Reichs- 215 arboretum. Von ihm und den allgemeinen Bedürfnissen gingen solche technischen Errungenschaften wie die industrielle Herstellung von Zucker und anderen Produkten aus. Um sich weiteren Nutzen der so nötigen Hölzer zu sichern, hat man geradewegs große Wälder angelegt, welche wissenschaftlich betreut und 220 geerntet werden. Sie haben z.B. Deutschland ein gewisses nicht unangenehmes Aussehen gegeben. Ferner dürfen wir des einfachen Gartens nicht vergessen in seinen mannigfachen Formen und pflanzlichen Zusammensetzungen. In ihrer intensiven Kultur kommen die obengenannten Stockwerke der verschiedenen 225 Pflanzendecken wohl am besten zum Ausdruck, denn wir finden darin nicht nur allerhand Baumsorten sondern auch viele Sorten von Nutzsträucher und allerhand Stauden wie Gemüse, Blumen und Beeren. Je näher der Mensch seiner Behausung bleibt, desto intensiver betreut er den ihm zur Verfügung stehenden 230 Erdboden und die mit ihm verbundene Pflanzenwelt. Je weiter er sich von ihr entfernt, desto mehr ist es sein Bestreben, Quantität zu erzielen.

212 **nach und nach** gradually
225 **zum Ausdruck kommen** to be expressed
230 **zur Verfügung stehen** to be at the disposal of

CHAPTER 15

DAS WILDE TIER UND DER MENSCH

Eine der interessantesten Studien auf dem Gebiete der Landschaftskunde befaßt sich mit den Wechselbeziehungen zwischen Tier und Mensch und besonders dem wilden Tier und dem Menschen, durch das Medium der Landschaft gesehen. In diese hineinversetzt erscheint das Tier dem Beobachter als verschiedenen Regionen angehörend. So sehen wir deutliche Abstufungen nicht nur in den Gattungen, Arten und Familien der Tiere innerhalb einer bestimmten Landschaft sondern auch von Landschaft zu Landschaft. Das Tier in der Waldlandschaft ist ganz anderer Art als das, welches sich auf der offenen Steppe, Savanne oder Prairie vorfindet. Ebenso ist das Tier auf den Hochgebirgen anders als das in den entgegengesetzten Regionen, dem Wasser oder sogar den Polgebieten. Und endlich muß noch die Kreatur unter dem freien Himmel, d.h. in der Luft genannt werden. Überall wurde und wird es auch noch heute vom Menschen, seinen Werken und Einflüssen berührt oder gar verfolgt. Ein besonderes Kapitel gebührt nun dem Tier in denjenigen Landstrichen, welche der Mensch sich urbar gemacht hat, oder über die sich seine Herrschaft in irgendwelcher Weise erstreckt. Sogleich drängen sich uns eine Menge Fragen auf; z.B. wer hat den gegenseitig größeren Einfluß ausgeübt, der Mensch oder das Tier? Daß [1] diese Frage nicht immer einseitig zu beantworten ist, beweisen die großen Tierwanderungen, welche von dem Leming, verschiedenen Raupensorten und einer ganzen Anzahl von Insektenarten periodisch ausgeführt werden, zur Genüge. Man könnte sich auch fragen, inwiefern das Tier sich dem allgemein stärkeren Menschen und seinen Werken angepaßt hat; ob es sich während [2] des Vorganges einer etwaigen Anpassung in irgend einem Maße physiologisch oder seelisch geändert hat; oder in welchem Maße sich der Mensch das Tier zu seinen eigenen Zwecken nutzbar gemacht hat. In

25 **zur Genüge** sufficiently*

alledem müssen wir uns dessen bewußt sein, daß das Erscheinen des Menschen die Oberfläche unseres Planeten stellenweise ganz gründlich verändert hat; daß die Landschaft, so wie wir sie heute vor unseren Augen haben, also gar nicht die ursprüngliche gewesen ist. Nehmen wir [3] den Fall an, der Mensch hätte sich nicht zu 35
seiner gegenwärtigen Stellung als „Krone der Schöpfung" emporgeschwungen, sondern er wäre ein den anderen ähnliches Geschöpf geblieben. Es wäre anzunehmen, daß das von der Natur erhaltene Gleichgewicht durch des Menschen Gegenwart nicht gestört worden wäre. Es gäbe keine Felder, Städte, industrielle Anlagen, 40
welche in so weitgehendem Maße das Landschaftsbild beeinflussen. Daß das Gleichgewicht unter den Tieren ein ganz anderes wäre, daß ihre Verbreitung ganz anders aussehen würde, daß sie ihre seelische Einstellung folglicherweise nicht hätten ändern brauchen, all dieses ist wohl ohne weiteres klar. Nun aber hat der Mensch 45
ganze Arten ausgerottet, andere bis zur Gefahr der Ausrottung gebracht. Er hat sie ihren altgewohnten Wohnsitzen enthoben, sie in Gegenden verdrängt, wo sie sich nicht zu Hause fühlen; er hat sie in Einzelfällen gezähmt und sie sich zu Haustieren gemacht. Andere Arten hat er gezwungenerweise an Schutz- 50
parke gewöhnt oder sie so in ihren natürlichen Revieren eingezwängt, daß er sie periodisch durch sogenannte Jagdgesetze und -gebräuche dezimiert, bis sie zu halbgezähmten Tieren geworden sind. Durch seine Eingriffe in die Naturgesetze hat er es so weit gebracht, daß er gewisse Arten von einem Erdteil nach dem 55
anderen verpflanzt, daß er manche Landstriche gänzlich der Tierwelt entvölkert. Anderseits aber hat er es auch fertig gebracht, daß gewisse Insektenarten sich durch seiner Hände Werk so gewaltig zu vermehren vermögen, daß sie ihm zu großen Gefahren geworden sind. Sehen wir uns das Problem ein wenig 60
genauer an, so erkennen wir sofort die eine Seite desselben: den Einfluß, den das Kulturland auf das Tier gehabt hat und noch hat. Erstens hat sich ganz bestimmt eine Änderung der Lebensgewohn-

32 **in alledem müssen wir uns bewußt sein, daß** in all this, we must be conscious of the fact that
45 **ohne weiteres** easily
54 **er hat es so weit gebracht, daß** he achieved that
57 **er hat es auch fertig gebracht, daß** he also brought it about that
60 **sehen wir uns das Problem ein wenig genauer an, so** if we look at the problem a little more closely

heiten des Tieres gezeigt. Es kann nicht geleugnet werden, daß z.B. einige Tierarten ihren Lebensunterhalt leichter zustande bringen, seit der Mensch sich in und neben ihren Revieren breit gemacht hat. Das Reh und der Hirsch lieben es, am Abend aus den Wäldern auf die bebauten Felder zu kommen und dort die viel saftigere und massenhafter zu findende Saat oder sonstige Nutzpflanzen zu verzehren. Überall, wo dies geschieht, hat der Mensch den Schrei erhoben, das Wild tue ihm zu großen Schaden an. Schlimmer als Rehe und sonstiges Damwild sind Wildschweine, die den Boden zerwühlen und dergestalt Schaden anrichten. In anderen Erdteilen könnte man den durch Elefanten oder Flußpferde angerichteten Schaden anführen. Es ist noch gar nicht lange her, seit wir hier in Amerika unter den ungeheuren Taubenschwärmen zu leiden hatten, ebenso wie der Farmer heutzutage wieder unter den großen sich zur Südwanderung fertig machenden Starenschaaren zu leiden hat. Raubtiere halten sich nicht mehr an freies Wild, sondern entwickeln leicht die Gewohnheit, sich ihre Mahlzeiten unter den viel leichter erreichbaren Haustieren wie Rindern oder Schafen zu holen. Sie werden daher erst recht als Raubtiere gehaßt und vom Menschen planmäßig verfolgt. Einige Arten, wie z.B. der Fuchs oder der amerikanische Prairiewolf, haben sich aber nicht verdrängen lassen. Im Gegenteil, sie haben sich den neuen Verhältnissen so gut anpassen können, daß sie sich ihr früheres Revier wieder zurückerobern. Auch kleine Säugetiere und Vögel können in dieser Beziehung genannt werden. Man denke nur daran, wie die Ratte sich auch unter dem größten Vernichtungsdruck unter den Menschen und in seinen Siedlungen behauptet, oder wie es der Sperling verstanden hat, sich zu einem ausgesprochenen Stadt- und Zivilisationsvogel zu entwickeln. Ein anderes Beispiel hierzu liefert das amerikanische Rotkehlchen.

Der Einfluß der Kulturlandschaft macht sich aber auch in einer Änderung des tierischen Seelenlebens bemerkbar. Jagdtiere sind nicht nur unter der Pflege des Menschen größer und stärker geworden, sondern haben oft haustierähnliche Eigenschaften

64 **es kann nicht geleugnet werden, daß** it cannot be denied that

73 **Schaden anrichten** to inflict damage

85 **im Gegenteil** on the contrary

88 **in dieser Beziehung** in this respect

angenommen. Der Hirsch nähert sich oft der menschlichen Siedlung und liebt es, die künstlich angelegten Apfelgärten zu besuchen 100 oder gar mitunter auf der Weide unter dem Vieh zu grasen. Ohne Zweifel ist es dieser Zug der Vertrautheit, welcher den Menschen zuerst veranlaßt hat, Zähmungsversuche zu machen. Und wo einst Millionen von Bisons die amerikanischen Prairien durchzogen, folgten ihnen die ungeheuren Rinderherden, bis auch diese 105 wieder den großen Schafherden oder in günstig gelegenen Landstrichen weitläufigen Farmen Platz machen mußten. Das Damwild ist scheuer geworden, denn es wird von Zeit zu Zeit gejagt; ebenso geht es mit denjenigen Raubtieren, die sich auf Kosten des Menschen erhalten. Anderseits aber sind die Sinne des Schafes 110 verstumpft, wohl auch die des Rindes. Hingegen haben sich die Sinne des Hundes ohne Zweifel verschärft. Ein zweiter Einfluß, der übrigens schon oben angedeutet worden ist, ist der auf den Körperbau des Tieres. Nicht nur werden möglichst große Körperausmaße erstrebt, sondern man hat, dem menschlichen Ge- 115 schmack Rechnung tragend, allerlei Sports planmäßig entwickelt. Man erstrebt möglichst großen Fettansatz oder größere Fleischmengen; man zielt auf eine möglichst große Eierproduktion hin oder auf eine Kombination von Eierproduktion und Fleischertrag. Hirsche tragen heutzutage größere Geweihe als früher, denn sie 120 werden, wohl auch nicht vollständig zufriedenstellend, während der Winterszeit mit Futter und Mineralien versehen.

So scheint der Mensch in gewissem Maße, wenn auch vielleicht unbewußt, planmäßig und zu gleicher Zeit auswählerisch vorgegangen zu sein. Einige Tierarten hat er zurückgewiesen, an- 125 dere bekämpft er. Einige scheint er in seiner Umgebung zu dulden, andere hat er an sich herangezogen. In gewissen Fällen gibt er sich sogar mit Kreuzungsversuchen ab, die sich nicht immer nur auf Haustiere zu erstrecken brauchen. Das Pferd hat er mit dem Zebra gekreuzt, den Löwen mit dem Tiger, einhei- 130 mische minderwertige Rindersorten verbessert er durch Kreuzungen mit anderen fremden Arten, eines Teils, um sie wegen ihrer größeren Fleisch- Milch- oder sonstiger Erträge aufzu-

107 **Platz machen** to make room for
109 **auf Kosten des** at the expense of the
116 **Rechnung tragen** to make concessions to
123 **in gewissem Maße** to a certain degree
132 **eines Teils** partly

züchten, anderen Teils aber auch, um sie in einem sonst ungünstigen Klima besser gedeihen zu lassen. Man erinnere sich 135
nur hier an die erfolgreichen Kreuzungen zwischen dem indischen Zeburind und gewissen Rinderarten hier in den Vereinigten Staaten, besonders im Südwesten oder im Staate Florida. In verhältnismäßig neuer Zeit ist dann auch noch das Züchtungsverfahren verschiedener Sorten von Pelzträgern hinzugekommen, 140
welche früher fast gänzlich dem freien Zustande der Natur entnommen wurden, nun aber zu Hunderttausenden auf besonders dazu eingerichteten Farmen für den Pelzmarkt gezüchtet werden.

Aber nicht immer kann der Mensch das Tier beherrschen. Manchmal steht [4] er ihm machtlos gegenüber. Das ist z.B. der 145
Fall, wenn gewisse Arten von Heuschrecken ihren natürlichen Rundlauf beendet haben und dann in ungeheuren Schwärmen an Grünernten Schaden anrichten. Oft wäre so etwas nicht möglich, hätte der Mensch nicht durch sein Pflügen ungeheure Landstrekken aufgelockert, um so im Boden den Insekten einen viel gün- 150
stigeren Brutschrank zu bieten, als sie es sonst hätten. Dasselbe kann von Bakterien und sonstigen Schädlingen gesagt werden, welche in unseren Obstgegenden zu Hause sind und oft die Ernten um ein Großes beeinträchtigen. Im Großen und Ganzen aber ist der Mensch erfolgreich geblieben in seinem Kampf gegen die Tier- 155
welt, und er lernt immer systematischer, die noch zu beherrschenden Tierarten irgendwie zu kontrollieren.

138 **in verhältnismäßig neuer Zeit** in relatively recent times
148 **so etwas** something of the sort
153 **zu Hause sein** to be native to
154 **um ein Großes** largely
154 **im Großen und Ganzen** by and large

CHAPTER 16

AUS DER GESCHICHTE DER MEDIZINISCHEN WISSENSCHAFT

Über die Geschichte der medizinischen Wissenschaft können Bände geschrieben werden. Es wäre[1] also ein fast erfolgloses Unternehmen, wenn wir innerhalb weniger Paragraphen auch nur das anführen wollten, was für den Fortschritt dieser Wissenschaft maßgebend ist. Was wir aber dennoch tun können, ist, 5
einige Zeitpunkte und Entwicklungen zu erwähnen, welche zusammengenommen die medizinische Wissenschaft in ihrem historischen Verlauf kennzeichnen. Es sei[2] zunächst erwähnt, daß die Wurzeln oder vielmehr deren Anfänge in der grauen geschichtlichen Vorzeit nicht mehr zu erkennen sind. Der Name selbst 10
läßt erkennen, daß sie als Wissenschaft, d.h. als organisiertes und zusammengefaßtes Wissensgebiet ins alte Griechenland zu setzen ist. Ars medicina bedeutet ärztliche Kunst oder Heilkunde und behandelt die Gesundheit wie Krankheit des Menschen und neuerdings auch die des Tieres, in welchem Falle wir dann von 15
Veterinärmedizin sprechen. Eine noch so oberflächliche Untersuchung der Wissensgebiete, welche alle unter dem Namen Medizinalwissenschaft gedeckt sind, läßt ersehen, daß diese keineswegs ein in sich geschlossenes Gebiet sondern aus einer ganzen Anzahl Gebiete zusammengesetzt ist. So erkennt man erstens die theo- 20
retische und angewandte Medizin; dann schließt man diesen medizinische Nebenfächer und diesen wiederum sog. Ergänzungsfächer an. Neuerdings haben sich nochmals Sondergebiete, wie die Orthopädie, Urologie und Lichtbehandlung aus schon bestehenden Zweigen losgelöst. Theoretische Medizin ist ent- 25
weder experimentell oder beschreibend, wie z.B. die Anatomie oder die Toxikologie; zu den angewandten Zweigen rechnet man,

15 **in welchem Falle** in which case
16 **eine noch so oberflächliche Untersuchung** even a very superficial investigation
18 **(es) läßt ersehen, daß** (it) shows that

sagen wir, die Chirurgie, zu den Nebenfächern die Zahnheilkunde, zu den ergänzenden Fächern die Bakteriologie. Ohne Zweifel werden sich in der Zukunft noch weitere Zweige entwickeln. 30

Ganz der modernen Geisteseinstellung entsprungen ist diese so hoch entwickelte[3] Wissenschaft nicht, denn es ist erstaunenswert, daß wir so manche angewandte ärztliche Behandlung schon unter den sogenannten primitiven Völkern und Völkergruppen vorfinden. An Hand von in Ausgrabungen gefundenen Schädeln, 35 z.B. hat man feststellen können, daß der vorgeschichtliche Mensch schon eine Art von Chirurgie betrieben haben muß. Löcher an gewissen Schädelstellen sind kunstgerecht mit Instrumenten gebohrt worden, vielleicht mit der Absicht, inneren Druck zu erleichtern. Auch heute noch haben primitive Völker bestimmte 40 Tränke oder auch Abführmittel, Umschläge und Einreibungen, welche alle als Heilmittel angewandt werden. Der Arzt war und ist auch heute noch bei diesen Stämmen der bekannte Medizinmann; oft verbindet er das Priesteramt mit dem des Arztes. Daß das Heilen schon in vorgeschichtlicher Zeit von außerordentlich 45 hoher Bedeutung gewesen sein muß, beweist manche Aufzeichnung in Keilschrifttexten, die man unter den Überresten der babylonischen und assyrischen Zivilisationen gefunden hat und die das Berufswesen der damaligen Ärzte zu regeln suchten. Auch da war der medizinische Beruf mit dem Priesteramt eng ver- 50 bunden und machte sogar von der Astrologie Gebrauch. Man dachte sich die Gesundheit des Menschen als stark von kosmischen Einflüssen bedingt. Die Krankheit war oft Folge von dämonischen Kräften, und man übte deshalb die „angewandte“ Medizin in Gestalt von Dämonenbeschwörungen. Die obener- 55 wähnten Keilschrifttexte enthalten aber auch schon eine ganze Anzahl von Rezepten. In der ägyptischen Zivilisation ist die medizinische Wissenschaft ungleich höher entwickelt. Da kannte man schon den Unterschied von menschlicher und tierischer Behandlung, wohl weil das Tier im alten Ägypten so hohe Vereh- 60 rung genoß. Die Chirurgie, die Gynäkologie und die Pharmakologie waren als getrennte Wissensfelder bekannt. Auch in diesem

32 **es ist erstaunenswert, daß** it is astonishing that
35 **an Hand von** on the basis of
51 **Gebrauch machen von** to use
53 **Folge sein von** to be a consequence of
56 **eine ganze Anzahl von** a large number of

Falle waren oft der Priester, Sterndeuter und Arzt eine und dieselbe Person. Eine weitere Übersicht der alten Völker würde ebenfalls von fesselndem Interesse sein; wir wollen uns aber nun wenigstens mit einigen Worten der Erwähnung an das alte Griechenland selbst wenden, denn dort erfährt die medizinische Wissenschaft den ersten Anflug des Wissenschaftlichen. Bekannt sind die Tatsachen, daß Asklepias im 7. Jahrhundert zum alleinherrschenden Heilgott gemacht wurde; ferner, daß sich nach und nach unter dem Einfluß der verschiedenen philosophischen Schulen auch solche im Medizinalwesen ausbildeten. Das Wesentliche aber an der ganzen Geschichte ist, daß diese Philosophen die Natur selbst zum Gegenstand ihrer Untersuchungen machten und dieselbe so dem wirklichen Wesen der Medizin um ein Beträchtliches näher brachten. Das Magische wurde abgestreift, das Reelle wurde betrachtet. Die andere für uns so wichtige Errungenschaft der altgriechischen Medizinalkunst ist in dem Corpus hippocraticum enthalten, dem ersten Sammelwerk über das medizinische Praktikum. Es trägt den Namen des noch heute hoch verehrten Vaters der medizinischen Wissenschaft, Hippokrates. Zum erstenmal befinden wir uns angesichts der Theorien, daß der Sitz von Gesundheit und Krankheit nicht in der Laune von Dämonen ist, sondern im menschlichen Körper selbst. Das klassische Altertum war also schon im Besitz entscheidender Tatsachen: dem Einfluß der Natur auf den Gesundheitszustand, dem Sitz von Krankheit und Gesundheit im Körper selbst und einer schon gewissermaßen systematischen Abhandlung über das Wesen von Krankheit und Gesundheit. Daß diese Ansichten von der Vier-Säftelehre getragen wurden, ist weniger wichtig; entscheidend ist die geistige Einstellung zum Problem. Das wirkliche Praktikum in der Bekämpfung der Krankheit ist nun auch schon etwas ganz Anderes als es früher der Fall war: man stellt sich nun auf Beobachtungen des Kranken und der Krankheit ein, um so ein Krankheitsbild, eine Diagnose, zu erhalten, auf Grund deren man zur Behandlung selbst überschreitet. Anders war es dagegen in Rom, wo man infolge des gesamten so hoch entwickelten Staatswesens eine noch weitere Entwicklung der medizinischen Wissenschaften hätte erwarten können. Statt dessen wird das ganze

63 **eine und dieselbe** one and the same 82 **angesichts der** in face of the

Problem in die Hand von Sklaven gelegt, die sich wohl der über- 100
lieferten Heilkunst der Griechen bedienten aber von selbst wenig
hinzufügten; d.h. bis der große Arzt Galen auftritt. Galen (130–
201? n. Chr.) scheidet also die römische Entwicklungsperiode in
zwei scharf von einander getrennte Abschnitte: die vorgalenische
und nachgalenische. Zwar hatte man auch in Rom ebenso gut 105
Schulen wie in Griechenland, sie konnten aber nicht in demselben
Maße beitragen wie die Griechen. Das meiste, was man von
ihnen sagen kann, beschränkt sich auf die engere und wirksamere
Verknüpfung einzelner[4] medizinischer Wissenschaftszweige wie
der Anatomie, Physiologie und Heilmittellehre. Galens Lehrge- 110
bäude enthält auch Hinweise über experimentelle Arbeit und
Tiersektionen sowie Gedanken über den Blutkreislauf. Im
Großen und Ganzen aber werden hier die Grundlagen gelegt,
welche späteren Jahrhunderten zur Grundlage einer wirklich sich
voll entwickelnden Heilswissenschaft zu dienen bestimmt ist. 115

Was wir bisher betrachtet haben, befaßt sich ausschließlich mit
denjenigen Strömungen, die sich allmählich zur medizinischen
Wissenschaft selbst entwickeln werden. Nun kommt aber etwas
im Mittelalter hinzu, was für den weiteren Verlauf der Dinge von
größter Bedeutung ist. Unsere Zeit selbst ist in derselben Hin- 120
sicht gekennzeichnet: die Errichtung besonderer Schulen an
bestimmten Orten, wo die Wissenschaft, hier die medizinische,
gepflegt wird. Diese Schulen bilden nicht nur Sammelpunkte
für Ärztepersönlichkeiten sondern auch für Gedanken und eine
nun schneller wachsende Literatur. Das klingt schon recht 125
modern an. Die erste Schule dieser Art ist die in Salerno im
südlichen Italien, wo zuerst zwar nur überlieferte Kunst angewandt und diskutiert wird, zumal die, welche durch die Araber
vom Morgenland an das Abendland überliefert wird. Die Chirurgie aber erlebt dort einen bedeutenden Aufschwung. Andere 130
Schulen, nun werden sie Universitäten genannt, werden in Bologna, Padua, Paris, und anderwärts gegründet. Man schreitet
nun an eine programmatische, wenn auch noch rohe, Ausbildung
der Ärzte. Viel Philosophie ist in den damaligen medizinischen
Anschauungen enthalten, und man nennt sie deshalb die scho- 135
lastische Medizin, zumal wird deren folgerichtige Entwicklung
stark durch das Kirchendogma gehindert, aber die Verbindung
medizinischer Ausbildung mit bestimmten Universitäten kann

dennoch als das Verdienst der mittelalterlichen Phase angesehen werden. 140

Von nun an ist es in der Skizzierung unseres Entwicklungsbildes ratsam, den weiteren Verlauf nach Jahrhunderten einzuteilen, weil sich ja nun einerseits die medizinische Geschichte viel schneller entwickelt, und auch weil andererseits die neuere Entwicklung so reichhaltig wird, daß man der Übersicht halber 145 einer klaren Organisierung folgen sollte. So kommen wir denn ins 16. Jahrhundert, das deshalb bemerkenswert ist, weil in seinem Verlauf zwei Erscheinungen besonders klar hervortreten: die kritische Reinigung der vielen überlieferten technischen Werke durch das Bemühen, das dem humanistischen Verfahren eigen war, 150 und die Vertiefung des wissenschaftlichen Interesses in die immer schneller wachsenden Naturwissenschaften. Das heißt, das 16. Jahrhundert schreitet nicht nur auf theoretischen sondern auch auf praktischen Grundlagen mächtig weiter. Personifiziert wird dieses Übergangsstadium in der prächtigen Persönlichkeit von 155 Paracelsus, dem vielleicht auch das Verdienst zuzusprechen ist, daß er die ersten wirklichen Anfänge der organischen Chemie geliefert hat. Er sucht Medikamente für die Bekämpfung der einzelnen Krankheiten in den Pflanzen der ihn umgebenden Welt und verficht seine Ansichten mit Wort und Tat. Das folgende 160 Jahrhundert aber kann erst als das große Jahrhundert der großen Entdeckungen angesehen werden, nicht aber ohne die Hilfe, welche der medizinischen Wissenschaft aus der Physik und Chemie erwächst. Große anatomische Entdeckungen werden von Malpighi, de Graaf, Leeuwenhoek und anderen gemacht. Harvey 165 (1578–1657) entdeckt den Blutkreislauf, und teils als dessen Folge werden große Fortschritte auch in der angewandten Medizin verzeichnet, obwohl die Chirurgie wohl noch zu kurz dabei abkommt. Das 18. Jahrhundert baut sich dann auf dem Experimentellen des vorigen auf und sieht die Gründung solcher berühmten 170 Schulen wie der Wiener medizinischen Klinik. Sie hat sich in der Folgezeit und bis in die Jetztzeit hinein Weltruf erworben und hat Ärzte aus allen Ländern und Weltteilen angelockt. Die medizinische Literatur wird durch das große Handbuch Hallers,

141 **von nun an** from now on
156 **ihm ist das Verdienst zuzusprechen, daß** his merit is that
168 **sie kommt zu kurz dabei ab** it comes off second best

das alle damaligen bekannten physiologischen Kenntnisse zusam- 175
menfaßt, bereichert. Die pathologische Anatomie wird von
Morgagni (1682–1771) gegründet. Die Chirurgie und Geburts-
hilfe verwenden die Erfahrungen der Anatomie und Physiologie
und entwickeln sich mächtig. Spezialgebiete der medizinischen
Wissenschaften beginnen, sich abzuspalten und auszubilden, so die 180
Kinderheilkunst. Als gegen Ende des Jahrhunderts endlich die
französische Revolution ausbricht und sich behauptet, ist das
internationale Zeitalter für das gesamte medizinische Wesen
vorbei, denn die einzelnen Länder fangen nun an, ihre eigenen
Wege zu gehen. Daß die politische Nationalisierung in Europa 185
das Ihre dazu beigetragen hat, kann natürlich nicht bezweifelt
werden.

Die letzte Entwicklungszeit kann entweder unter dem 19. und
20. Jahrhundert zu einer Einheit zusammengefaßt und als die
Neuzeit betrachtet werden, oder man könnte diese Periode wie- 190
derum in Einzelabschnitten betrachten. Allgemein aber kann
man sich damit zufrieden geben, wenn man dieselben in eine
Vor- und Nach-Virchow Periode einteilt. Die vielen philosophischen Strömungen, darunter solche von politischer, literari-
scher und pseudo-wissenschaftlicher Natur, haben viel Verwirrung 195
verursacht. Dann aber kam das Jahr 1839 und mit ihm die Entdeckung der Zelle als lebentragendes Element durch Schwann
in der Biologie. Damit war auf einmal große Klarheit geschaffen,
denn man wandte sich nun dem Kern der ganzen Sache selbst zu:
der einzelnen Zelle als dem Sitz aller pathologischen Erscheinungen 200
der Krankheiten. Virchow baute das so neuerworbene Wissen zu
seiner bekannten Zellularpathologie aus und schuf dadurch eine
Anschauungsweise, die sich heute noch am stärksten fühlbar
macht. Nimmt man noch dazu die Entdeckung der Welt der
Bazillen und Mikroben, am besten durch Koch und Pasteur 205
gekennzeichnet, so kann man sich eine lebhafte Vorstellung vom
Kommenden machen. Entdeckung folgt auf Entdeckung: die
Röntgenstrahlen kommen 1895, Radium 1898; Wassermann gibt
der Welt seine bekannte Blutuntersuchung auf Syphilis im Jahre
1907; Ehrlich und Hata erscheinen 1909 mit dem Salvarsan, und 210
Banting und Best 1921 mit dem Insulin. Die Physiologie wird
zur Grundlage des klinischen Verfahrens. Die Chemie wird der
Medizin immer wichtiger; sie gibt uns die Untersuchungen und

Isolierung sowie den Gebrauch der verschiedenen Vitamine und Hormone. Die Psychologie endlich liefert ihre eigenen Beiträge. 215 In immer engere Felder oder Wirkungsbezirke wird die medizinische Wissenschaft geteilt, eine Tendenz, in der wir heute noch stecken und welche eine immer stärkere und fachmännischere Ausbildung des künftigen Arztes erfordert.

CHAPTER 17

DIE TUBERKULOSE

Unter den vielen die Menschen wie Tiere befallenden Krankheiten ist die Tuberkulose eine der wenigen, über welche die medizinische Wissenschaft gut Bescheid weiß. So ist es denn auch nicht verwunderlich, daß sie, verglichen mit anderen Krankheiten, in den letzten Jahrzehnten immer mehr an Wichtigkeit verloren hat und heutzutage fast ganz kontrollierbar geworden [1] ist. Diese allgemeine Beobachtung hält aber nur für die sog. zivilisierten Länder Stich, denn wenn wir zahlenmäßige Vergleiche zwischen, sagen wir, einerseits dem Weißen und anderseits dem Neger anstellten, so würden wir sofort das häufigere Vorkommen dieser Krankheit unter den Negern bemerken. Man könnte natürlich auch andere Rassengruppen, wie z.B. Indianer u.a.m. zu solch einem Vergleich heranziehen und würde ein ähnliches Mengenverhältnis in Augenschein nehmen können. Untersuchten wir zudem noch die Verbreitung der Tuberkulose nach Ständen und Beschäftigung, so träte eine weitere Tatsache hervor: unter gewöhnlichen, d.h. Handarbeitern ist Tuberkulose sechs mal so häufig wie bei Berufsleuten. Mit anderen Worten, wenn wir 28,3 Todesfälle pro 100 000 männlichen Angestellten annehmen — nur auf Tuberkulose bezogen — so ist das genaue zahlenmäßige Mengenverhältnis bei gewöhnlichen Handarbeitern auf 183,1 zu setzen. Ein weiterer Einblick in die Lage bringt die Annahme nahe, daß der Prozentsatz der Todesfälle, die direkt auf Tuberkulose zurückzuführen sind, proportional mit dem Grad der beruflichen Ausbildung abnimmt. Man könnte also sagen, Tuberkulose ist eine Berufskrankheit.

3 **gut Bescheid wissen** to be well informed
7 **sie hält Stich für** it holds true for
14 **in Augenschein nehmen** to observe
18 **mit anderen Worten** in other words
22 **ein weiterer Einblick in die Lage** another look into the situation

Das ist aber noch lange nicht die ganze Geschichte, denn je genauer wir uns die Sachlage ansehen, desto mehr Auskunft erhalten wir darüber. So hat man im Laufe der Zeit feststellen können, daß Tuberkulose vorwiegend eine Jugendkrankheit zu sein scheint, denn die meisten Todesfälle kommen im Alter von neunzehn bis fünfundzwanzig Jahren vor. Von da an fallen sie allmählich und ziemlich gleichmäßig ab, um im Alter von 75 bis 80 Jahren verschwindend klein zu werden. Das Umgekehrte ist der Fall mit Krankheiten wie Herzkrankheit, dem Krebs, der Lungenentzündung, Nierenentzündung und anderen. So kommen die weitaus meisten Todesfälle, die auf Herzkrankheit beruhen, im Alter von 65 bis 75 Jahren vor, während der Krebs sich besonders im Alter von 50 bis 70 Jahren hervortut. Eine genauere Studie dieser verschiedenen Krankheiten würde ohne Zweifel ebenfalls ergeben, daß das Berufsleben viel mit dem Erscheinen und Verlauf derselben zu tun hat. Art des Berufslebens, Ausführung desselben sowie die notwendigerweise damit verbundene Lebenshaltung müssen unbedingt als beiträgliche Ursachen angesehen werden. Eine andere bedeutsame Beobachtung liegt darin, daß beide Geschlechter unterschiedlich von der Tuberkulose betroffen werden. Im männlichen Geschlecht macht sie sich besonders im Zeitraum von 35 bis 40 Jahren bemerkbar, während das weibliche Geschlecht besonders schwer in den frühen Zwanzigern (vom 20. bis 25.) zu leiden hat. Man hat dafür verschiedene Erklärungen geliefert, welche alle ohne Zweifel ihre gute Begründung haben. Sehen wir aber von diesen beiden ebengenannten kurzen Zeitspannen ab, so bleibt dennoch die Tatsache, daß das männliche Geschlecht allgemein eine ungemein größere Anzahl von Todesfällen dieser Art zeigt als das weibliche. Andere Befunde von Bedeutung beziehen sich darauf,[2] daß das Leben in der Stadt der Verbreitung dieser Krankheit weit günstiger ist als das Leben auf dem Lande; daß sie keine erbliche Eigenschaft hat; daß sogar die Neigung zu ihr nicht vererbt wird, sondern daß sie vielmehr Ansteckungskrankheit ist; d.h. daß sie von einer Person zur anderen übertragen wird. Das erklärt wohl auch die Erscheinung, daß sie vorwiegend „Familienkrankheit" ist, denn als eine besonders eng verknüpfte Gruppe bietet die Familie ihr weit mehr Gelegenheiten sich fortzupflanzen als unter anderen freien Menschengruppen.

32 **von da an** from there on

Was wissen wir über den geschichtlichen Hintergrund dieser Krankheit? Hippokrates, der große griechische Arzt, welcher übrigens von 460 bis 377 v. Chr. lebte, erkannte die durch sie verursachte Gesundheitsstörung und nannte sie phthisis. Dieses Wort bedeutet „dahinschwindend". Die Deutschen nannten diese Krankheit lange „Schwindsucht", die Krankheit des Dahinschwindens, und in der angelsächsischen Welt war sie ebenso lange unter dem Namen „consumption" bekannt, was eigentlich dieselbe Bedeutung hat. Hippokrates aber wußte nicht, was die Ursache dieser Krankheit war; also konnte er auch keine genauen Heilmittel angeben. Dennoch aber verschrieb er gutes Essen und sonstige leichte Gesundheitsmaßnahmen. So blieb die Sache bis ins achtzehnte Jahrhundert, als es Bayle (1774–1816) glückte, die verschiedenen Entwicklungsstadien der einzelnen Tuberkeln bis zu deren Losbruch aus der Lunge zu verfolgen. Eine andere wichtige Entwicklung ging zeitlich Hand in Hand: die Erfindung des Stethoskops durch Laennec, einen Franzosen. Mittels dieses Instruments war es ihm möglich, verschiedene Brusttöne zu unterscheiden und sie so mit bestimmten Gesundheitszuständen in Verbindung zu bringen. Dadurch begründete er die medizinische Methode der Diagnose, eine der wichtigsten Handhabe des neuzeitlichen Mediziners. Die eigentliche Geschichte aber beginnt erst, als man während des „goldenen Zeitalters" der europäischen Wissenschaften in der zweiten Hälfte des neunzehnten Jahrhunderts die Welt der Bakterien entdeckte, sie fachgemäß untersuchte und erforschte. Die Namen Koch und Pasteur sind zu bekannt, als daß wir uns eingehend mit diesen Männern beschäftigen wollen. Sei es genug zu sagen, daß Koch 1882 den Tuberkelbazillus entdeckte und auch bewies, daß die Tuberkulose nur durch ihn allein übertragen werden kann. Die Isolierung dieses Krankheitserregers ist eine der großen Errungenschaften der modernen medizinischen Wissenschaft, und wir verdanken den Rückgang der Krankheit an sich fast ausschließlich dieser Entdeckung sowie den Arbeiten, die sich im folgenden darauf stützten. Gelöst aber war das Problem noch nicht, denn es stellte sich heraus, daß es nicht nur eine Art von Tuberkulose gibt, sondern auch noch eine zweite, die sich an das Rind heftet. Folgende

92 **sei es genug zu sagen, daß** suffice it to say that

99 **es stellte sich heraus, daß** it was found that

Forschungen führten dann zur Erhitzung der Kuhmilch bis zu einem gewissen Grad, was wir heute mit dem Namen Pasteurisieren bezeichnen. Damit war eine der großen Ansteckungsgefahren beseitigt, und es blieb nunmehr Aufgabe der Wissenschaft, 105 auch die erste Ansteckungsquelle zu beseitigen, die der Übertragung von Mensch zu Mensch. Der erste große Fortschritt in dieser Richtung wurde dann von dem Forscher Dr. Nägeli, einem Schweizer, gemacht. Er fand nämlich, daß auf Grund von Hunderten von Leichenuntersuchungen weitaus die größte Anzahl der 110 Gestorbenen charakteristische Lungennarben aufwiesen, die von Tuberkeln herrührten. Nägeli stand nun vor der Frage, ob Tuberkulose die Neigung habe, selbst auszuheilen, oder ob sie sich nur bis zu gewissen Entwicklungsstadien hinziehe, um dann in einen Ruhestand zu gehen. Da kam ihm ein anderer Arzt zu 115 Hilfe, ein Dr. von Pirquet, welcher das vorher von Koch angewandte Verfahren, Patienten auf das Vorhandensein von Tuberkulose zu prüfen, dergestalt verbesserte, daß er schon durch das bloße Einritzen eines Tropfens Tuberkulins in die Haut des Armes und die darauf folgende Abwesenheit oder Anwesenheit einer 120 roten Geschwulst an der Einimpfungsstelle auf die Krankheit selbst schließen konnte. Es zeigte sich demzufolge, daß man wohl positiv darauf reagieren konnte, aber die Krankheit selbst nicht zu haben brauchte. Das heißt, es war wohl möglich, daß man den Tuberkelbazillus in sich beherberge aber dennoch nicht davon 125 krank zu sein brauche. Positive Bestätigung fand dies ferner durch die Anwendung von Wilhelm Röntgens sogenannten X-Strahlen, mittels derer man die Lungen photographieren und so von Pirquets Annahme bestätigen konnte.

Die nächste Aufgabe, die sich der medizinischen Wissenschaft 130 ergab, war eine Annäherung an die Heilung der Tuberkulose selbst. Der geschichtlich erste wichtige Vorschlag kam von George Bodington, der 1840 unbedingte Ruhe und frische Luft verschrieb. Neunzehn Jahre später eröffnete Dr. Hermann Brehmer das erste Sanatorium im Schwarzwalde. Und damit 135 betrat die Heilkunde denjenigen Weg in der Behandlung der Schwindsucht, den sie bisher immer noch beibehalten hat. Wollen wir uns aber noch weiter mit dem Problem dieser Krankheit

112 **er steht vor der Frage** he is faced with the problem 128 **mittels derer** by means of which

beschäftigen, so müssen wir uns zunächst fragen, wie sie von einer Person zur anderen übertragen werden kann. Man hat verschiedene Arten der Übertragung feststellen können: die Gewohnheit des Ausspuckens, das Übertragen des Bazillus' durch das Medium von Tischgeräten, durch Kuhmilch oder durch unmittelbaren Kontakt mit einer erkrankten Person. Das Eindringen des Bazillus' allein aber genügt noch nicht, um die Krankheit selbst hervorzurufen, denn die Widerstandskraft der in Frage kommenden Person mag entweder so groß sein, daß er isoliert wird, oder er wird zufällig sofort wieder aus dem Körper entfernt. Unter Widerstandskraft brauchen wir hier nicht gerade nur an den allgemeinen Gesundheitszustand denken; es kann auch sein, daß die wandernden weißen Blutzellen den Eindringling sofort unschädlich machen. Wird er aber nicht wieder entfernt und setzt er sich an einem günstigen Platz fest, so hat seine Vernichtungsarbeit auch schon begonnen. Denn er ist mit einer außerordentlichen Vermehrungsfähigkeit ausgestattet und vermehrt sich schneller als die weißen Blutzellen. Es ist demnach klar, daß ganz bestimmte Bedingungen gegeben sein müssen, welche die Übertragung erst ermöglichen. So ist die Ansteckungsgefahr besonders für Kleinkinder groß, denn sie kommen widerwillen in körperliche Berührung mit den sie umgebenden Erwachsenen. Ein zweiter Ansteckungsherd ist dann auch in der von den Kindern besuchten Schule zu suchen, denn dort häufen sich die körperlichen Berührungspunkte. Und zuletzt wäre noch hinzuzufügen, daß das sogenannte Übergangsalter für Knaben und Mädchen, aber besonders für die letzteren, gefährlich ist, denn es scheint, die körperlichen und wohl auch seelischen Anstrengungen sind dann besonders groß. Aus dem Gesagten ist es dann wieder ersichtlich, daß man auf unbedingte Sauberkeit der Person und Umgebung achten muß sowie auch auf genügende Ruhe, um dem Körper die Widerstandsfähigkeit nicht zu beeinträchtigen.

Was die frühen Anzeichen oder Symptome der Krankheit anbetrifft, so kann man nicht mit Bestimmtheit sagen, daß sie immer unzweideutig auf die Anwesenheit und Verbreitung des schädlichen

146 **in Frage kommend** respective
150 **es kann auch sein, daß** it may also be that
163 **es wäre noch hinzuzufügen, daß** there would still be added the fact that
167 **aus dem Gesagten ist es dann ersichtlich, daß** from what has been said it is clear that

Bazillus' hindeuten, denn sie können ebenso gut auf andere körperliche Beschwerden weisen. Ja, anfänglich [3] sind gar keine 175 Anzeichen zu bemerken. Der Bazillus hat sich eben noch nicht weit genug im Körper, vor allem in der Lunge, ausgebreitet, um dem Organismus beschwerlich zu werden. Die weißen Blutzellen sind noch in zu großer Anzahl im Kampf mit dem Tuberkelbazillus begriffen. Treten aber später Anzeichen auf, so kön- 180 nen sie zweierlei Art sein, und zwar sind sie entweder ganz örtlich zu finden, oder der ganze Körper ist davon mitgenommen. Das erste allgemein gültige Anzeichen ist körperliche Müdigkeit, die aber wieder, wie schon angedeutet, auch auf andere gesundheitliche Mängel hinweisen kann. Verdauungsstörungen können sich 185 ebenfalls bemerkbar machen; dazu kommt dann noch anhaltender Gewichtsverlust. Auch dieser braucht nicht notwendigerweise auf Schwindsucht hinzudeuten, denn er kann auch Symptom des gefürchteten Krebses sein. Schließt sich aber darnach anhaltender Husten, und besonders blutender Husten an, so 190 hat man das erste bestimmt auf Schwindsucht weisende Zeichen. Es ist natürlich nicht immer der Fall, daß diese sich immer auf die Lunge legt. Ganz im Gegenteil: andere Körperteile können ebenso davon befallen werden. Oft werden die Wirbelsäule oder die großen Gelenke der Hüften, gewisse Drüsen im Genick, oder 195 die Eingeweide befallen. Man hat auch Tuberkulose der Haut, der Nieren, der verschiedenen Sinnesorgane und sogar der Knochen festgestellt. Ganz allgemein gesprochen erkennt man drei bestimmte Stadien an: die frühe, mittlere und fortschrittliche Tuberkulose, und es kann gesagt werden, daß, je eher die 200 ersten Anzeichen festgestellt werden, umso sicherer eine eventuelle Heilung des Patienten bewirkt werden kann.

Dank dem Bemühen des Mediziners, des sozialen Arbeitens einzelner Gesellschaften sowie der menschlichen Gesellschaft überhaupt ist man nun der Krankheit derart auf den Leib ge- 205 rückt, daß fast überall effektiv unterhaltene und unterstützte Gesundheitsprogramme in Gestalt von Schuluntersuchungen, Massen-Röntgenuntersuchungen unter der minder begünstigten Bevölkerung und Sanatorien bestehen. Das heißt, seitdem es möglich geworden ist, den Erreger der Krankheit genau in seinem 210

198 **ganz allgemein gesprochen** generally speaking

203 **dank dem** thanks to the

205 **auf den Leib rücken** to attack

Wesen und seiner Lebensweise kennenzulernen, ist man programmatisch gegen ihn verfahren und auch in diesem Unternehmen siegreich hervorgegangen. Hauptsächlich werden Sanatorien dem Patienten nur deswegen zur Verfügung gestellt, um ihm das zu bieten, wofür er, sich selbst überlassen, wenig oder keine Sorge tragen würde: absolute Ruhe und gute Pflege. Nicht nur der Körper sondern auch das Gemüt muß Ruhe haben. Seelische Anstrengungen wie Furcht, Kummer und Sorgen ziehen entsprechende Körperanstrengungen nach sich, und diesen muß der Kranke enthoben werden. Ist die Krankheit aber schon zu weit fortgeschritten, und ist deshalb die gewöhnliche Pflege in einem Sanatorium aussichtslos, so kann noch in anderer Weise verfahren werden: die betroffene Lunge des Kranken kann operativ in den Ruhestand gesetzt werden, sodaß sie nun nicht mehr die anstrengende Arbeit des Atmens zu verrichten braucht. Es ist dem Arzt nämlich bekannt, daß jedesmal, wenn die Lunge einatmet und sich dadurch ausdehnt, die Kontaktfläche desjenigen Lungenteils, welches unmittelbar mit der Außenwand des Tuberkels in Berührung steht, von dieser gewaltsam losgelöst wird; ein folgendes Ausatmen läßt die Berührungsfläche der Lunge wieder auf den Tuberkel hinabfallen. Das heißt mit anderen Worten, die Kontaktstelle bleibt eine ständige Wunde, welcher die Gelegenheit genommen ist, sich von selbst auszuheilen. Der Zweck eines operativen Eingriffs ist also, der Kontaktstelle die Gelegenheit zu geben, sich ruhig zu verhalten, damit eine Heilung der Wunde bewerkstelligt werden kann. Die Operation selbst kann in verschiedener Weise ausgeführt werden. Mittels einer Nadel kann die Brustwand von außen her durchbrochen werden. Durch die so entstandene Öffnung wird dann gerade soviel Luft zwischen Lunge und Brustkorb eingeführt, daß der dadurch entstandene Druck den Innendruck ausgleicht. Folglicherweise atmet die betroffene Lunge nicht mehr sondern übergibt der anderen Lunge diese Arbeit. Oder aber man kann, falls es nötig sein sollte, einen Dauerzustand dieser Art dadurch erhalten, daß man betreffende Stücke der Rippen entfernt, um so den atmosphärischen Außendruck dauernd auf die betroffene Lunge einwirken zu lassen. Manch-

214 **zur Verfügung stellen** to place at the disposal of

228 **in Berührung stehen mit** to be in contact with

mal ratet der Arzt auch zur Unterbrechung des die betroffene Lunge kontrollierenden Nerven, indem man ihn an einer günstigen Stelle durchschneidet. Gelegentlich wird Klimawechsel empfohlen, obwohl dies nicht immer notwending ist. Das Wichtige am ganzen Problem aber ist, daß man nun weiß, wie man an den Einzelfall herantreten soll, und folglicherweise, wie man der ganzen Sachlage im allgemeinen zu begegnen hat. Dasselbe kann man z.B. noch nicht vom Krebs sagen, obwohl man gerade in letzter Zeit auch dort große Fortschritte verzeichnen konnte.

CHAPTER 18

DER KREBS

Das Gebiet der Krebsforschungen kann kaum als unabhängige Wissenschaft bezeichnet werden, denn es setzt sich aus einer ganzen Anzahl von Einzelwissenschaften zusammen und entlehnt einer jeden das, was es für nötig hält, um selbst ans Ziel zu kommen: die Ausrottung einer der gefürchtetsten Krankheiten, vor der die Menschheit je gestanden hat. Die klinische Medizin, die Chirurgie, Pathologie, Strahlenphysik, Vererbungslehre, Biochemie, die Immunologie und Endokrinologie, jede trägt dazu bei, die Arbeit des Krebsforschers erfolgreich zu gestalten. Der Krebs selbst ist wohl eine der geschichtlich ältesten Krankheiten, jedenfalls, was deren Beobachtung anbelangt. Man hat Aufzeichnungen darüber, die bis 1500 v. Chr. zurückgreifen. Aktives Interesse vom ärztlichen Standpunkt aber erscheint erst,[1] nachdem Virchow zwischen 1850 und 1860 seine berühmten Untersuchungen über die Pathologie der Zellen unternommen und sich darin besonders mit der Pathologie des bösartigen Zellengewächses beschäftigt hatte. So kann man die moderne Krebsforschung in zwei Abschnitte teilen: die Zeit zwischen 1850 und der Wende des 20. Jahrhunderts, während welcher man sich besonders mit den klinischen und anatomischen Erscheinungen des Krebses befaßte, d.h. mit der beschreibenden Seite des Problems, und die Zeit seit 1900, die dadurch gekennzeichnet ist, daß sie sich der analytischen d.h. Laboratoriumforschung bedient. Die Zahl der Gründungen, die sich ausschließlich mit diesem Problem befassen, wächst von Jahr zu Jahr. Um nur einige der bekanntesten zu nennen: In London besteht das Cancer Hospital, in Heidelberg das Samariterhaus, in New York die Rockefeller Foundation, und gegenwärtig wird sogar auch die breite Öffent-

8 **sie trägt dazu bei, zu** it contributes to

11 **was anbelangt** as regards

22 **sie ist dadurch gekennzeichnet, daß** it is characterized by the fact that

lichkeit mit in den Kampf um die Krebsausrottung hineingezogen. 30

Wie schon oben erwähnt, ist der Krebs neben Herzkrankheit heute die gefürchtetste Krankheit. Ein noch so oberflächlicher Einblick in zahlenmäßige Aufstellungen zeigt schon, daß die Sachlage hier noch ernster aufzufassen ist als bei der Tuberkulose, und die volkserzieherischen Bemühungen, die man gegenwärtig 35 an den Tag legt, beweisen, daß man versucht, den Krebs ebenso auszumerzen wie die Tuberkulose. Ferner wird uns aber bei dieser Einsicht klar, daß wir es hier nicht mit einer Krankheit zu tun haben, die alle Lebensalter gleichmäßig befällt; im Gegenteil, die Altersverbreitung ist ebenso kennzeichnend wie die der 40 Schwindsucht. Diese ist vorwiegend eine Jugendkrankheit, jene eine Alterskrankheit. Befassen wir uns ein wenig weiter mit dieser höchst interessanten statistischen Deutung. 1932 gab es in den Vereinigten Staaten 106 Todesfälle unter je 100 000 Einwohnern. In Holland, Dänemark und der Schweiz aber 45 stand die Zahl noch höher. Kann man deshalb sagen, daß ein Volk mehr als das andere von dieser schrecklichen Krankheit angegriffen wird? Ferner steht es fest, daß gewisse Rassen weniger darunter leiden als die weiße, so z.B. die Neger in den Südstaaten der Union. Kann man sagen, daß diese Aussage, 50 vorausgesetzt sie ist gut begründet, wirklich den Tatsachen entspricht? Man hat auch beobachtet, daß gewisse Bevölkerungsklassen und besonders gewisse Arbeiterklassen mehr darunter zu leiden haben als andere. Ist es somit möglich, die Verbreitung des Krebses so zu umschreiben, daß man ein wesentlich charak- 55 teristisches Bild davon bekommt und vielleicht so auch einen versprechenderen Angriffspunkt zur Bekämpfung des Krebses hat? Auf alle diese Fragen kann nur mit einem Nein geantwortet werden. Denn erstens hat man entgültig festgestellt — d.h. wenn wir die erste Frage beantworten wollen — daß die 60 erwähnten europäischen Staaten einen höheren Prozentsatz des Krebsvorkommens aufweisen, weil bei [2] ihnen ärztliche Betreuung weit allgemeiner ist als bei uns, weil bei ihnen post mortem Untersuchungen mehr gepflegt werden als bei uns, und weil letztlich bei ihnen solche Betreuung und Untersuchungen nicht 65

31 **wie schon oben erwähnt** as already mentioned above

36 **an den Tag legen** to exhibit

so sehr auf bestimmte Volksklassen beschränkt sind als bei uns. Wir wollen damit sagen, daß, wenn unsere Mediziner damals — 1932! — ebenso allgemein und intensiv vorgegangen wären, wir vielleicht dieselben oder ähnlich hohe Zahlenwerte erhalten haben würden. Zur Beantwortung der zweiten Frage, ob gewisse 70 Rassen weniger vom Krebs befallen werden als die weiße, ist darauf hinzuweisen, daß, so weit, sagen wir, die Neger in den Südstaaten sich ärztlicher Untersuchung unterzogen haben, ein weit kleinerer Prozentsatz von Krebserkrankungen bemerkt worden ist. Es ist aber allgemein bekannt, daß nur ein ver- 75 schwindend kleiner Prozentsatz von Negern in den genannten Gebieten sich ärztlicher Betreuung bedient; kommt er aber nach den Nordstaaten, wo es übrigens besseres medizinisches Können und bessere Heilsanstalten gibt, und bedient er sich derselben in demselben Maße wie der Weiße, so schnellt das 80 zahlenmäßige Vorkommen des Krebses unter ihnen zu demselben statistischen Niveau hinauf wie bei dem Weißen. Ungefähr dasselbe läßt sich[3] zur Beantwortung der letzten Frage sagen, nur mit dem Vorbehalt, daß gewisse Arten von Arbeiten wirklich dem Krebsvorkommen günstiger sind als andere. Im Großen 85 und Ganzen aber muß bemerkt werden, daß die so oft gehörten Aussagen, daß der Krebs gewisse Völker oder Rassen oder auch Volksklassen bevorzuge und andere verschone, keine Gültigkeit haben. Dagegen scheint der Krebs eine unter allen Völkern und Rassen gleich weit verbreitete Krankheit zu sein, die sich 90 wohl hie und da an gewisse Beschäftigungen mehr als an andere heftet, aber sonst auch alle Volksklassen gleich stark befällt. Dies ist die erste wichtige Feststellung; die andere beruht auf einem Vergleich zwischen Krebsvorkommen und dem anderer Krankheiten auf die verschiedenen Perioden des einzelnen Lebens- 95 alters bezogen: je älter der Mensch wird, umso größer ist die Möglichkeit, daß er vom Krebs angegriffen wird. Krebs ist demnach eine Alterskrankheit, und das ist natürlich umso wichtiger, je klarer wir im Auge behalten, daß die Lebensspanne sich in den letzten zwei oder drei Dezennien bis zu 70 Jahren für 100

67 **wir wollen damit sagen, daß** with this, we wish to say that
71 **es ist darauf hinzuweisen, daß** it must be pointed out that
84 **mit dem Vorbehalt, daß** with the reservation that
88 **Gültigkeit haben** to be valid

Frauen und 65 für Männer verlängert hat. Deshalb auch das relativ häufigere Vorkommen dieser Krankheit während der hohen Altersperiode. Es kann auch noch hinzugefügt werden, daß je mehr die allgemeine Bevölkerung sich der medizinischen Hilfsmittel bedienen wird, desto größer der allgemeine Erkrankungsprozentsatz ebenfalls wird. Die Natur dieser Krankheit aber macht das Problem der Bekämpfung zum Problem des Einzelnen. Wie, das werden wir sofort sehen. 105

Wenden wir uns nun der Krankheit, ihrem Ursprung, ihren Erscheinungsformen und endlich ihren Bekämpfungsmethoden selbst zu. Da es der medizinischen Wissenschaft nicht gelungen war, sich dieser Krankheit wie so vielen anderen mit den relativ einfachen Mitteln der symptomologischen Beschreibung und den darauf folgenden therapeutischen Angriffsweisen zu nähern — denn man war und ist sich ja auch heute noch über vieles darüber betreffs des Krebses im Unklaren — galt es zunächst, das gesamte Krankheitsbild aufs gründlichste zu erforschen. Und eine der wichtigsten und wertvollsten Angriffsmethoden ist es noch heute, die Krankheit in Versuchstieren so zu erzeugen, daß sie ein möglichst treues Abbild der menschengetragenen Krankheit ist. Rein äußerlich gesehen unterscheidet man zwei allgemeine Arten von Krebs: diejenige Sorte, die auf der Hautoberfläche zum Vorschein kommt und die man carcinoma nennt. Diese Sorte kommt wenigstens zehnmal so häufig vor wie die andere, die man sarcoma nennt und die sich im Inneren des Körpers festsetzt. Diese beiden Sorten werden der Einfachheit halber in viele Unterarten eingeteilt, je nach dem Sitz, den sie im oder am Körper selbst haben. Abgesehen von dieser Zweiteilung kann man auch von einer anderen Zweiteilung sprechen, je nachdem die Krebserscheinung bösartig oder nicht bösartig ist. So ist man nach langwieriger Forschungsarbeit endlich zur Einsicht gekommen, daß ein Krebs nichts anderes ist als eine oder mehrere Zellen, die sich von ihrem ursprünglichen Sitz im Zellgewebe eines bestimmten Körperorgans losgerissen haben und nach einem anderen ihnen fremden Körperteil gewandert sind. Um diese Erscheinung recht zu bewerten, muß man sich vor Augen 110 115 120 125 130 135

119 **möglichst treu** as true as possible
120 **rein äußerlich gesehen** superficially
128 **abgesehen von** aside from
131 **zur Einsicht kommen** to realize

halten, daß jeder Körperteil in vorgeburtlicher Zeit aus gewissen Arten von Zellen aufgebaut ist. Eine Anzahl derselben Zellen verbinden sich während der Entwicklungszeit zu einzelnen Zellgeweben; diese wieder zu Organen und diese wiederum zum ganzen Organismus, d.h. dem fertigen Körper. Sind nun bestimmte anhaltende Reize vorhanden, die dauernd auf ein und dasselbe Gewebe einwirken, so entsteht eine Empfindlichkeit der betroffenen Zellen oder Gewebe den Reizen gegenüber; einzelne Zellen, lösen sich aus der Reizstelle aus, um den Reizen zu entgehen, und wandern nun durch die Lymphgefäße oder den Blutkreislauf anderen Stellen zu, wo sie sich unter Umständen festsetzen. Das Eigentümliche nun bei der ganzen Sache ist, daß derart vertriebene Zellen in ihrer neuen Umgebung nicht umkommen sondern sogar von den dort einheimischen Zellen großgefüttert werden und sich so zu einem Krebs entwickeln. Das erklärt auch die Tatsache, daß ein Krebs an sich keinen Schmerz hervorruft, und daß Schmerzen erst dann in Erscheinung treten, wenn der nun immer größer wachsende Krebs das Nervensystem berührt und dieses an einer gegebenen Stelle durch Druck, usw. beeinflußt. Ebenso erklärt dies die Erscheinung, wonach Krebs nicht nur an einer einzigen Stelle des Körpers selbst zur Erscheinung tritt, sondern auch durch seine eigenen wandernden Zellen sog. Ausläufer in andere Körperteile schicken kann. Es ist klar, daß unter solchen Umständen ein Krebs nicht leicht zu entdecken ist, denn er kann an sich sehr klein sein und braucht anfangs keine Symptome hervorzurufen. Diese entstehen oft nur in den Endstadien der Entwicklung und deuten dann oft darauf hin, daß eine Heilung ausgeschlossen ist. Die Frage um die Ursachen einer Zellenwanderung ist auch heute noch nicht gelöst. Daß sie unter dauerndem Reiz stattfinden kann, ist bewiesen worden, denn gerade hier scheint die Erklärung zu liegen, warum gewisse Beschäftigungen mehr den Gefahren der Krebsbildung ausgesetzt sind als andere. Es ist aber auch festgestellt worden, daß solche Zellenwanderungen noch vor der Geburt, d.h. während der Fötusentwicklung stattfinden. Das hat man z.B. bei gewissen Erscheinungen des Nierenkrebses vorgefunden. Nierenkrebs ist übrigens eine der ganz wenigen Krebsarten, die das Kindesalter

153 **in Erscheinung treten** to appear 163 **es deutet darauf hin, daß** it points to the fact that

heimsuchen. Im Laufe der Zeit hat der Mediziner eine ganze Reihe von Stoffen zu einer Liste zusammengestellt, die krebs- 175 fördernd sind. Es ist also möglich geworden, auf besonders gefährliche Berufe oder Beschäftigungen hinzuweisen und wenigstens so dem Krebs entgegenzuarbeiten. Daß es andere beiläufige Ursachen in der Krebsbildung gibt, ist hinreichend bewiesen worden. So hat man darauf hinweisen können, daß unter den 180 vielen Reizstoffen, unter denen Teer einer der aktivsten ist, auch Anilin zu rechnen ist. Ferner kommen auch die oft angewandten Röntgenstrahlen dazu. Zu lange angewandt rufen auch sie Hautreiz hervor, die in gegebenem Falle erst nach Jahren als Krebs erscheint. Die Röntgenstrahlen selbst sind daran 185 natürlich nicht schuld sondern vielmehr die Reize selbst. Radium verhält sich ähnlich wie die Röntgenstrahlen. Eine häufige Ursache des Krebses ist auch in Geschwüren zu suchen, besonders inneren Geschwüren, die sich an und in den Weichteilen des Körpers befinden, so z.B. im Magen oder dem Darm. Jedes- 190 mal aber hat man es mit langanhaltenden Reizen zu tun, die sich früher oder später derart auswirken. Bei Männern entwickelt sich oft ein Krebs an den Lippen, der oft darauf zurückzuführen ist, daß diese durch Rauchen und den damit verbundenen Angewohnheiten, wie z.B. dem Anheften einer Zigarette 195 an die Unterlippe, irritiert werden. Aus alledem gehen zwei weitere Tatsachen hervor: der Krebs ist nicht erblich, weder ist er ansteckend.

Was sind nun die Erscheinungsarten des Krebs? Um diese Frage zu beantworten, müssen wir uns die verschiedenen Körper- 200 teile ansehen, die davon befallen werden. Es wäre in dieser Beziehung nicht ratsam, alle Körperteile anzuführen sondern nur einige derselben, die besonders klare Krebsformen zur Schau tragen. Zu diesem Zweck wählen wir die Haut, das Gehirn, die Lippen, den Magen und den Darm. Der Hautkrebs führt den 205 Namen E p i t h e l i o m a und besteht aus zwei scharf von einander getrennten Arten: der des Gesichtes und der auf der übrigen Hautoberfläche. Die erstere Art erscheint besonders im Alter von 50 Jahren und darüber und macht sich dadurch bemerkbar,

185 **schuld daran sein** to be blamed for
203 **zur Schau tragen** to exhibit
209 **sie macht sich dadurch bemerkbar, daß** it is recognized by the fact that

daß sich auf einer etwas erhöhten Fläche ein Schorf bildet, der 210
immer nach einer gewissen Entwicklung abfällt. Endlich entwickelt sich die betroffene Stelle zu einem Geschwür. Gewöhnlich nicht sehr gefährlich und sonst durch chirurgische Eingriffe beseitigt, kann er dennoch höchst gefährlich werden, wenn er auf den Augenlidern erscheint. Kommt er aber auf anderen 215
Hautoberflächen vor — und dann ist er unter dem Namen Schwammgewebe bekannt — so ist das eine andere Sache, denn diese Art ist höchst gefährlich, sogar von Anfang an. Eine Krebserscheinung im Gehirn ist glücklicherweise verhältnismäßig selten, ist aber dafür fast ganz unheilbar; denn erstens 220
macht sie sich nur im fortgeschrittenen Stadium bemerkbar, und zweitens sendet sie derart verzweigte Ausläufer in das benachbarte Hirngewebe aus, daß sogar ein operativer Eingriff nie das störende Gewächs entfernen kann. Dagegen kann gesagt werden, daß nicht alle Krebsgewächse im Gehirn sich schädlich erweisen, 225
denn sie können jahrelang im Ruhezustand verharren. Chirurgische Eingriffe in diese Art des Krebses laufen oft in Lähmung anderer Gliedmaßen aus, denn es ist fast unmöglich, daß ein operativer Eingriff das den Krebs umgebende Hirngewebe unberührt läßt. Lippenkrebs ist schon erwähnt worden, und es mag 230
nur noch hinzugefügt werden, daß, obwohl Erleichterung durch eine Operation möglich ist, diese dennoch Entstellungen mit sich bringt. Ungefähr die Hälfte aller Krebsfälle kommen im Magen vor. Die Hälfte derselben verteilen sich auf Männer und ungefähr ein Drittel auf Frauen. Unglücklicherweise ist 235
diese Art höchst schwer der Diagnose zugänglich. Ebenso ziehen sich Untersuchungen darüber unangenehm lange hin, und man ist neuerdings dazu übergegangen, Röntgenphotographie als zuverlässigste Diagnose anzuwenden. Magenschmerzen unmittelbar nach einer Mahlzeit werden als eines der ersten Kenn- 240
zeichen angesehen, und es hat sich oft bestätigt, daß solch ein Krebs sich aus einem Magengeschwür langsam entwickelte. Soweit es heute bekannt ist, scheinen Strahlen- und Radiumbehandlungen noch erfolglos zu sein. Der Sitz eines Krebses im Darm ist fast immer auf den Dickdarm beschränkt, er ist 245

217 **das ist eine andere Sache** that is something else

237 **man ist neuerdings dazu übergegangen, zu** one has recently turned to

weit weniger häufig als der Magenkrebs und ist ungefähr gleichmäßig auf Männer wie Frauen verteilt. Allmähliche Auszehrung des Kranken, wenn nicht auf Tuberkulose hinweisend, ist Hinweis auf das mögliche Bestehen eines Krebses im Darm. Dann aber ist es schon fast zu spät mit der Behandlung, und wenig kann 250 für den Kranken getan werden. Natürlich gibt es Sorten, die sich besonders auf das eine oder andere Geschlecht legen; so kommt der Brust- und der Gebärmutterkrebs nur bei Frauen vor, während der Lippenkrebs sich vorwiegend bei Männern vorfindet. In neuerer Zeit hat man noch andere Arten fest- 255 stellen können, die man früher nicht kannte.

Was ist nun nach all dem Gesagten über die Behandlung zu sagen? Zunächst ist zu erwähnen, daß eine frühe Feststellung des Vorhandenseins eines Krebses eine unbedingte Grundlage für eine Erfolg versprechende Behandlung sein muß. Auch heute 260 noch bildet das operative Entfernen das beste Vorgehen. Solch ein Entfernen wird entweder mit dem Messer oder dem elektrischen Schnittfunken unternommen, ist aber in den meisten Fällen nur für oberflächliche Krebse anwendbar. Wegen der mit einer Gehirnsoperation verbundenen Gefahr hat man auch ver- 265 sucht, einen dort sitzenden Krebs mit einem dazu geeigneten Saugverfahren herauszuziehen. Stets aber sind solche Einzelverfahren nur auf Einzelfälle anwendbar, und es ist wohl möglich, daß damit gute Ergebnisse erzielt werden. Radium und Röntgenbestrahlungen sind noch immer am wirksamsten; man muß 270 aber auch hier äußerst vorsichtig vorgehen; denn erstens können nur bestimmte Sorten von Krebs dieser Behandlung unterworfen werden, dann aber ist auch die weitere Gefahr damit verbunden, daß Gewebe, durch welche die Röntgenstrahlen gehen, später infolge der anhaltenden Reizung selbst in Mitleidenschaft gezogen 275 werden könnten. Radium wird oft bei Innenkrebsen gebraucht, hilft aber auch da wenig, wenn sie schon zu weit fortgeschritten sind. Dagegen sind die Röntgenstrahlen auch nicht immer wirksam; denn, obwohl sie zeitweilige Besserung bringen, kommt es doch häufig genug vor, daß der Krebs später wieder erscheint. 280 Zum Schluß soll auch noch angeführt werden, daß gerade unsere

275 **infolge der** in consequence of the

Jetztzeit sich in sehr starkem Maße diesem Problem zugewandt hat, besonders seit man viele neue chemische Stoffe gefunden hat, die bestimmte Wirkungen auf das Krebsgewächs haben. Ähnlich wie bei der Schwindsucht muß aller Erfolg aber von der Erziehung 285 des Einzelnen abhängen.

CHAPTER 19

DIE CHEMIE

Die Chemie ist die Wissenschaft der Zerlegung und Zusammensetzung der Materie. Was die Herkunft des Wortes *Chemie* selbst anbetrifft, so herrscht in dieser Beziehung noch Unklarheit, und es ist zu bezweifeln, ob diese Frage je gelöst werden wird. Von ungemeiner Wichtigkeit ist die Lösung dieses Rätsels zwar nicht, denn man hat einige interessante Anhaltspunkte, von welchen ein jeder das Geheimnis der Lösung selbst enthalten mag. So vermutet Webster, *Chemie* sei eine Abkürzung des Wortes *Alchemie*, während anderseits angenommen wird, das Wort stamme aus dem Griechischen *chymos*, welches die Bedeutung von *Saft* oder auch *Flüssigkeit* habe. Daraus soll sich dann der Begriff der *Tinktur* entwickelt haben. Die interessanteste Erklärung, wohl auch diejenige, welche am wahrscheinlichsten klingt, geht auf das ägyptische *chēmi*, schwarz, zurück. Im Altertum war Ägypten auch als das *schwarze Land* bekannt. Da man nun aber [1] weiß, daß das alte Ägypten die Heimat einer sehr hoch entwickelten Chemie in unserem Sinne war, wenigstens für damalige Verhältnisse, ergeben sich aus dieser Tatsache zwei Möglichkeiten: *chēmi* kann sich entweder auf die schwarze Bevölkerung beziehen, d.h. Ägypten ist das Land der Schwarzen, oder es besteht die Möglichkeit, daß die *schwarze*, d.h. geheime Kunst damit gemeint sei. Warum? Weil unter anderen chemischen Errungenschaften einige davon, besonders das Einbalsamieren nur von bestimmten dazu auserwählten Gruppen geübt werden konnte. Wahrscheinlich bestand darin eine enge Verknüpfung mit der Priesterschaft. Wie schon erwähnt besaß [2] das alte Ägypten eine relativ hoch entwickelte Chemie. Es kannte Farbstoffe und deren Zusammensetzung, wußte, wie man

4 **es ist zu bezweifeln, ob** it must be doubted that

Glas, klares und gefärbtes, herstellte, besaß die Kenntnisse, künstliche Edelsteine herzustellen und war mit anderen Errungenschaften vertraut, welche das Abendland erst nach langem Bemühen erwarb, wie der Herstellung der Emaille. Die größte Errungenschaft, an die jeder in Verbindung mit diesem alten Kulturland denkt, ist natürlich die Reihe von Konservierungsmitteln, die bei der Einbalsamierung Verwendung fanden.

Man sollte denken, daß beide, Griechenland und Rom, in ihrem Aufschwung die schon vorhandenen chemischen Kenntnisse um ein Bedeutendes bereicherten. Dem war aber nicht so. Dieses Verdienst ist den auch anderweitig geistig rührigen Arabern zuzuschreiben. Als diese dann im siebenten Jahrhundert in Europa einfielen und ihre Herrschaft in Spanien begründeten, brachten sie auch unter anderen Wissensgebieten die Chemie mit, stießen damit aber fast sofort auf den Widerstand der christlichen Kirche. Deren dictum war es ja, alles Nachfragen in die Geheimnisse der Natur zu verpönen, denn an seiner statt war ja schon längst der Wunderglaube getreten. Ganz unterdrücken konnte man die junge Chemie natürlich nicht, und wo diese sich zu behaupten wußte, wurden von ihr ebenfalls Wunder erwartet. So erhielt das Wort chēmi dann auch die Bedeutung der schwarzen Kunst, die nicht nur geheim sondern auch verboten und den Lehren der Kirche zuwider war. Einige Berechtigung dazu hatte man zwar, denn unter dem nun verbreiteten Glauben, man könne wirklich mit den Mitteln der Chemie allerlei Wunder vollbringen, ging man dazu über, allerhand phantastische Experimente auszuführen: man versuchte, künstliche Menschen zu schaffen, oder ein Elixir zu brauen, das das Leben verlängern könnte; oder man erstrebte, den bekannten Stein der Weisen zu finden, mit dessen Hilfe man dann imstande sein wollte, unedle Metalle in Gold zu verwandeln. So war es natürlich nur allzumöglich, daß die so vielversprechende junge Wissenschaft im Laufe der Zeit entartete und sich den Namen der Alchemie zulegte. Frisches Blut wurde ihr aber zugeführt, als man sie im späteren Mittelalter mit den schon bestehenden Anfängen der medizinischen Wissenschaften verband. Die ersten modernen Anfänge aber sind erst mit dem Erscheinen von R. Boyle zu

35 **Verwendung finden** to be applied 38 **dem war aber nicht so** but this was not so

erkennen. Und auch er hätte wenig darin erzielen können, wenn sich nicht durch alle Jahrhunderte hindurch, als die Chemie noch die schwarze Kunst war, trotz allem die Grundlage der Chemie als Wissenschaft herausgearbeitet hätte: das Experiment. R. Boyle (1627–1691) ist als der erste rein wissenschaftlich arbeitende Chemiker anzusehen. Andere gutbekannte Namen folgen bald, wie Priestley, Scheele und Cavendish. Zugleich aber erhielt die sich erneut erhebende Wissenschaft auch theoretischen Aufschwung mit der sog. Phlogistontheorie, welche indirekt Anlaß wurde [3] für die Aufstellung und Erweiterung der quantitativen Chemie. Denn sie befaßte sich mit dem Gedanken, daß bei der Verbrennung dem brennenden Stoff ein sog. Phlogiston entweiche. Ein sog. Phlegma bleibe zurück. Anderseits sollte es auch möglich sein, den ursprünglichen Stoff wieder durch Zuführung des Phlogistons aufzubauen. Und es war gerade Lavoisier (1743–1794), welcher experimentell fand, daß ein Körper nach der Verbrennung schwerer ist als vorher, daß ihm also nichts entweicht, sondern daß ihm ein Etwas zugeführt wird. Er nannte dieses neues Etwas Oxygène und berechnete den Gewichtsgewinn durch einfaches Abwiegen des Brennstoffes vor und nach dem Verbrennen. Daraus entstand die quantitative Analyse der Chemie.

Und weil wir uns nun mit der Bezeichnung quantitativen Analyse beschäftigen, wenden wir uns der mannigfaltigen Aufteilung zu, die wir in der Chemie vor uns haben. Die Chemie ist ein außerordentlich weitverzweigtes Gebiet und enthält so viele streng von einander getrennte Felder, daß es uns nur von Vorteil sein kann, etwas darüber zu erfahren. Im allgemeinen teilt man das Gesamtgebiet der Chemie in zwei große Unterabteilungen ein: die reine und die angewandte Chemie. Die erstere unterscheidet wiederum eine ganze Anzahl ihr untergeordneter Studienfelder wie die anorganische und organische Chemie, die analytische und synthetische Chemie, die theoretische (allgemeine) und die physikalische Chemie. Eine jede dieser Abteilungen ist dann wieder in Unterabteilungen eingeteilt. So die anorganische Chemie, welche sich mit den Stoffen aus dem Mineralbereich beschäftigt und darunter wiederum zwei Hauptabteilungen unterscheidet: Metalle und Nichtmetalle, zu welch letzteren auch

103 **welch letztere** which latter

die Metalloide zu zählen sind. Ein weit größeres Studiengebiet wird in der organischen Chemie untersucht. Diese ist 105
die Chemie der Kohlenstoffverbindungen und — ganz allgemein gesagt — versucht aliphatische und aromatische Verbindungen zu zerlegen und zusammenzusetzen. Jene Gruppe behandelt Fette und ihre Derivate, welche alle auf der Verbindung CH_4 oder dem Methan aufgebaut sind; diese behandelt die Benzolderivate, 110
welche sich auf die chemisch sehr schwer zu zerreißende ringförmige Atomkette C_6H_6 stützt. Es sei daran erinnert, daß die Synthese hier außerordentliche Triumphe gefeiert hat, denn die Möglichkeit, künstliche Stoffe aufzubauen, ist fast unendlich. Die derart bisher theoretisch und praktisch zusammengesetzten 115
Verbindungen sind zahlenmäßig bis in die Hunderttausende gestiegen. Was die analytische und synthetische Chemie bezwecken, ist ja allgemein bekannt; wir wollen uns deshalb nicht weiter damit befassen. Aufschlußreich ist wiederum die Unterabteilung der physikalischen Chemie, denn sie setzt sich aus der Thermo-, 120
Photo-, Elektro- und Kolloidchemie zusammen. Es ist natürlich unmöglich, besonders heutzutage, wenn wir schon bestehende Wissensgebiete in immer engere Wissenschaften zerlegen und dieselben selbstständig machen, die Chemie von anderen großen Wissenschaften fernzuhalten. Besonders eng berührt sie sich mit 125
der Physik, was auch schon die Bezeichnung Physikalische Chemie zeigt. Wärmemessungen, die bei dem Vorgang einer chemischen Reaktion gemacht werden müssen, stützen sich auf physikalische Methoden; Untersuchungen über das elektrische Wesen des Atoms und den Einfluß der Elektrizität in chemischen 130
Verfahren arbeiten mit physikalischen Werten, usw.

Sprechen wir aber nun von der angewandten Chemie, so können wir nicht umhin, auf die weitesten Bereiche unseres Wissens und Könnens hinzuweisen. Fast jedes Gebiet sucht bei der Chemie um Hilfe. Arbeitet die Chemie, sagen wir, in der Geologie und Mine- 135
ralogie, so sprechen wir von der Mineralchemie; wendet sie sich der Boden- und Düngeranalyse zu, so beschränkt sie sich ohne Zweifel auf landwirtschaftliche Fragen und wird Agrikulturchemie genannt. In der Physiologie befaßt sie sich mit Untersuchungen über chemische Umsetzungen im tierischen Körper und der 140

134 **um Hilfe suchen** to look for assistance

chemischen Beschaffenheit der verschiedenen Körperteile. Man wendet sie besonders in der Nahrungsmittelforschung an und in der Biochemie hat man gerade in den letzten Jahren in den Entdeckungen der Vitamine und Hormone, ihrem Wesen, ihrer Funktion und Wirkung im Körper großartige Erfolge erzielt. In einer Anzahl von Feldern findet sie mittels des Mikroskops gute Anwendung; da kennt man sie unter dem Namen Mikrochemie. Ja, in letzter Zeit hat man besondere Seiten der Chemie so ausgebaut, daß sie sich nur besonderen Problemen angepaßt hat. Die Petroleumindustrie hat ihre Petroleumchemie, und in der Biochemie hat sich jetzt schon und unter unseren Augen die Chemie der Vitamine und Hormone abgespaltet. Die weitere Geschichte und Entwicklung der Chemie als Wissenschaft ist in ihren Errungenschaften seit dem 16. und besonders 17. Jahrhundert klar zu erkennen. Wir müßten uns mit den einzelnen Forschern und ihren Beiträgen auseinandersetzen, wollten wir die einzelnen Entwicklungsfäden bis in die Jetztzeit hinein verfolgen. Es sei nur erwähnt, daß die organische Chemie ihren eigentlichen Ausgang von Paracelsus nimmt, welcher schon im 16. Jahrhundert die Pflanzenwelt als die Quelle vieler Heilmittel ansah. Eine neue Epoche wurde für sie dann eingeleitet, als F. Wöhler im Jahre 1828 zum erstenmal künstlichen Harnstoff, ein typisch tierisches Stoffwechselprodukt zusammenstellte. Ferner sei noch hinzugefügt, daß die Begründer der Strukturlehre in der organischen Chemie solche Männer waren wie Kékulé und Frankland. Wie auch in anderen Gebieten der Wissenschaft, so erwies sich das 19. Jahrhundert als besonders ergiebig, denn das Jahr 1853 sah die Erzeugung des synthetischen Fettes; Hofmann stellte 1858 zum erstenmal künstliche Anilinfarben her, und 1890 erschien dann auch der synthetische Frucht- und Traubenzucker. Auf dem theoretischen Gebiet erwies sich die genaue Feststellung der Natur des Moleküls und des Atoms von grundlegender Bedeutung. Man schritt erstens dazu über, die Materie in bestimmte Kategorien einzuteilen. So schied man Gemische, in denen sich einzelne Bestandteile in beliebig großen Mengen vorfanden, und welche wiederum im flüssigen oder festen Zustand vorkommen können, von bestimmten chemischen Verbindungen, in denen man be-

158 **ihren Ausgang nehmen** to start 166 **sich als ergiebig erweisen** to prove profitable

sondere Bestandteile nur nach gewissen Gewichtsprozenten erkannte. Daneben sah man eine bestimmte in dem Molekül vorhandene Anordnung der Atome und kam so zu der Annahme, 180
daß verwandte organische Verbindungen bestimmte unveränderliche Atomkomplexe besäßen. Diese Ansicht wurde besonders vom bekannten Organiker Liebig vertreten. Diese unveränderlichen Atomkomplexe waren die sog. Radikale der einzelnen Verbindungen. 185

Damit kommen wir aber auf das Gebiet des Atoms, seines Wesens und seiner Wirkung an sich und in einer Verbindung. Hier berühren wir natürlich auch die Grundlagen der Chemie, erkennen aber auch, wie nahe diese der Physik verwandt sind. Es soll unterlassen bleiben, an dieser Stelle die Atomtheorie selbst zu 190
besprechen. Das ist eine Wissenschaft für sich. Erwähnt aber werden muß, wie der Atombegriff sich herausgebildet hat. Man hatte nämlich erkannt, daß das kleinste Teil eines Stoffes als Molekül bezeichnet werden sollte. Da eine chemische Verbindung aber aus einer ganzen Reihe von Elementen bestehen kann, und 195
diese irgendwie mit einander in anderer Weise als in einem bloßen Gemisch gesetzmäßig verbunden sind, so nahm man weiterhin an, daß ein Molekül wieder in kleinere Teile gespalten werden kann. Diesen allerkleinsten Teil — wir sind ja in dieser Hinsicht heute schon viel weiter gekommen — nannte man ein Atom. Es 200
wäre nun doch geschichtlich höchst interessant, wenn wir uns mit den verschiedenen Atomvorstellungen im Laufe der Jahrhunderte befassen könnten. Das aber wäre zu weitläufig. Anstatt dessen geben wir die bisher übliche Definition eines Elements: Ein Element ist ein Stoff, der sich nicht mehr in einfachere zer- 205
legen läßt. Ganz anders sieht solch eine Definition innerhalb der Atomtheorie aus. Für uns genügt sie aber. Demnach ist eine chemische Verbindung ein Stoff, der sich durch bestimmte unter besonderen Bedingungen vorgenommene Verfahren in Elemente zerlegen läßt. Hat man dann einmal das kennzeichnende Ge- 210
wichtsverhältnis einer Verbindung, so ist es möglich, daraus eine Formel und zuletzt auf Grund einer Reaktion auch eine Gleichung aufzustellen. Äußerlich sieht solch eine Gleichung auch ziemlich einfach aus, nimmt aber, wenn man sich den Reaktionsvorgang analytisch vorstellt, auch ein viel komplizierteres Aussehen an. 215

191 **für sich** in itself

Dabei sei noch erwähnt, daß ein chemischer Vorgang gar nicht stattfinden könnte, wenn das einzelne Atom, d.h. Element, nicht mit einer bestimmten Wertigkeit ausgestattet wäre. Diese beruht auf der Fähigkeit des Elements, sich mit so und so vielen Wasserstoffatomen zu verbinden. 220

Seit die Atomtheorie in den letzten Jahren ja durch die Errungenschaft der Atombombe eine besondere Bedeutung erlangt hat, wollen wir uns dieselbe im nächsten Aufsatz näher betrachten.

219 **so und so viele** a given number of

CHAPTER 20

AUS DER GESCHICHTE DES PERIODISCHEN SYSTEMS

Eins der interessantesten Kapitel in der geschichtlichen Entwicklung der Chemie ist das Werden des periodischen Systems der Elemente. Noch ist wenig darüber geschrieben worden, und es würde sich gewiß lohnen, eine vollständige Abhandlung davon zu besitzen. Eines der bekanntesten Werke darüber ist heute das von E. Rabinowitsch und E. Thilo geschriebene Buch: Periodisches System, Geschichte und Theorie. Es wurde im Jahre 1930 von Ferdinand Enke in Stuttgart herausgegeben und ist ein wirklich aufschlußreiches Werk. Dr. E. Rabinowitsch lehrte zur Zeit des Verfassens (1929) an der Universität Göttingen und Dr. E. Thilo am Chemischen Institut der Universität Berlin. Beide sind bekannte Schulen und haben bedeutende Wissenschaftler hervorgebracht. Ein Überblick über das Inhaltsverzeichnis liefert schon Aufschluß über die Art und Weise, wie die Verfasser vorgegangen sind. Der Einteilung nach ist ihr Vorgang äußerst einfach. Sie teilen den Inhalt in fünf Teile ein. Der[1] erste behandelt die geschichtliche Entwicklung des natürlichen Systems der Elemente, eine Behandlung des Inhaltstoffes, die uns bis in die altindische Philosophie zurückführt. Der zweite Teil beschäftigt sich mit den Bestandteilen der Atome, so wie sie zu jener Zeit den Physikern und Chemikern bekannt waren. Neuerdings ist man ja im Großen und Ganzen darüber hinausgegangen, indem[2] man sich besonders den Bestandteilen des Protons durch die Kernphysik zugewandt hat. Im Wesentlichen aber haben die neueren Ergebnisse der Kernforschung wenig an den Tatsachen geändert. Der dritte Teil befaßt sich mit dem Atommodell, der vierte mit dem Aufbau des periodischen Systems

3 **es würde sich lohnen, zu** it would be profitable to

14 **Aufschluß liefern über** to give information about

24 **im Wesentlichen** essentially

und der letzte endlich mit der Periodizität der chemischen Eigenschaften. Das Werk ist 302 Seiten stark und trägt die Widmung: „Unserem gemeinsamen Lehrer Herrn Professor Dr. Paneth in 30 Dankbarkeit gewidmet".

Da [3] der erste Teil ja meistens von altbekannten Persönlichkeiten und ihren Errungenschaften spricht, alles Tatsachen, welche jedem Schüler bekannt sein sollten, wollen wir uns ihm zuwenden, denn auch hier finden wir eine höchst einfache aber 35 bezeichnende Einteilung vor. Dieser Teil enthält fünf Kapitel wie folgt: Die Lehre von den Elementen. Die Lehre von den Atomen. Die Bestimmung der Atomgewichte. Die Vorgeschichte des periodischen Systems. Die Entdeckung des periodischen Systems. Es ist also ganz und gar dem Gesichtspunkt 40 der geschichtlichen Entwicklung nach orientiert. Am interessantesten ist wohl die Tatsache, daß die Verfasser bis in die indische Philosophie zurückgehen, um darin die Wurzeln der Chemie und besonders der Urstoffe, der Elemente, zu suchen. Sie greifen auf die bekannten Veden zurück, die klassischen 45 altindischen Werke, welche während der zwölften, elften und zehnten Jahrhunderte v. Chr. geschrieben wurden. Darnach sind die Urstoffe als Äußerungsformen des allesbeherrschenden geistigen Prinzips anzusehen. Das heißt, die alten Inder betrachteten die sie umgebende Natur nicht objektiv, so wie wir es heut- 50 zutage gewohnt sind, sondern als Ergebnisse einer besonderen Welterschaffung, die von einem großen universalen Geist ausgegangen ist, ungefähr so wie die christliche Religion sich zu Jehova und der biblischen Erschaffung der Welt stellt. Und ähnlich wie auch die christliche Anschauung betrachteten die 55 alten Inder das Weltgeschehen, d.h. den fortlaufenden Strom der Weltereignisse, als immer neue Schöpfung dieses Allgeistes. Die Veden geben uns auch Aufschluß, was und wer dieser Allgeist ist. Sie nennen ihn tad ekam, was man am besten vielleicht mit Jenem Einen übersetzen kann. Tad ekam selbst ist nicht 60 Gottheit, kann aber die Gestalt vieler Götter annehmen, und indem er es tut, schafft er das „Urwasser". Man vergleiche das mit der alttestamentlichen Ansicht, die man im ersten Buch Moses, Kapitel I, Vers 2 findet: „Und die Erde war wüst und leer, und es war finster auf der Tiefe; und der Geist Gottes schwebte 65

53 **ungefähr so wie** about like

auf dem Wasser". (Luthers Übersetzung.) Gegenstände entstehen, indem tad ekam nun in das Wasser fährt und dessen Gestalt und Beschaffenheit ändert. Das Wesentliche hier ist immer, daß das geistige Prinzip eine größere Bedeutung hat als diese erste Form der Materie. 70

Ein entschiedener Fortschritt ist in denjenigen Werken verzeichnet, die man mit dem Namen Upanischaden versehen hat. Diese wurden ungefähr um 500 v. Chr. geschrieben und bezeichnen das geistige Prinzip mit dem Namen Brâhman oder Aman. Darin sind Erde und Feuer schon getrennt. Weiter aber geht die 75 indische Philosophie nicht. Um den nächsten Fortschritt festzustellen, müssen wir uns in die altgriechische Philosophie begeben. Da erscheint Wasser als das erste Element (Ilias und Odyssee). Bei Hesiod (um 850 v. Chr.) ist es die Erde, welche aus dem Urstoff entstanden ist, und bei Pheretrides von Syros 80 (um 544 v. Chr.) erscheinen schon Feuer, Wind und Wasser. Der große Philosoph Empedokles (490–430 v. Chr.) fügte dann die Erde als viertes Element hinzu. Aristoteles (384–322 v. Chr.) ergänzte nach dem Vorbilde Platos diese Reihe der Elemente durch den Äther, die quinta essentia des Mittelalters. Von 85 nun an schreiten wir auf schon bekannteren Pfaden dahin, denn wir kommen bald zur Alchemie. Sind wir als moderne Menschen oft geneigt, die Alchemisten und ihr Tun ein wenig von obenher zu betrachten, so tun wir ihnen ein Unrecht an. Denn erstens arbeiteten sie mit der damals noch wenig bekannten Materie und 90 wenigen Elementen; zum andern aber haben sie der Wissenschaft einen Beitrag geliefert, den man nicht hoch genug geschichtlich einschätzen kann. Es war der erste Trieb zum Experimentieren, der uns so wichtig scheint. All ihr Experimentieren ging von täglicher Beobachtung aus, und zwar davon, daß Stoffe sich 95 verwandeln ließen. Das ist schon rein wissenschaftliche Einstellung, und ihr Verfahren, solche Verwandlungen selbst herbeiführen zu wollen, ist schon wissenschaftliches Wollen. Daß sie niedere Stoffe in edlere verwandeln wollten, ist natürlich; denn erstens ist die Verfolgung der Wissenschaft ja fast gänzlich vom 100 praktischen Gesichtspunkt aufzufassen, zum andern aber war die

68 **das Wesentliche hier ist immer, daß** the important thing here is always that

89 **ein Unrecht antun** to do an injustice

Werteinschätzung des Mittelalters, das ja gerade mit dem Erscheinen des Geldes als ökonomische Erscheinung zu tun hatte, ganz auf die edlen Metalle eingestellt. Nach und nach aber entwickelte sich der Begriff des Elements aus der Erfahrung heraus. 105
So genügten bald die vier bekannten Elemente nicht mehr und man fügte ihnen noch drei weitere hinzu: Quecksilber,* Salz und Schwefel. Allmählich also beginnt sich die Anzahl derjenigen Stoffe zu vermehren, denen man eine bestimmte Funktion im Experimentieren mit der Materie zugeteilt hatte. 110

Die beiden ersten Namen, welche man endgültig mit dem modernen Beginn der Chemie als Wissenschaft verknüpft hat, sind die von Joachim Jungius (1587–1657) und Robert Boyle (1627–1691). Das eigentliche Ziel der Alchemisten, nämlich die Umwandlung der Metalle, erwies sich im Laufe der Zeit als unerreichbar, wenigsten mit den von ihnen angewandten Hilfsmitteln. 115
Da erschienen nun kritische Geister, die sich die Frage stellten, warum das denn eigentlich so sei. Sie sammelten und studierten das auf Grund der Erfahrung gewonnene Tatsachenmaterial. Besonders waren es Jungius, Boyle und Lavoisier. Während von 120
den beiden erstgenannten Boyle der bekanntere ist (The Sceptical Chymist, 1661), schrieb Jungius schon im Jahre 1642 in seinen Disputationen über die Prinzipien der Stoffe, Hamburg, daß die letzten Bestandteile aller Stoffe selbst stofflicher Natur wären, und daß es keine Prinzipien im aristotelischen Sinn 125
gäbe. Besonders aber hob er hervor, daß diese letzten Bestandteile nur durch systematisch und vorurteilslos durchgeführte experimentelle Zerlegungen aller bekannten Stoffe erkannt werden könnten. Mit andern Worten, wir haben hier einen klar ausgesprochenen Begriff über das Wesen der Wissenschaft und der 130
Chemie im besonderen. Wichtiger aber noch als das ist die Ahnung, daß man zu den Urbestandteilen der Stoffe durch Zerlegung kommen kann. Die Idee der Elemente scheint damals schon bestanden zu haben. Natürlich sind das nur rein naturphilosophische Betrachtungen von Seiten Jungius', und es war 135
Boyle beschieden, zum objektiven Experimentieren überzugreifen.

105 **aus der Erfahrung heraus** from experience

117 **sich die Frage stellen, warum** to ask oneself the question why

* Siehe Atomgewichtstabelle am Ende des Kapitels.

So findet man in seinem schon angeführten The Sceptical Chymist alle wesentlichen Bestandteile der neuzeitlichen Elemente: den Atombegriff und die Idee des Moleküls.

Von nun an geht es schnell über die Phlogistiker und Lavoisier (1743–1794) zur Entdeckung der einzelnen Elemente. Die Entdeckung der meisten fällt in die Zeit zwischen Lavoisier und Mendelejeff. Bei einigen kann das Datum der Entdeckung nicht genau angegeben werden, wie z.B. das des Fluor, Titan, Niob, Uran, u.a.m. Wieder andere sind erst nach der Aufstellung des periodischen Systems entdeckt worden, so z.B. Gallium, Skandium, u.a. Man müßte eigentlich erwarten, daß der Weg zu Mendelejeff und dem periodischen System über die Lehre von den Atomen geht; dem ist aber nicht so. Statt dessen, wollten wir diese verfolgen, so müßten wir wieder mit dem Altertum anfangen. Der Weg zu Mendelejeff führt über Gassendi und D. Bernoulli im 17. Jahrhundert und Dalton (1766–1844), J. L. Proust (1755–1826), J. B. Richter (1762–1807), über W. H. Wollaston (1766–1828), J. Berzelius (1779–1848) und St. Cannizaro (1826–1910), alle im 18. und 19. Jahrhundert, mit Ausnahme von Cannizaro, welcher bis in das gegenwärtige Jahrhundert hineinragt. Alle diese Wissenschaftler haben sich eingehend mit dem Atombegriff beschäftigt. Die letzte und praktische Definition eines Elements kann angegeben werden, indem wir Paneth anführen. Er sagt: „Ein chemisches Element ist ein Stoff, der durch kein chemisches Verfahren in einfachere zerlegt werden kann".

Einiges sollte nun auch über die Vorgeschichte des periodischen Systems der Elemente gesagt werden. Wären Elemente untereinander vollkommen unabhängig, so wären keine inneren Beziehungen unter ihnen zu erwarten. Es wäre also aussichtslos, ein System aufzustellen, welches verwandte Eigenschaften darzustellen sucht. Das war auch der Gedanke, welcher die chemischen Wissenschaftler nach Lavoisier beherrschte. Trotzdem starb aber der Gedanke an eine gesamte Einheit der Materie nicht ganz aus. Man beschäftigte sich nicht mehr praktisch damit, behielt ihn aber bei. Der erste, welcher nach solch einem einheitlichen System suchte, war der um 1786 wirkende

147 **man müßte eigentlich erwarten, daß** one would have to expect that

155 **mit Ausnahme von** with the exception of

N. H. Marne. Marne war eigentlich Phlogistiker. Sein wirklicher Name war Johann Bernhard Herrmann. Im Jahre 1786 veröffentlichte dieser eine Schrift Über die Anzahl der Elemente, 175 in welcher er an den aristotelischen und alchemistischen Elementschriften scharfe Kritik übte. Sein Beitrag zur Systematik der Elemente kann kurz zusammengefaßt werden, indem man sagt, daß er diese einer unendlichen Stufenreihe nach anordnete und zwar nach fortlaufenden Zahlen. Er scheint aber auch schon eine 180 Ahnung davon zu haben, daß ein einfaches Zahlenverhältnis für die Eigenschaften der Elemente gelte, also eine Ahnung, daß es doch innere Beziehungen zwischen den vielen vermuteten Elementen gebe. Dreißig Jahre später drückte W. Prout (1786–1850) den Gedanken aus, alle Elemente Lavoisiers und Daltons 185 seien durch die Kondensation von Wasserstoff entstanden. Wäre dies der Fall, dann müßten ihre Gewichte auch in einem bestimmten Verhältnis zu dem des Wasserstoffs stehen; sie müßten bestimmte Vielfache des Wasserstoffgewichtes sein. Berzelius bestritt diesen Gedanken, und so begann man einen Streit, der erst 190 100 Jahre später geschlichtet werden konnte. Ein weiterer entschieden praktischer Fortschritt wurde durch J. W. Döbereiner (1780–1849) gemacht. Dieser fand nämlich, daß das Atomgewicht der Strontianerde (SrO) fast genau das arithmetische Mittel aus den Atomgewichten der Kalkerde (CaO) und der Baryt- 195 erde (BaO) ist. Mit dieser Entdeckung hatte man zum erstenmal eine der sog. Triaden vor sich. Später, und zwar im Jahr 1829, schrieb Döbereiner eine Abhandlung, worin er neben der obengenannten Triade noch die von Cl, Br, J; Li, Na, K; und S, Se, Te angab. Der Titel dieser Abhandlung lautet: Versuch zu einer 200 Gruppierung der elementaren Stoffe nach ihrer Analogie.

Während verschiedene Forscher (unter anderen Kremers, 1852; Lenssen, 1857) versuchten, diesen Anfang einer Gruppierung der Elemente zu einer allgemeineren Klassifizierung zu gebrauchen, stieß M. Pettenkofer in einer anderen Richtung vor. 205 Man hatte nämlich gefunden, daß besondere homologe Reihen unter den chemischen Verbindungen bestehen, deren Einzelglieder sich in ihrem Molekulargewicht um bestimmte Beträge vermehrten. Diesen Gedanken wandte Pettenkofer nun an die sogenannten Äquivalentgewichte der Elemente an und zeigte, 210

177 **Kritik üben** to criticize

daß es wirklich solche Beziehungen gibt. Er veröffentlichte diese Resultate in der Schrift: Über die regelmäßigen Abstände der Äquivalentzahlen der sogenannten einfachen Radikale (1850). Darin veröffentlicht er auch in tabellenartiger Anordnung diese Werte. 215

W. Odling (geb. 1829) war der nächste, der sich dann eingehend mit dieser Frage befaßte. Auch er veröffentlichte eine solche Anordnung, tat es aber mit allen damals bekannten Elementen mit Ausnahme von Wasserstoff und Kohlenstoff. Er ordnete alle Elemente in einzelne Familien an und gruppierte diese in Tabellenform. 220 Man erkennt schon eine gewisse Ähnlichkeit mit dem heute bestehenden System. J. H. Gladstone ordnete diese in seiner Schrift: Über die Beziehungen zwischen den Atomgewichten analoger Elemente (1853) nach Größe ihres Atomgewichts an. Er gebrauchte aber dazu noch die alten Werte, wie 225 sie Berzelius gegeben hatte, und so konnte das Bild der periodischen Gesetze noch nicht entdeckt werden. Endlich aber wurden die Werte Berzelius' von J. A. Newlands (um 1865) durch die von Cannizaro ersetzt. Das war das sog. Oktavengesetz, welches auf den Gesetzen von Gay-Lussac, Avogadro, Dulong und Petit be- 230 ruht. Und mit der Anwendung dieses Gesetzes beginnt nun endlich die eigentlich moderne Arbeit an dem periodischen Gesetz, so wie wir es heute kennen.

ATOMGEWICHTSTABELLE (1949)

Element	Chemisches Symbol	Atomgewicht	Atomnummer
Aktinium	Ac	227,0	89
Alabamin	Vi	224,0	87
Aluminium	Al	26,97	13
Antimon	Sb	121,76	51
Argon	A	39,944	18
Arsen	As	74,91	33
Barium	Ba	137,36	56
Beryllium	Be	9,02	4
Blei	Pb	207,21	82
Bor	B	10,82	5
Brom	Br	79,916	35
Chlor	Cl	35,457	17

Element	Chemisches Symbol	Atomgewicht	Atomnummer
Chrom	Cr	52,01	24
Dysprosium	Dy (Ds)	162,46	66
Eisen	Fe	55,85	26
Eka-Jod	Ab	221,0	85
Emanation	Em	222,00	86
Erbium	Er	167,2	68
Europium	Eu	152,0	63
Fluor	F	19,00	9
Gadolinium	Gd	156,9	64
Gallium	Ga	69,72	31
Germanium	Ge	72,60	32
Gold	Au	197,2	79
Hafnium	Hf	178,6	72
Helium	He	4,003	2
Holmium	Ho	164,94	67
Illinium	Il	146,0	61
Indium	In	114,76	49
Iridium	Ir	193,1	77
Jod	I	126,92	53
Kadmium	Cd	112,41	48
Kalium	K	39,096	19
Kalzium	Ca	40,08	20
Kassiopeium	Cp	174,99	71
Kobalt	Co	58,94	27
Kohlenstoff	C	12,010	6
Krypton	Kr	83,7	36
Kupfer	Cu	63,57	29
Lanthan	La	138,92	57
Lithium	Li	6,940	3
Magnesium	Mg	24,32	12
Mangan	Mn	54,93	25
Masurium	Ma	96,0	43
Molybdän	Mo	95,95	42
Natrium	Na	22,997	11
Neodym	Nd	144,27	60
Neon	Ne	20,183	10
Nickel	Ni	58,69	28
Niobium	Nb	92,91	41
Osmium	Os	190,2	76
Palladium	Pd	106,7	46
Phosphor	P	30,98	15
Platin	Pt	195,23	78
Polonium	Po	210,0	84
Praseodym	Pr	140,92	59

Element	Chemisches Symbol	Atomgewicht	Atomnummer
Protoaktinium	Pa	231,0	91
Quecksilber	Hg	200,61	80
Radium	Ra	226,05	88
Rhenium	Re	186,31	75
Rhodium	Rh	102,91	45
Rubidium	Rb	85,48	37
Ruthenium	Ru	101,7	44
Samarium	Sm (Sa)	150,43	62
Sauerstoff	O	16,000	8
Schwefel	S	32,06	16
Selen	Se	78,96	34
Silber	Ag	107,880	47
Silizium	Si	28,06	14
Skandium	Sc	45,10	21
Stickstoff	N	14,008	7
Strontium	Sr	87,63	38
Tantal	Ta	180,88	73
Tellur	Te	127,61	52
Terbium	Tb	159,2	65
Thallium	Tl	204,39	81
Thorium	Th	232,12	90
Thulium	Tu (Tm)	169,4	69
Titan	Ti	47,90	22
Uran	U	238,07	92
Vanadium	V	50,95	23
Virginium	Vi	224,0	87
Wasserstoff	H	1,0080	1
Wismut	Bi	209,00	83
Wolfram	W	183,92	74
Xenon	Xe	131,3	54
Ytterbium	Yb	173,04	70
Zäsium	Cs	132,91	55
Zerium	Ce	140,13	58
Zink	Zn	65,38	30
Zinn	Sn	118,70	50
Zirkonium	Zr	91,22	40

CHAPTER 21

DIE ATOMBOMBE

Die praktische Anwendung der Kenntnisse, welche wir über die Struktur des Atoms besitzen, in der Wüste New Mexicos sowie über Japan, ist von solch großer Wichtigkeit für den Einzelnen wie für die Allgemeinheit, daß der geschichtliche und wissenschaftliche Hintergrund dieser Entwicklung einer Behandlung unterzogen werden soll. Es sei nur noch vorausgesetzt, daß die verschiedenen Einzelheiten über die technische Seite der Bombe schon lange im Besitz der Allgemeinheit sind, daß diese, wenigstens so wie sie hier dargestellt sind, keine Staatsgeheimnisse sind, und daß jedermann sie für sich selbst lesen kann, wenn er zu den der Öffentlichkeit bereitgestellten Quellen greift.

In unserer Studie ist es natürlich unumgänglich notwendig, daß wir uns einer gewissen Folgerichtigkeit der Darstellung befleißigen, und so wollen wir zuerst sehen, was die allgemeine Grundlage der Entdeckung ist, wie Energie im Atom freigesetzt wird, wie das Zyklotron entstand,[1] wie Einsteins Energiegleichung angewendet wurde, und wie endlich die gewünschten Ergebnisse erzielt wurden. Was den Namen Atombombe betrifft, so ist zu sagen, daß er einer besonderen Art von Bombe gegeben wurde, die ihre explosiven Kräfte durch die Befreiung von Atomenergie erhält. Diese Befreiung ist allgemein bekannt unter dem Namen Atomzertrümmerung und stellt gegenwärtig die gewaltigste Waffe dar, welche die Menschheit je zu Zerstörungszwecken entwickelt hat. Die Behauptung wird gemacht, daß die ersten primitiven Atombomben, welche auf Hiroschima und Nagasaki niedergingen, je eine Sprengkraft von 20 000 Tonnen Dynamit besaßen.

Das ganze Atomzertrümmerungsverfahren ist auf der Uranspaltung von O. Hahn und F. Straßmann begründet und in fol-

5 **einer Behandlung unterziehen** to treat

6 **es sei nur noch vorausgesetzt, daß** let it be said in advance that

10 **zu Quellen greifen** to have recourse to sources

genden Jahren in den Vereinigten Staaten unter Mithilfe Kanadas und Englands voll entwickelt worden. Die Uranspaltung selbst wurde zum erstenmal 1939 in Deutschland erzielt. Sechs Jahre später wurde die erste Versuchsbombe in New Mexico losgelassen. Das genaue Datum ist der 16. Juli 1945. Die Bombardierung Hiroshimas und Nagasakis fand am 6. August 1945 resp. 9. August desselben Jahres statt. Um der ganzen Geschichte auf den Grund zu kommen, müssen wir bis ins Jahr 1896 zurückgreifen, denn in jenem Jahre wurde die Radioaktivität gewisser Elemente durch A. H. Becquerel entdeckt. Vier Jahre später untersuchte Lord Rutherford dieselbe Erscheinung, und im Jahre 1905 stellte sich Einstein vor die Aufgabe, die Gesetze von der Erhaltung der Materie und der Energie in sein neues Gesetz der Gleichwertigkeit zu gestalten. Praktisch bedeutete dies die Umsetzung der Materie in Energie und ist uns als Relativitätstheorie bekannt. Das neue Gesetz beruht auf der Beobachtung, daß die Masse der Materie zunimmt,[2] wenn man ihr eine immer größere Geschwindigkeit zuteilt. Nun stellte sich Einstein vor, daß die einzelnen Partikel der Materie nicht aus Materie sondern aus stark zusammengeballten Energiebündeln bestehe. In solcher Gestalt besäße die Materie eine gewisse Elastizität, wodurch Massenzunahme und damit auch letzten Endes Freiwerden von Energie möglich werde. Einsteins berühmte Gleichung für diesen Vorgang lautet

$$E = mc^2.$$

E bedeutet hier die Energie in Ergs ausgedrückt, m ist die Masse der Materie in Gramm und c die Geschwindigkeit des Lichtes in Sekundenzentimetern.

Betrachten wir uns Lord Rutherfords Atomvorstellung. Er kam zu dem Gedanken, daß ein einzelnes Atom aus einem Kern, dem sogenannten Nukleus, bestehen müßte. Zu dieser einfachen aber an sich neuen Vorstellung fügte Bohr die Idee der Elektronen hinzu, leichter Partikel, die um den Kern des Atoms in derselben Weise kreisen wie die Planeten um die Sonne. Die Atomtheorie entwickelte sich bald bis zu dem Punkt, wo man erkannte, daß der Kern des Atoms selbst nicht mehr einfacher

35 **auf den Grund kommen** to explore

sondern zusammengesetzter Natur ist. Man erkannte neue 65
Bestandteile, das Proton und das Neutron, als dem Nukleus
angehörend. Die um den Kern kreisenden Elektronen aber stellte
man sich in Gestalt von elektrisch negativ geladener Partikel-
wolken vor. Das Proton selbst ist positiv elektrisch geladen und
zwar von derselben Stärke wie die Summe der negativen Elek- 70
tronen; das Neutron aber hat keine elektrische Ladung. Wasserstoff (H) hat das einfachste Atom; sein Kern besitzt nur ein
einziges Proton; alle anderen Elemente haben einen komplizier-
teren Kern, der sich aus Protonen und Neutronen zusammensetzt.
Die Zahl der Protonen in einem Kern stellt die gesamte positive 75
Ladung dar und ist als Atomnummer bekannt. Die Gesamtan-
zahl der Protonen und Neutronen ist als die Massennummer
bekannt. Atome, welche dieselbe Atomnummer aber verschiedene
Massennummern besitzen, sind Isotope desselben Elements.

Was kann nun auf Grund des bisher Gesagten über die Befreiung 80
der Atomenergie bestimmt werden? Nun, man weiß, daß das
Atomgewicht des Kerns kleiner als das gemeinsame Gewicht der
Protonen und Neutronen ist. Dieser Unterschied ist die sogenannte „Massendifferenz“ und beruht auf der Neigung der einzelnen Partikel, sich in den Kern hineinzudrängen. Die Gesamt- 85
masse des Kerns muß also kleiner sein als vor dem Hineindrängen
der Partikel und dieser Massenverlust muß nach Einstein von
einem Energieverlust begleitet sein. Diese Energiemenge muß
also „frei“ werden. Ferner muß nach dem Gesetz Coulombs die
Kraft, welche im Kern zwischen elektrisch geladenen Partikeln 90
herrscht, die Protonen auseinander treiben, denn sie sind positiv
geladen, und positiv geladene Teilchen stoßen einander ab. Also
muß es im Kern noch eine andere Kraft geben, die denselben
zusammenhält. Die Neutronen kommen [3] ja nicht in Betracht,
da sie weder positiv noch negativ geladen sind. Die Kraft nun, 95
welche beide, Protonen und Neutronen im Kern zusammenhält,
wird als „Bindekraft“ bezeichnet und ist mathematisch gleich der
schon erwähnten Massendifferenz dividiert durch die Zahl der
in ihr enthaltenen Partikel oder Teilchen. Alle Elemente sind
sich in dieser Hinsicht nicht gleich sondern sie unterscheiden sich 100
wesentlich gerade durch diese Bindekraft. Folge unserer Betrach-

68 **in Gestalt von** in the form of

101 **Folge ist, daß** the consequence is that

tungen bis zu diesem Punkt ist, daß die Umänderung eines Kerns in einen anderen durch größere Bindekraft ausgezeichneten Kern in einen weiteren Massenverlust, d.h. einen weiteren Energieverlust auslaufen muß. Dieser Energieverlust ist nun die schon 105 erwähnte Energiebefreiung. Auf Grund des nun Bekannten ist es möglich, Energie auf zwei verschiedenen Weisen frei zu setzen: erstens durch den Aufbau sehr leichter Kerne zu schwereren, und zweitens durch die Zerlegung schwerer Kerne zu leichteren. Die unter der ersten Möglichkeit genannte Synthese geht bekanntlich 110 im Inneren der Sterne vor sich, ist aber hier nicht anwendbar, denn die Temperatur- und Druckbedingungen, unter denen dieser Vorgang im Sterneninneren vor sich geht, können mit unseren Mitteln nicht wiedergegeben werden. Also bleibt uns nur noch der letztere Vorgang übrig: die Zerlegung schwerer Kerne zu 115 leichteren. Dieser Vorgang nun unterliegt der ganzen Atombombenentwicklung. Es ist also eine Frage der Zertrümmerung schwerer Atome. Versuche dieser Art sind schon oft unternommen worden, und zwar nicht nur in Deutschland oder den Vereinigten Staaten. In dieser Hinsicht ist die Entwicklung der 120 Atombombe der des Radars sehr ähnlich: sie wurde von einer ganzen Reihe von Wissenschaftlern aus verschiedenen Ländern unternommen und stellt deshalb mehr eine wissenschaftliche Entwicklung als eine Entdeckung dar. Zuerst muß noch einmal Lord Rutherford genannt werden, der 1919 Stickstoff (N) mit 125 alpha-Teilchen aus Radium bombardierte. Es ergaben sich Protonen, welche durch das Bombardieren aus dem Stickstoffkern herausgerissen worden waren und welche tatsächlich Wasserstoffisotope waren. Ihm war der Versuch geglückt, ein Element in ein anderes umzuwandeln. Die dadurch gegebene Gleichung ist 130

$${}_{7}N^{14} + {}_{2}He^{4} \longrightarrow {}_{8}O^{17} + {}_{1}H^{1},$$

wobei die Unterschrift die Atomnummer bezeichnet und die Überschrift die der Masse. Damit war allen anderen Physikern, die sich mit der Atomstruktur beschäftigten, die Möglichkeit geboten, ebenfalls an den Vorgang der Atomzertrümmerung mit 135 einiger Aussicht auf Erfolg heranzutreten. Im Laufe der folgenden Versuche aber wurde es immer klarer, daß man zu einer

114 **übrig bleiben** to remain

126 **es ergaben sich für ihn** he obtained

solchen Zertrümmerung weit schwerere Geschosse brauchte, als es die alpha-Teilchen aus Radium darstellten. Man war wieder vor die Notwendigkeit gestellt, die Geschosse schwerer zu gestalten; also ging man daran, die Geschwindigkeit der vorhandenen alpha-Teilchen so zu erhöhen, daß sich durch Massengewinn auch eine größere Durchschlagskraft ergab. Diese Beschleunigung der alpha-Teilchen (auch als Heliumkerne bekannt) oder der der Protonen (auch als Wasserstoffkerne bekannt) gelang nun 1929 Ernest O. Lawrence, dem bekannten amerikanischen Physiker. Er erreichte sein Ziel mittels des Zyklotrons, einer Maschine, welche den Protonen durch stetig gesteigerte Beschleunigung in einem starken magnetischen Feld zunehmende Masse, das ist zunehmendes Gewicht, das ist zunehmende Durchschlagskraft, verleiht. Und als es 1932 den Wissenschaftlern J. D. Cockroft und E. T. Walton gelang, Protonen mit den Kernen von Lithium zu verbinden, sodaß diese wiederum in zwei gleiche Teile zerfielen, ergaben sich als neue Produkte Heliumatome, daneben aber auch eine gewisse Menge freigewordener Energie. Die hierdurch gegebene Gleichung lautet

$$_{3}Li^{7} + {}_{1}H^{1} \longrightarrow {}_{2}He^{4} + {}_{2}He^{4}.$$

Die Unterschrift hier ist wieder als die Atomnummer und die Überschrift als Massennummer zu bezeichnen. Hierauf folgte 1932 die Entdeckung des Deutrons, des sog. schweren Wasserstoffs, dessen Atomgewicht das doppelte des gewöhnlichen ist. Ebenso sei noch die Entdeckung des Positrons genannt, eines Atomteilchens, das die Masse eines Elektrons besitzt, dagegen aber elektrisch positiv geladen ist. Es ist ein positives Elektron und entnimmt seinen Namen „Positron“ dieser Bezeichnung. Auch nicht zu vergessen ist die wichtige Entdeckung der künstlichen Radioaktivität durch Irene Curie und F. Joliot im Jahre 1934. Diese Forscher fanden nämlich, daß es möglich ist, gewisse Elemente weniger stabil zu gestalten, wenn man sie mit Atomteilchen beschießt. Ihre Kerne nehmen unter solchen Umständen die Geschosse in sich auf und halten sie verschieden lange fest. Nach einiger Zeit aber geben sie den Geschossen wieder ihre Freiheit zurück, indem sie dieselben wieder ausstrahlen. Dieser Vorgang wird als künstliche Radioaktivität bezeichnet und beruht oft auf der Umwandlung eines Neutrons innerhalb eines Kerns in

ein Proton und ein Elektron unter der Begleiterscheinung einer elektrischen Ausstrahlung. Manchmal verwandelt sich ein Proton in ein Neutron und ein Positron mit ebenderselben elektrischen Ausstrahlung als Begleiterscheinung. Ein weiterer Fortschritt in der Beschießung der Atomkerne wurde durch Enrico Fermi im 180
Jahre 1934 erzielt, als er nämlich feststellte, daß es möglich ist, die Geschwindigkeit der Geschoßteilchen dadurch herabzusetzen, daß er sie durch Paraffin hindurch laufen ließ. Ebenfalls stellte es sich heraus, daß ein mit schnellen Geschossen getroffener Kern nicht ganz so lange stabil blieb, als wenn man die verlangsam- 185
ten Geschosse dazu verwendete. Unter letzteren Verhältnissen dauerte die Vereinigung beider Teilchen weit länger. Dieser „Neutronenfang“ wurde seinerseits wieder Anlaß zur Kernzertümmerung. Mittels dieses „Neutronenfangs“ wurde es Fermi dann auch möglich, Uran (Nr. 92) in ein neues Element, Uran 190
(Nr. 93) zu verwandeln. Wir sehen, die Umwandlung der Elemente nimmt immer größeren Umfang an, und von nun an verdanken wir es einigen Zufällen, daß die Atomforschung sich in der rechten Richtung weiterentwickelte. Die schon erwähnten Forscher O. Hahn und F. Straßmann erreichten den Wendepunkt in 195
der anscheinend sich noch immer im Dunkeln befindenden Entwicklung, als es ihnen im Januar 1939 gelang, Barium (Ba) als ein Nebenprodukt ihrer Atomzertrümmerungsforschung zu erhalten. Diese Errungenschaft gelangte hierher nach den Vereinigten Staaten und zwar durch Vermittlung Bohrs. Nach Bespre- 200
chungen mit Einstein, kam man u.a. zu dem Schluß, daß es sich hier um die Spaltung von Uran in zwei annähernd gleich große Bariumteile handelte. In das periodische System versetzt ergab sich aber die erstaunenswerte Tatsache, daß man es mit einer Umwandlung am Ende der periodischen Tafel, wo die Bindekraft am 205
schwächsten ist, nach der Mitte der Tafel zu tun hatte, wo die Bindekraft am stärksten ist. Mathematische Berechnungen zeigten nun, daß die durch diese Umwandlung frei gewordene Energie 200 000 000 Elektronvolt betragen mußte. Man war dem Geheimnis der Atombombe auf die Spur gekommen. Es handelte sich nun nur 210
noch darum, die energiebefreiende Reaktion eine ständige zu machen. Man mußte noch die Kettenreaktion herstellen und

kontrollieren. Um wieder zu dem Uran zurückzukehren: weitere Forschungen ergaben, daß wenigstens zwei hierfür in Frage kommende Uranarten existierten: Uran mit der Massennummer 238 und ein anderes mit der Massennummer 235. Bohr und Wheeler zeigten nun versuchsweise, daß das erstere Uran von den verlangsamten Neutrongeschossen nicht beeinflußt wird, anders war es der Fall mit der letzteren Sorte, die man auch als reines Uran oder mit dem Namen Plutonium bezeichnete. Es ist in gewöhnlichem Uran (238) in nur verschwindend kleinen Mengen enthalten. Mit der Verbreitung dieser neuen Erkenntnis begann nun die gesamte Welt, fieberhaft an dem Projekt der Bombenherstellung zu arbeiten. Zudem wurde das bisher notwendige Wissen Allgemeineigentum, und es blieb den Bemühungen der Vereinigten Staaten und der Hilfe Englands und Kanadas vorbehalten, als erste Großmacht aus diesem Wettlauf siegreich hervorgegangen zu sein.

Aber nun zu der Kettenreaktion. Dieselbe hängt von der Anzahl der frei gewordenen Neutronen ab und was aus ihnen im folgenden wird. Es gibt für sie drei Möglichkeiten: sie können erstens ganz entweichen oder zweitens durch den Neutronenfang der Spaltung vorbehalten werden; oder aber sie können drittens die erwünschte Spaltung verursachen. Die Anzahl der spaltungverursachenden Neutronen wird mit den nicht spaltungverursachenden verglichen und daraus der Multiplikationsfaktor gewonnen. Wollen wir eine Kettenreaktion unterhalten, so muß dieser Faktor größer als eins sein; zudem spielt die Größe und Form der Uranmasse eine Rolle. Hier ergeben sich wieder zwei Möglichkeiten, je nachdem man die schnellen oder langsamen Neutronengeschosse anwendet. Diese ergibt unter Benutzung gewöhnlichen Urans (einer Mischung von Uran 234, 235 und 238) Energie, die sich für industrielle Zwecke eignet. Wendet man aber jene an und zwar nur unter Benutzung des reinen Urans (Nr. 235), so ist das Ergebnis die Befreiung der gewünschten explosiven Kräfte. Das sind die Kräfte der Atombombe.

Natürlich ist die Sache nicht so einfach, wie sie hier auseinandergesetzt worden ist. Es ergeben sich darin solch große Schwierig-

213 **um wieder . . . zurückzukehren** let us return again to

225 **es blieb ihnen vorbehalten, zu** it was their merit to

241 **unter Benutzung** using

keiten, und ebenso enthält der gesamte Vorgang so viele geheimgehaltene Verfahren, daß wir darauf nicht weiter eingehen können. 250
Eins aber kann noch gesagt werden: die Uranspaltung selbst setzt nur die sog. schnellen Neutronengeschosse frei, während man für eine fortgesetzte Reaktion nur die verlangsamten Neutronen gebrauchen konnte. Auf Veranlassung Fermis und L. Szilards schloß man Klumpen Urans (Nr. 235) in eine Substanz ein, 255
welche die Verlangsamung der schnellen Neutronen ermöglichte. Folgerichtig aufgebaut ergibt dieses Hilfsmittel den sog. Atombrenner, oder, wie man hier in Amerika sagt, den „pile". Im Februar 1940 gelang es A. O. Nier zum erstenmal, reines Uran (Nr. 235) mittels der Massenspektographie zu erhalten. 260

Von da an arbeitete man hier in den Vereinigten Staaten noch vier Jahre, ehe man zum Endergebnis aller Versuche und Forschungen gelangte, die sich um die Befreiung der Atomenergie drehten. Wie schon gesagt, arbeiteten die Vereinigten Staaten, England und Kanada zusammen. Es ist ferner bekannt, daß die 265
Kosten der ersten Atombombe sich auf $2 000 000 000 beliefen. Diese kolossale Errungenschaft schuf natürlich eine ganze Reihe anderer Probleme, wie z.B. die Internationalisierung der Atomenergie, die Verwendung der Bombe selbst als Verteidigungs- und Angriffswaffe, die fortlaufende Verbesserung der Bombe, 270
u.s.w. Wir wollen uns aber damit nicht befassen, da all dieses ganz neue Problemkreise anschneidet.

250 **darauf eingehen** to discuss

CHAPTER 22

RADAR

Eine der wichtigsten Erfindungen, die das Neuzeitalter hervorgebracht hat und die sich sofort einen hervorragenden Platz im Haushalt des Krieges und Friedens gesichert hat, ist Radar. Wir wollen uns infolgedessen ein wenig näher damit beschäftigen. Sei es aber im Voraus gesagt, daß die Unmenge von Einzelheiten, die man sonst in Verbindung mit solch einer Erfindung, oder sagen wir Entwicklung, erwartet, nicht geliefert werden kann; denn, wenn man auch die allgemeinen Grundzüge in Kenntnis gebracht hat, so sind doch viele technische Einzelheiten immer noch Staatsgeheimnis. Wie lange es dauern wird, bis alles der Öffentlichkeit bekannt gegeben wird, weiß niemand. Daß aber nicht nur die Vereinigten Staaten sondern auch andere Länder an der Entwicklung teilgenommen haben und im Verlaufe besonders des zweiten Weltkrieges ihr eigenes Radar zu sogenannten Netzen ausgebildet haben, ist jedermann bekannt. Aus dem, was bekannt ist, wollen wir uns demnach ein Bild dieser technischen Errungenschaft machen, indem wir kurz ihre Vorgeschichte bis zum zweiten Weltkrieg, Herkunft des Namens Radars, seine technischen Grundlagen, den sog. Radiospiegel, die Anfänge des neuzeitlichen Radars, seine Funktion sowie Anwendung im Krieg und Frieden erwähnen. Hinsichtlich des ersten Punktes, nämlich der Vorgeschichte des Radars, ist zu sagen, daß, wenn man eine ordentliche Geschichte dieser Entwicklung schreiben wollte, man eigentlich bis auf den großen italienischen Wissenschaftler Marconi zurückgehen müßte; denn wie gesagt,[1] ist Radar nicht die Erfindung eines einzigen Geistes sondern die Entwicklung einer ganzen Anzahl von Entdeckungen, Erfindungen und Beobachtungen. Seine Anwendung ist wohl modern, seine Grundlagen aber sind so alt wie die Entwicklung des Radios selbst. Es ist auf

4 **sei es aber im Voraus gesagt, daß** but let it be said in advance that 8 **wenn auch** even though

der Erscheinung der Ultrakurzwellen aufgebaut, und führten wir den Gedanken dieser Erscheinung in der wissenschaftlichen Literatur zu seinem Ursprung zurück, so fänden wir Anzeichen davon schon in den Schriften Hertz' und Marconis. Beide stellten ja bekanntlich Versuche mit Ultrakurzwellen an. Neben diesen beiden hervorragenden Forschern wären dann auch noch andere, wie Tesla, Thomson, Braun, Edison, De Forest, Kenelly, Heaviside, Taylor, Tuve, Zworkin, Wolf, u.a.m. zu nennen. Das erste wichtige Datum ist wohl das Jahr 1886, denn es war in jenem Jahr, als Hertz elektromagnetische Wellen benutzte und dadurch der Maxwellschen Theorie, daß es Ätherwellen gäbe, Anerkennung verschuf. Zugleich aber bewies er auch experimentell, daß diese elektromagnetischen Wellen von einer glatten oder sogar unebenen Oberfläche ähnlich einem Lichtstrahl zurückgeworfen werden. Die Reflektierung eines Wellenstrahles von einer ihr fern gelegenen Oberfläche ist die erst zu behaltende Tatsache.

Schenken wir der dieser Entwicklung zu Grunde liegenden Notwendigkeit ein wenig unsere Aufmerksamkeit. Daß sie etwas Kriegsgeborenes ist, haben wir schon erwähnt. Dazu kommt noch, daß es sich besonders um die Detektion von feindlichen Flugzeugen handelte, welche sich hier so fruchtbar auswirkte. Während des ersten Weltkrieges benutzte man nämlich noch die altmodischen Laut- oder Schallfänger, um das Herannahen feindlicher Flugzeuge zu konstatieren. Wie bekannt ist dieser Schallfänger auf dem Prinzip der Fortpflanzung von Schallwellen aufgebaut. Der Schall pflanzt sich mit einer ungefähren Stundengeschwindigkeit von 1000 km fort. Moderne Flugzeuge sind aber nicht viel langsamer. Die unangenehme Tatsache stellte sich also heraus, daß der früher gebrauchte Schallfänger den modernen Anforderungen nicht mehr genügte. Man mußte etwas Sensitiveres haben. Schalldetektion war veraltet; man wandte sich also den in der Ultrakurzwelle liegenden Möglichkeiten zu und begann, ernstlich mit demjenigen Problem zu arbeiten, das uns heute unter dem Namen Radar bekannt ist.

Der Name Radar wurde zum erstenmal von Commander S. M. Tucker gebraucht. Da dieses Wort also amerikanischen

33 **Versuche anstellen** to experiment
40 **Anerkennung verschaffen** to procure recognition for
46 **zu Grunde liegen** to be basic to
48 **dazu kommt noch, daß** to this may be added the fact that

Ursprungs ist, müssen wir, um es zu erklären, auch auf englische Wörter zurückgreifen. Die einzelnen Buchstaben in diesem Wort RA–D–A–R haben die folgende Bezeichnung: RA bezeichnet das Wort „Radio", D bezeichnet „Detektion" (oder „Direction-finding"), A bezeichnet das Wort „And" und das Schluß-R bedeutet 70 „Ranging". Das Wort selbst verrät schon die Funktion des Gesamtapparats; nämlich ein Radioimpuls, der von einer überaus starken Quelle in den Raum hinausgeworfen und dort von irgendeinem Gegenstand wieder zurückgeworfen wird, kehrt in Form eines Echos wieder zur Sendestelle zurück. Wiederaufgefangen 75 gibt er durch Berechnungen kund, was für ein Gegenstand er im Raum getroffen hat, und wo und wie weit derselbe sich von der Sendestelle befindet. Radar kann also einigermaßen einem Scheinwerfer verglichen werden, der den Himmelsraum abspielt und sich mit seinem Lichtfinger an ein etwaiges Flugzeug heftet, 80 um es von nun an festzuhalten. Nun kommt eine weitere Tatsache hinzu: die Entdeckung des sogenannten Radiospiegels, des „Heaviside layer's", durch Sir Oliver Heaviside, der diesen 1902 ungefähr hundert km über der Erdoberfläche vorfand. Dieser Radiospiegel ist dafür verantwortlich, daß ein ausgeschleuderter 85 Kurzwellenstrahl ähnlich einem Lichtstrahl gebrochen und wieder zur Erde zurückgeworfen wird. Marconi machte ähnliche Beobachtungen. Aber es war erst Nikola Tesla, der die praktische Anwendung für diese Tatsache fand. Die Engländer besaßen schon vor dem Beginn des zweiten Weltkrieges eine wohl noch ein- 90 fache aber dennoch wirksame Art von Radar. 1936 gab es in England fünfzehn derselben, und als endlich der Krieg ausbrach, hatte man schon ein ganzes System davon. Es ist aber eigentlich nicht ganz richtig, wenn wir die Entfernung dieses Radiospiegels von der Erdoberfläche als genau auf 100 km einsetzen, denn 95 tatsächlich schwankt die Entfernung zwischen 80 und 200 km. Die Höhe desselben wurde natürlich dadurch festgestellt, daß man den Zeitraum maß, welchen die Strahlen brauchten, um [2] wieder zur Sendestelle zurückzukehren. Die Geschwindigkeit des Schalles zu messen, hatte sich früher als ziemlich einfach erwiesen, 100 anders aber war es mit den Kurzstrahlenwellen. Die Antwort auf diese Frage wurde mittels der sogenannten Kathodenröhre gegeben. Man kann also sagen, Radar stützt sich auf die beiden großen Tatsachen der Aussendung eines Elektronenstromes und

dessen Rückkehr zur Sendestelle, wo der inzwischen verflossene 105
Zeitraum mittels der Kathodenröhre gemessen wird.

Wie [3] ist man nun auf den Gedanken gekommen, elektromagnetische Wellen für diese Zwecke zu verwenden? Wie schon so oft, ist man auch hier von Naturbeobachtungen ausgegangen. In diesem Falle haben gewisse Tiere den Beobachtungsgegenstand 110
geliefert. Es handelte sich nämlich um die Fledermaus. Man weiß, daß diese imstande ist, äußerst hohe Schallwellen auszusenden, um sich in ihrem raschen Flug vor dem Zusammenprall mit Gegenständen in ihrer näheren Umgebung zu schützen. Treffen diese Schallwellen, welche übrigens bis 50 000 Schwingungen pro 115
Sekunde besitzen, einen in der Nähe befindlichen Gegenstand, so werden sie von demselben wieder zurückgeworfen, und kehren infolge ihrer großen Geschwindigkeit fast gleichzeitig wieder zur Fledermaus zurück. Die fein entwickelten Sinnesorgane derselben reagieren darauf, und die Fledermaus ändert ihre Flugrichtung, 120
ehe sie mit dem Gegenstand zusammenprallt. Radar kann mit derselben Situation verglichen werden. Es ist übrigens auch interessant hier zu bemerken, daß es nicht nur eine einzige Art von Kurzstrahlwellen gibt sondern eine ganze Anzahl. Das erklärt auch die Tatsache, wonach es uns kürzlich geglückt ist, den Radio- 125
spiegel zu durchbrechen und solche Strahlen weit in den Weltraum hinauszuschleudern. Vor einiger Zeit hat man sie sogar bis an den Mond geworfen, von wo sie wieder zur Sendestelle zurückgeschleudert wurde.

Wir sprachen oben von der sogenannten Kathodenröhre, welche 130
dazu gebraucht wurde, die Entfernung des gesuchten Gegenstandes von der Sendestelle zu messen. Beschäftigen wir uns etwas damit. Die Kathodenröhre geht auf Karl F. Braun zurück. Zwar entwickelte er sie nicht bis zur höchsten Vollkommenheit, aber er gebrauchte sie in Form des bekannten Oscilloskops. 135
Andere Forscher wiederum verbesserten sie und wandten sie für ihre eigenen wissenschaftlichen Zwecke an. Unter denjenigen, die Entscheidendes zur Entwicklung dieser Röhre beigetragen haben, sind Sir William Crooks und von Röntgen. Zu ihrer Zeit aber war der Kathodenstrahl noch nicht kontrollierbar, und es 140
war eben Braun, der gerade dieses erreichte. Kathodenstrahlen sind Ströme negativ geladener Partikel, welche von negativ geladenen Elektroden, auch Kathoden genannt, ausgesandt

werden. Und Braun gelang es, einen engen Strom von Elektronen zu erzeugen, den er dazu verwendete, Voltänderungen wahrzunehmen und zu messen. Die daraus entwickelten Kathodenstrahlenröhren aber waren noch nicht genügend, um Radar zu erzeugen; man brauchte dazu eine weit stärkere Quelle, die Elektronenröhre, um die kurzwelligen Strahlen in den Raum hinauszuwerfen. Wie geschah dies nun? Der Strom, der von der Kathodenröhre ausging, schwang horizontal im Raum und wurde mit den ebenfalls ausgehenden Radiowellen so synkronisiert, daß er das zurückkehrende Echo aufwies. Aus allem Gesagten ist zu sehen, daß der gesamte Radarapparat aus vier Hauptbestandteilen besteht: dem Kurzwellensender, dem Empfänger, dem Kathodenröhrenanzeiger und einem richtungsbestimmenden Antennensystem. Alle müssen synkronisiert werden, um wirksam zu werden. Zu gleicher Zeit, wenn die Kurzwellen den Sender verlassen, bewegt sich die Kathodenröhre in horizontaler Richtung und zieht eine ebenfalls horizontale Linie über das Sichtfeld des Ableseapparats. Sobald nun das Echo wieder aufgefangen wird, erscheint in der Linie ein sogenannter Buckel, dessen Lage auf dem linierten Sichtfeld dann die Entfernung des getroffenen Gegenstandes angibt. Die Sache ist natürlich viel komplizierter, als es hier angegeben ist. Im allgemeinen ist das aber der Grundzug.

Je nach Verwendung gibt es verschiedene Arten von Radarapparaten. Eine Art hat bewegliche Antennen, die weitere Gegenstände anzeigen. Bewegt sich der getroffene Gegenstand, so wird jegliche neue Lage ebenfalls angezeigt durch die veränderte Lage des „Buckels" auf dem Sichtfeld. Ein Synkronisieren der Antennen kann sogar die genauen Umrisse des getroffenen Gegenstandes angeben.

Aus dem notwendigerweise Wenigen, was über die Entwicklung des Radars gesagt worden ist, geht ohne Zweifel hervor, daß es sich um eine äußerst wichtige Einrichtung handelt. Wenn wir zudem noch im Auge behalten, daß die ganze Entwicklung in ihren entscheidenden Komponenten unter Kriegsdruck vor sich gegangen ist, so können wir ebenfalls leicht glauben, daß ihre Anwendung zuerst für Kriegszwecke stattgefunden hat. So wurde sie, wie jetzt jedermann weiß, zur Hauptabwehrwaffe gegen Flieger- und Bombenangriffe und hat sich tatsächlich auch so wirksam

166 **je nach** depending on

bewiesen, daß man mit Recht sagen kann, sie hat entscheidend in den Verlauf des Krieges eingegriffen. Natürlich war und ist dies nicht der einzige militärische Gebrauch davon; im Gegenteil, es ist durchaus möglich, Radar auch in einem sich bewegenden 185 Flugzeug anzubringen, oder vielleicht auf einem Schiff oder sogar in Verbindung mit Artilleriefeuer, um dasselbe auf Richtung und Entfernung einzustellen. Die Anwendung im Frieden zu friedlichen konstruktiven Zwecken ist vielleicht ebenso wichtig wie die im Kriege; und es ist vielleicht eine nicht zu weit greifende Aus- 190 sage, daß Radar den Beginn eines neuen Zeitalters bezeichnen kann. Schon heute können Flugzeuge, Raketen und Bomben, derart kontrolliert, ihren Zielen zugeschickt werden. Da es zu jeder Tageszeit angewendet werden kann, und da Wetterzustände keinen Einfluß auf die Wirksamkeit des Radars haben, kann man 195 es in der Handelsmarine, in allerlei Unfallversicherungsvorrichtungen in Häfen wie auch auf dem Lande anwenden. Die Möglichkeit ist groß, daß es bald wirksame Anwendung im Autoverkehr sowie dem Eisenbahnwesen finden wird. Ja, man hat daran gedacht, Radar zum Auffinden von allerlei Erzlagern zu 200 gebrauchen. Zwar ergeben sich in dieser Beziehung einige Schwierigkeiten, wie z.B. der Einfluß der Tiefe, in der ein Lager sich befinden könnte, oder auch die Art und Feuchtigkeit von Erdschichten über solchen Lagern; aber ohne Zweifel ist es nur noch Frage der Zeit, bis man auch diese Probleme gelöst hat. Es ist 205 natürlich unmöglich, daß solch eine staunenswerte Entwicklung wie diese ganz ohne Gegner geblieben sein sollte. In der Tat haben sich deren eine Anzahl gefunden und haben behauptet, Radar beeinflusse Klima und Wetter ungünstig, verursache gesundheitliche Schäden oder sei für verheerende Stürme verantwortlich. 210 Manche dieser Einwendungen sind als grundfalsch bewiesen worden; andere werden immerwährender Prüfung unterworfen und werden sich ohne Zweifel ebenso falsch erweisen. Aber welche große Erfindung oder Entwicklung in der Technik ist ganz ohne Kritik geblieben?

207 **in der Tat** indeed

APPENDIX

TRANSLATION HINTS AND POINTS

These notes refer to the reading selections in Part II. The numbers are correlated to the superior figures that appear in the text.

[Chapter 11]

1. **nach:** In technical German, **nach** ordinarily means *according to.* Two other meanings for the word are also frequently met with. When a sequence is implied, **nach** may mean *after.* When a geographical destination is indicated, **nach** may mean *to.*
2. **deren: dessen:** When preceded by a comma, or by a comma which in its turn is followed by a preposition, e.g., . . . , **deren** — . . . , **in deren,** either **deren** or **dessen** means *whose* or *in whose.* Otherwise it is a demonstrative pronoun and means *his, her, its,* or *their.*
3. **werden:** This verb functions in three different ways: (a) As an independent verb. In this case it means *to become* or any appropriate tense form of *to become.* (b) As an auxiliary verb that forms the future tense. In this case it means *shall* or *will.* (c) As an auxiliary verb that forms the passive voice. In this case it means *is being, are being,* or in the past tense of the passive voice, *was being, were being.*
4. **man sehe . . . an:** A third person singular present tense subjunctive. This is equivalent to an indirect imperative (a command) and may be translated in either of two ways: (a) By omitting the subject **man** and using the verb form as a direct imperative. E.g., *look at.* . . . (b) By using *should.* E.g., *one should look at.* . . .

[Chapter 12]

1. **dieser:** When **dieser** or any form of it appears at the beginning of a statement without being accompanied by a noun, it means *the latter.* Likewise, a form of **jener** similarly used means *the former.*
2. **wenn . . . auch:** This construction is basic to a whole series of **auch** expressions. It means *even though* or *although.* Other expressions that belong to this group are set out below.

wer . . . auch	whoever
was . . . auch	whatever
wo . . . auch	wherever
wie . . . auch	in whatever manner

3. **sein:** Any form of **sein,** when used with a **zu**-infinitive, results in a corresponding form of *is to be* + past participle or *must be* + past participle.

4. **also:** This word never means *also;* on the contrary it means *therefore.* The following words are also similarly used: **darnach, folglich, demgemäß,** and **somit.**

[Chapter 13]

1. **sich:** When used as a reflexive pronoun, **sich** must be translated when the equivalent English verb requires it. When not, it may be omitted. It is frequently used as the equivalent for *is.* E.g., **Es befindet sich dort.** *It is found there.*

2. *if:* When a sentence begins with a finite verb, unless it is a question or a command, the translation must begin with *if.* This is always true when such a clause is followed by a main clause which may often be begun with *so.*

3. **je:** When **je** occurs alone, it may usually be translated by *each.* When in the form **je nachdem,** it may be translated by *depending upon.* When used in a comparison, this word appears as **je . . . desto** or **je . . . umso.** The latter construction may also occur in the reverse order. E.g., **umso . . . je.**

[Chapter 14]

1. **als:** This word has three principal functions. (a) As a subordinating conjunction with the meaning *when.* (b) As a comparative connective with the meaning *than.* (c) When accompanied directly by a noun, it may mean *in the role of* or *in the function of.*

2. **es:** When followed by a finite verb and a nominative, **es** may be omitted in translation. Sometimes it may be translated by *there.*

3. **repeated preposition:** Occasionally a prepositional phrase will begin and end with a preposition. The terminal preposition may not be the same as the initial one, though it has the same meaning. Usually the function of the terminal preposition is to emphasize the initial one. It may be omitted in translation.

4. **ganz:** This word is one of a group, all of which express *very.* The others are **sehr, äußerst, recht,** and **höchst.**

[Chapter 15]

1. **daß:** When a statement begins with the word **daß,** it must be translated by *the fact that.*

2. **während:** When this word is followed by a noun in the possessive case, it means *during.* When the entire verb is found at the end of the clause, **während** must be translated by *while.*

3. **let us:** When an inverted first person plural of the present tense occurs in a main clause or a simple sentence, it must be translated by *let us.*

4. **sein:** The idea of *to be* may also be expressed by a suitable form of **stehen, stecken,** or **sich befinden.**

[Chapter 16]

1. **would:** When the past tense of a subjunctive verb occurs in the main clause or in a simple sentence, the translation is *would* + the infinitive of the verb represented by the past subjunctive. E.g., **käme** *would come.* Likewise, a pluperfect subjunctive in a similar position becomes *would have* + past participle. E.g., **wäre gekommen** *would have come.*

2. **es sei(en):** When this subjunctive verb form is followed by a past participle, it is an imperative (command) and must be translated by *let us* + the infinitive of the verb represented by the past participle. E.g., **es sei daran erinnert, daß . . .** *let us recall that. . . .*

3. **adverb adjective series:** When, in a series of adjectives, one of them has no ending, it is an adverb to the following adjective and must be so translated. E.g., **ein vollkommen mißglückter Versuch** *a completely unsuccessful experiment.*

4. **ein:** The student should thoroughly master the series of words set out below.

ein	a, an	**vereinigt**	united
eins	one	**einzeln**	single, singly
einig	united, in agreement	**vereinzelt**	individual(ly)
einige	some, several	**eigen**	own (*adj.*)
einzig	only (*adj.*)	**eigentlich**	actual(ly), proper(ly)

[Chapter 17]

1. **geworden:** This word, which is the past participle of **werden,** means *become.* When the form **worden** follows a past participle, it always means *been.* The tense of the auxiliary verb **sein,** which appears as **ist, sind, war,** or **waren,** indicates the present or pluperfect passive.

2. **dadurch, daß . . . :** This construction is characteristic of an entire series of similar ones. All are identical except for the fact that the preposition varies. Other members of the series are **davon, daß . . . , darauf, daß . . . , darin, daß . . . ,** and so on. These are translated by *through the fact that . . . , upon the fact that . . . , in the fact that . . . ,* and so on.

3. **there:** Inversion, especially when it occurs in a rather lengthy clause or statement, may often be easily solved by inserting the word *there* directly before the finite verb.

[Chapter 18]

1. **erst:** This word functions in several different ways. (a) As an adjective. E.g., **das erste Experiment** *the first experiment.* (b) As an adverb of order. E.g., **Erst besprechen wir dieses Experiment.** *First we shall discuss this experiment.* (c) With the meaning of *not until.*

E.g., **Wir analysieren dieses Experiment erst morgen.** *We shall not analyze this experiment until tomorrow.* (d) When directly followed by a noun, it often has the meaning *only* or *as*. E.g., **Erst Koch gelang es, ...** *Only Koch succeeded. . . .* (e) In its adverbial form, **erstens,** it means *firstly*. E.g., **Erstens muß dieses Experiment wiederholt werden.** *Firstly, this experiment must be repeated.*

2. **bei:** This word has three principal functions. (a) When used with statistical data either expressed or implied, it means *at*. (b) When used in expressing an idea that involves the progression of an action it means *during*. (c) Otherwise it means *in the case of*.

3. **sich lassen:** When this reflexive verb appears with an infinitive, it must be translated by *can be* + the past participle of the verb indicated by the infinitive. E.g., **Das läßt sich berechnen.** *This can be calculated.* The past tense of this construction uses **ließ.** The plural uses the verb forms **lassen** and **ließen.**

[Chapter 19]

1. **aber:** When this word is removed from its initial position in the statement, it receives added emphasis and means *however*.

2. **besaß:** The verb **besitzen** is a synonym of **haben.** It may be translated by a suitable form of the latter verb.

3. **Verb missing at the end:** Contrary to all classroom rules to the effect that in a main clause all verb forms except the finite verb stand at the end, the student will sometimes find that the verb forms at the end of the clause have been removed from that position and brought nearer to the finite verb form.

[Chapter 20]

1. **der:** This word chiefly functions in three ways. (a) As a definite article. (b) As a relative pronoun; in this function it may be replaced by **welcher.** (c) When it occurs as neither the definite article nor the relative pronoun but as a very emphatic demonstrative pronoun.

2. **indem — in dem:** The word **indem** — written as one word — is a subordinating conjunction. It may be translated in two different ways: (a) By using the preposition *by* + the present participle in *-ing*. (b) By using the phrase *in that* + a finite verb form. The phrase **in dem** is a relative pronoun construction. It may be translated by *in which* or *in whom*.

3. **da:** When this word is directly followed by a finite verb, it is an adverb. As such it causes inversion and must be translated by *there* or *then*. When, on the contrary, the finite verb stands at the end of the clause, **da** is a subordinating conjunction. It must then be translated by *because* or *since*.

[Chapter 21]

1. **stehen:** This verb is the root word of a series of **stehen** compounds that are important in technical German. The student should master the principal compounds such as **bestehen** *to exist*, **bestehen aus** *to consist of*, **entstehen** *to originate*, **verstehen** *to understand*, and many others.

2. **nehmen:** This verb also forms many important compounds such as **zunehmen** *to increase*, **abnehmen** *to decrease*, **annehmen** *to assume*, **vornehmen** *to undertake*, **aufnehmen** *to take up*, *to absorb*, **übernehmen** *to take over*, and many others.

3. **kommen:** Important compounds of this verb include **bekommen** *to receive*, **vorkommen** *to occur*, **ankommen** *to arrive*, **überkommen** (*adj.*) *traditional*, and many others.

[Chapter 22]

1. **Missing subject:** Whenever a statement appears without a subject, it is safe to assume that the subject is to be understood. In such a case the subject is usually the pronoun **es**. Thus, in translating, either *it* or *there* must be used.

2. **um:** When a clause begins with the word **um** and there is a **zu**-infinitive at the end, it is part of the **um-zu**-construction and must be translated *in order to*. . . . If there is no **zu**-infinitive at the end of the clause, then **um** is a preposition that must be translated by *around* or *about*.

3. **wie:** This word functions in several different ways. (a) As a comparative connective having the meaning *as*. (b) As a direct or indirect question word having the meaning *how*. (c) As a subordinating conjunction having the meaning *as*.

TECHNICAL EXPRESSIONS

The following expressions occur frequently enough in technical German to warrant the student's special attention. They are not necessarily idiomatic. Since it is very difficult to classify them alphabetically in a satisfactory manner, the attempt has been made to make them clearly recognizable by printing the key words in boldface type.

A

Es ist **abhängig** von . . .	It is dependent upon . . .
Es kam zum **Abschluß.**	It was concluded.
vor **Allem**	above all
in **Anbetracht** des	in consideration of the
von **Anfang** an	from the beginning
Man ist darauf **angewiesen, zu** . . .	One is dependent upon . . .
Es wird in **Angriff** genommen.	It is being started.
Es gab den **Anlaß** dazu, zu . . .	It provided the occasion for . . .
Es wurde **Anlaß** zu . . .	It became the cause of . . .
in **Anlehnung** an . . .	with reference to . . .
Es gab **Anregung** zu . . .	It stimulated . . .
Er vertritt die **Ansicht,** daß . . .	He is of the opinion that . . .
Aufgabe des Arztes ist es, zu . . .	It is the task of the physician to . . .
Die **Aufgabe** fällt ihm zu, zu . . .	It is his task to . . .
Es war ihm **aufgefallen,** daß . . .	His attention was drawn to the fact that . . .
unter **Aufwand** von . . .	with the expenditure of . . .
Er fand den **Ausdruck** für . . .	He found the expression for . . .
Es nimmt seinen **Ausgang** von . . .	It begins with . . .
Es ist **ausgeschlossen,** daß . . .	It is impossible that . . .
Es gibt **Auskunft** darüber.	It furnishes information about (the matter).
Er macht die **Aussage,** daß . . .	He makes the statement that . . .
nach **außen** hin	externally
ein **Auszug** daraus	an excerpt from it

B

Die **Bedeutung** liegt darin, daß . . .	The significance lies in the fact that . . .
Es ist **bedeutungsvoll,** daß . . .	It is significant that . . .
unter der **Bedingung,** daß . . .	under the condition that . . .

unter gewöhnlichen **Bedingungen**	under ordinary conditions
Es **befaßt** sich mit . . .	It deals with . . .
mit der **Begründung,** daß . . .	by reason of the fact that . . .
Er führt ein **Beispiel** an.	He cites an example.
Er liefert einen **Beitrag.**	He makes a contribution.
Wir werden zunächst **beleuchten,** wie . . .	We shall at first make clear how . . .
nach **belieben**	at one's pleasure
Er ist **berechtigt,** zu . . .	He is entitled to . . .
Es kommt in **Berührung** mit . . .	It comes into contact with . . .
Er weiß **Bescheid** über . . .	He is versed in . . .
Man muß sich darauf **beschränken,** zu . . .	One must limit oneself to . . .
Es ist von **Bestand.**	It is lasting.
Es **bewährt** sich so gut, daß . . .	It so well proves that . . .
Es muß **bewiesen** werden, daß . .	It must be proved that . . .
Er ist sich **bewußt,** daß . . .	He is conscious of the fact that . . .
in jeder **Beziehung**	in every respect
auf den ersten **Blick**	at first glance
auf dem **Boden** einer . . .	on the basis of a . . .
Es steht im **Brennpunkt** der . . .	It is at the center of the . . .

D

dadurch, daß . . .	by the fact that . . .
Es wird künstlich **dargestellt.**	It is produced synthetically.
dazu, daß . . .	to the fact that . . .
Es leistet **Dienste.**	It renders a service.
Es erschien im **Druck.**	It was published.

E

eigens für ihn	especially for him
Es gibt einen **Einblick** in . . .	It furnishes an insight into . . .
Es übt einen **Einfluß** aus über . . .	It exercises an influence upon . . .
Es tut **Einhalt.**	It stops.
Es steht im **Einklang** mit . . .	It is in accord with . . .
Es ist **einleuchtend,** daß . . .	It is clear that . . .
Es ist zu **Ende.**	It is at an end. (It has come to an end.)
letzten **Endes**	in the final analysis
Tatsächlich **ergibt** sich, daß . . .	It is actually found that . . .
Sobald **erkannt** ist, daß . . .	As soon as one realizes that . . .
Man **erkannte,** daß . . .	One realized that . . .
Man **erkennt** erst allmählich, daß . . .	One only gradually realizes that . . .
Es bereichert uns um wichtige **Erkenntnisse.**	It enriches us with important knowledge.

durch **Ermittlung** von . . .	by the inquiry of . . .
zum **erstenmal**	for the first time
Es ist **erwiesen,** daß . . .	It is proved that . . .

F

Dies ist der **Fall.**	This is the case.
nur in den dringendsten **Fällen**	only in the most urgent cases
Er **fand** vor allem, daß . . .	Above all, he found that . . .
Es **steht fest,** daß . . .	It is a fact that . . .
Es wurde ferner **festgestellt,** daß . . .	Furthermore, it was found that . . .
Es ist noch im **Fluß.**	It is still in a state of flux.
Die **Folge** davon ist, daß . . .	The consequence of this is that . . .
Wir werden im **Folgenden** sehen, daß . . .	We shall see from the following that . . .
Man zieht die **Folgerung,** daß . . .	One draws the conclusion that . . .
in der **Folgezeit**	subsequently
Es **fragt sich** nun, ob . . .	The question now is, if . . .

G

Man macht sich **Gedanken** über . . .	One wonders about . . .
im **Gegensatz** zu	in contrast to
Es **gelang** ihm nachzuweisen, daß . . .	He succeeded in proving that . . .
Man hat die **Gelegenheit,** zu . . .	One has the opportunity to . . .
mit einiger **Genauigkeit**	with some accuracy
von einem anderen **Gesichtspunkt** aus	from a different point of view
Zunächst **gilt** es, zu . . .	First, it is a question of . . .
bis zu einem gewissen **Grade**	up to a certain degree
im **Großen**	on a large scale
auf **Grund** von	on the basis of
im **Grunde** (genommen)	basically
Er legt es ihm zu **Grunde** . . .	He supports it with . . .
Es liegt darin **begründet,** daß . . .	It is based on the fact that . . .
Es wurde auf eine wissenschaftliche **Grundlage** gestellt.	It was put on a scientific basis.
Es ging **zugrunde.**	It perished.

H

Es ist zur **Hand.**	It is at hand.
Es **handelt** sich um . . .	It is a question of . . .
in der **Hauptsache**	chiefly
Nun **heißt** es, zu . . .	It is now a question of . . .
Es hat sich **herausgestellt,** daß . . .	It was found that . . .

Wie wichtig es ist, **geht** daraus **hervor,** daß . . .	Its importance is seen from the fact that . . .
mit **Hilfe** der . . .	with the aid of the . . .
in dieser **Hinsicht**	in this respect

I

Er ist **imstande,** zu . . .	He is capable of . . .
infolge der . . .	in consequence of the . . .

K

Es ist **kennzeichnend,** daß . . .	It is characteristic that . . .
Es ist dadurch **gekennzeichnet,** daß . . .	It is characterized by the fact that . . .
im **Kleinen**	on a small scale
Es **kommt** daher, daß . . .	It is due to the fact that . . .
Es **kommt** darauf **an,** zu . . .	It is a question of . . .
So **kommt** es, daß . . .	It so happens that . . .
Woher **kommt** es, daß . . .	What is the reason that . . .
Er macht eine **Krise** durch.	He undergoes a crisis.
vor **Kurzem**	recently

L

Man ist heute in der **Lage,** zu . . .	Today one is in position to . . .
ins **Leben** rufen	to bring to life
Es läßt sich nicht **leugnen,** daß . . .	It cannot be denied that . . .
in erster **Linie**	primarily

M

Er **machte sich** daran, zu . . .	He began to . . .
in weit höherem **Maße**	to a far greater extent
Er machte die **Mitteilung,** daß . . .	He brought out the information that . . .
Mittel zum Zweck	means to an end
Es steht im **Mittelpunkt** der . . .	It is at the center of the . . .
Die **Möglichkeit** ergibt sich, daß . . .	There is a possibility that . . .
Man wird vor die **Möglichkeit** gestellt, zu . . .	One is faced with the possibility of . . .

N

Er konnte **nachweisen,** daß . . .	He could prove that . . .
Es ist **naheliegend,** daß . . .	It is easy to infer that . . .
Er nahm **Notiz** von . . .	He took notice of . . .

R

mit **Recht**	rightly
Es kann keine **Rede** sein von . . .	There can be no discussion of . . .
eine **Reihe** von . . .	a series of . . .
mit **Rücksicht** auf . . .	with reference to . . .

S

Man **schätzt,** daß . . .	It is estimated that . . .
Man zieht den **Schluß,** daß . . .	One draws the conclusion that . . .
Er macht **Schule.**	He wins over followers.
es **sei** denn, daß . . .	unless
So viel ist **sicher,** daß . . .	This much is certain, that . . .
Er hat dafür keinen **Sinn.**	He has no aptitude for it.
im engeren **Sinne**	in a more limited sense
im tiefsten **Sinne** des Wortes	in the fullest sense of the word
im weiteren **Sinne**	in a broader sense
Man war jetzt **soweit,** daß . . .	One had now come to the point where . . .
Es **spricht** dafür, daß . . .	It emphasizes the fact that . . .
Er nimmt **Stellung** zu . . .	He assumes an attitude toward . . .

T

bis auf den heutigen **Tag**	until the present
Es ist damit nicht **getan.**	That won't do.
eine **Tat** ersten Ranges	a first-rate achievement
in der **Tat**	indeed
Tatsache ist, daß . . .	The fact is, that . . .
zum großen **Teil**	largely

U

Man **geht** dazu **über,** zu . . .	One proceeds to . . .
im **Übermaß**	in excess (excessively)
Er kam zu der **Überzeugung,** daß . . .	He came to the conviction that . . .
in größtem **Umfang**	to the greatest degree
Es war ein glücklicher **Umstand,** daß . . .	It was a fortunate circumstance that . . .
unter dem **Umstande,** daß . . .	under the circumstances that . . .
allem **ungeachtet**	irrespective of all

V

Er erwarb sich **Verdienste** um . . .	He deserved well of . . .
Er machte sich **verdient** um . . .	He earned merit for . . .
Es wurde **verfügt,** daß . . .	Arrangements were made that . . .

Es steht zur **Verfügung.**	It is available.
im **Vergleich** zu . . .	in comparison with . . .
im weiteren **Verlauf**	in the further course
Es ist **verständlich,** daß . . .	It is understandable that . . .
Es **kommt** nicht selten **vor,** daß . . .	It happens frequently that . . .
Er **nahm** sich nun **vor,** zu . . .	He now intended to . . .
schon im **voraus**	even in advance
Es hat zur **Voraussetzung,** daß . . .	The supposition is that . . .
Es steht im **Vordergrund.**	It is in the foreground.
Es macht einen **Vorgang** durch.	It goes through a process.
Es ist **vorhanden.**	It is available.
So konnte es **vorkommen,** daß . . .	So it could happen that . . .
von **vorneherein**	to begin with
Ausgehend von der **Vorstellung,** daß . . .	Starting with the idea that . . .

W

Es vollzieht sich ein **Wandel.**	A change occurs.
in ähnlicher **Weise**	similarly
in so tief gehender **Weise**	in such a profound manner
ohne **Weiteres**	without trouble
Es ist am **Werk.**	It is at work.
seinem **Wesen** nach	according to its nature
im wesentlichen	essentially
um seiner selbst **willen**	for its own sake
Es wird zur **Wirklichkeit.**	It becomes a reality.
eine **Wirkung** ausüben	to exert an influence

Z

zu keiner **Zeit**	at no time
Es ist kein **Zufall,** daß . . .	It is no mere accident that . . .
Er hatte **Zugang** zu . . .	He had access to . . .
Er machte es **zugänglich.**	He made it accessible.
zunichte machen	to destroy
Er bringt es **zustande.**	He accomplishes it.
Es wird ihm **zuteil.**	It falls to his lot.
Es unterliegt keinem **Zweifel,** daß . . .	There is no doubt that . . .

A LIST OF ABBREVIATIONS THAT ARE FOUND IN TECHNICAL GERMAN

a.a.O.	**am angeführten Orte**	in the before-mentioned place
abgk.	**abgekürzt**	abbreviated
Abh.	**Abhandlung**	treatise
Abschn.	**Abschnitt**	paragraph
a.D.	**außer Dienst**	off duty, retired
A.G.	**Aktiengesellschaft**	joint-stock company
allgm.	**allgemein**	in general
Anm.	**Anmerkung**	note
Anz.	**Anzeige**	advertisement
Art.	**Artikel**	article
Aufl.	**Auflage**	edition
ausgel.	**ausgelassen**	omitted
Bd.	**Band**	volume
bed.	**bedeutet**	signifies
beif.	**beifolgend**	herewith
betr.	**betreffs**	concerning
bez.	**bezüglich**	with reference to
b(e)zw.	**beziehungsweise**	respectively
C.	**Celsius**	centigrade
ca.	**circa**	about
cm	**Zentimeter**	centimeter
das.	**daselbst**	in the same place
dgl.	**dergleichen**	similarly
d.h.	**das heißt**	that is, i.e.
Dr. u. Vrl.	**Druck und Verlag**	publisher
ebds.	**ebendaselbst**	in the same place
Einl.	**Einleitung**	introduction
einschl.	**einschließlich**	inclusive (of)
entspr.	**entsprechend**	corresponding(ly)
Erl.	**Erläuterung**	explanation
ev.	**eventuell**	perhaps
F.	**Fahrenheit**	Fahrenheit (thermometer)
ff.	**folgende**	the following
F.f.	**Fortsetzung folgt**	to be continued
Forts.	**Fortsetzung**	continuation
Fußn.	**Fußnote**	footnote

g	Gramm(e)	gram
geb.	geboren	born
geh.	geheftet	stitched
gen.	genannt	mentioned
gest.	gestorben	died
gez.	gezeichnet	signed
gleichbd.	gleichbedeutend	synonymous
G.m.b.H.	Gesellschaft mit beschränkter Haftung	limited company
Gr.	Grad	degree
Grndr.	Grundriß	outline, compendium
hl.	heilig	saint
hrsg.	herausgegeben	edited, published
Hs.	Handschrift	manuscript, Ms.
Hsgbr.	Herausgeber	editor, publisher
i.a.	im allgemeinen	in general
i.b.	im besonderen	in particular
i.J.	im Jahre	in the year
kswgs.	keineswegs	in no wise
Kl.	Klasse	class
km	Kilometer	kilometer
l.	lies	read
l	Liter	liter
m.	merke, Meter	notice, meter
mg	Milligramm	milligram
mm	Millimeter	millimeter
n.A.	neue Ausgabe	new edition
näml.	nämlich	that is to say
namtl.	namentlich	especially
n.Chr.	nach Christus	A.D.
n.F.	neue Folge	new series
NNW	Nord-Nordwest	north-northwest
n(r)o., Nr.	Nummer	number
N.S.	Nachschrift	postscript, P.S.
o.	oben	above
org.	organisch	organic
p.	per, par, pro	per, par, pro
Pf.	Pfennig, Pfund	penny, pound
p.t.	pro tempore	for the time being

R.	**Réaumur**	Réaumur (thermometer)
r.	**rund**	around, about
resp.	**respektive**	respectively
rd.	**rund**	about, approximately
S.	**Seite**	page
s.	**siehe**	see
s.a.	**siehe auch**	see also
s.d.	**siehe dies (dort)**	see above
s.d.V.	**siehe das Vorige**	see above
sog.	**sogenannt**	so-called
s.o.	**siehe oben**	see above
s.u.	**siehe unten**	see below
s.Z.	**seiner Zeit**	at that time
teilw.	**teilweise**	partly
u.	**und**	and
u.a.	**unter anderm**	among other things
u.a.a.O.	**und am andern Orte**	and elsewhere
u.a.m.	**und andere mehr**	and other things besides
u.dgl.	**und dergleichen**	and similar things
urspr.	**ursprünglich**	originally
u.s.f.	**und so fort**	and so forth, et cetera, etc.
usw.	**und so weiter**	
z.B.	**zum Beispiel**	for example, e.g.
zuw.	**zuweilen**	at times
zw.	**zwischen**	between
z.Z.	**zur Zeit**	at the time
vgl.	**Vergleich(e)!**	compare

z.B.	**zum Beispiel**	for example, e.g.
zuw.	**zuweilen**	at times
zw.	**zwischen**	between
z.Z.	**zur Zeit**	at the time

VOCABULARY

GERMAN-ENGLISH VOCABULARY

The following vocabulary has been compiled to achieve a certain completeness within the range of a basic scientific word-list. The following items were omitted, however, because of obvious reasons:

1. Proper names.
2. Words with which the student should be familiar from his study of elementary German.
3. Words of foreign origin whose meanings are obvious. E.g., **Klassifizierung, elektrisch,** etc.
4. Compound words whose component parts, when put together, result in a clear meaning. E.g., **Agrikulturchemie, entgegenarbeiten,** etc.
5. Individual component parts of compound words whose meaning is clear. E.g., **Bekämpfungs (methode).** In such cases the student will have to look up only the unknown part of the word. E.g., **Bekämpfung.**

A

abbauen to reduce
das Abbild, –er image
abblasen (ä; ie, a) to blow off
der Abdruck, –e impression
das Abendland Occident
abendländisch Occidental
der Abfluß, ⁻sse drainage
das Abführmittel, — purgative
abgeben (i; a, e) to give off, to deliver, to discharge
abgesehen von aside from
die Abhandlung, –en treatise
der Abhang, ⁻e incline, hillside
abhängen von to be dependent on
abhängig dependent
die Abhängigkeit dependence
der Abkömmling, –e descendant
die Abkühlung cooling off
abkürzen to abbreviate
die Abkürzung abbreviation
der Ablauf, ⁻e course, expiration
ablegen to lay off
ablehnen to reject
ableiten to derive
ablenken to derive
die Ablenkung, –en deviation, deflection
ablesen (ie; a, e) to read off
ablösen to relieve
abnehmen (i; a, o) to take off, to decrease
abrunden to round off
abschließen (o, o) to conclude, to complete
der Abschluß, ⁻sse conclusion, completion

der Abschnitt, –e part, section
absehen von (ie; a, e) to disregard
die Absicht, –en intention
abspalten to split off
sich abspielen to come off
der Abstand, ⸗e distance
abstellen to stop
absterben (i; a, o) to die off
abstoßen (ö; ie, o) to repel
abstreifen to slough off
die Abstufung, –en gradation
der Absturz, ⸗e fall
abwechseln to change off, to alternate
die Abwehr defense
abweichen (i, i) to deviate
abweisen (ie, ie) to refuse, to reject
abwiegen (o, o) to weigh
die Achse axis, axle
der Affe, –n ape, monkey
ahnen to have a premonition
die Ahnung, –en premonition
die Alge, –n algae
allerdings to be sure
allerhand all sorts of
allgemein general
allgemeingültig generally valid
allmählich gradually
also therefore, thus
das Altertum antiquity
altmodisch old-fashioned
anbelangen to concern
anbringen (a, a) to attach
ändern to change
andersartig of a different kind
anderswo elsewhere
die Änderung, –en change
anderwärts elsewhere
anderweitig elsewhere
andeuten to indicate
anerkennen (a, a) to recognize
die Anerkennung, –en recognition
der Anfang, ⸗e beginning
anfänglich at the beginning
anfangs at the beginning
der Anflug, ⸗e beginning
die Anforderung, –en requirement
anführen to cite, to quote
die Angabe, –n statement, data
angeben (i; a, e) to indicate, to quote
angehören to belong
angelsächsisch Anglo-Saxon
angemessen stable
angesichts in the face of
der Angestellte, –n white-collar worker
angewandt applied
angewiesen auf dependent upon
die Angewohnheit, –en habit
angreifen (i, i) to attack
der Angriff, –e attack
die Angst, ⸗e fear
anhaltend continuous
der Anhaltspunkt, –e point of attachment
der Anhänger, — disciple
die Anhäufung, –en accumulation
anheften to attach
der Ankömmling, –e newcomer
die Ankunft arrival
die Anlage, –n plan, plant, arrangement
anlangen to arrive
der Anlaß, ⸗sse cause
anlegen to construct
die Anlegung, –en construction
die Anleihe, –n loan
annähernd approximately
die Annäherung, –en approximation
die Annahme, –n assumption
annehmen (i; a, o) to assume
die Anordnung, –en arrangement
anpassen to adapt
die Anpassung, –en adaptation
die Anregung, –en stimulation
sich ansammeln to collect
der Ansatz, ⸗e beginning
die Anschauung, –en viewpoint
der Anschein appearance

anscheinend apparently
anschließen (o, o) to connect with
der Anschluß, ⸚sse connection
anschneiden (i, i) to touch upon
die Ansicht, –en viewpoint
die Ansteckung contagion
anstellen to occupy
der Anstoß, ⸚e impulse, stimulus
anstrengend strenuous
die Anstrengung, –en exertion
der Anteil, –e share
der Antrieb, –e motive, urge
anwendbar applicable
anwenden to apply
die Anwendung, –en application
anwerben (i; a, o) to hire
die Anzahl, –en number
das Anzeichen, — symptom, sign
anzeigen to indicate
der Anzeiger, — indicator
anziehen (o, o) to attract
die Arbeit, –en work
die Art, –en type, kind, species
ärztlich medical
atmen to breathe
der Aufbau, –ten construction
aufbewahren to preserve
auferlegen to impose
die Auferstehung resurrection
auffallen (ä; ie, a) to be striking, to arouse attention
auffällig conspicuous
auffassen to consider
die Auffassung, –en concept, idea
auffinden (a, u) to find, to detect
die Aufgabe, –n task
aufgeben (i; a, e) to assign
aufhalten (ä; ie, a) to stay, to remain
die Auflockerung loosening
sich auflösen to dissolve
die Aufmerksamkeit attention
der Aufsatz, ⸚e essay
aufschließen (o, o) to unlock
aufschlußreich informative
der Aufschwung rise
das Aufsehen attention, excitement
aufspalten to split up
aufstellen to set up
die Aufstellung, –en erection
auftauchen to emerge
die Aufteilung division, distribution
auftreten (i; a, e) to appear
das Auftreten appearance
der Aufwand expenditure
der Augenschein appearance
augenscheinlich apparent
aufweisen (ie, ie) to show, to exhibit
aufwerfen (i; a, o) to throw up
die Aufwölbung, –en bulge
aufzeichnen to record
die Aufzeichnung, –en record
aufzüchten to improve by breeding
der Augenblick, –e moment
augenblicklich momentary
augenscheinlich apparent
ausarten to degenerate
der Ausbau, –ten development
ausbauen to develop
ausbeuten to exploit
die Ausbeutung exploitation
ausbilden to train
die Ausbildung training
ausbleiben (ie, ie) to fail to appear
ausbrechen (i; a, o) to break out
sich ausbreiten to spread
der Ausbruch, ⸚e outbreak
ausdehnen to extend, to expand
die Ausdehnung, –en extension, expansion
der Ausdruck, ⸚e expression
ausdrücken to express
ausdrücklich expressly
auseinandersetzen to expound, to dispute, to argue
ausfechten (i; o, o) to fight out
ausführen to carry out
ausführlich explicitly
die Ausführlichkeit explicitness
die Ausführung, –en execution

die Ausgabe, -n expense, edition
ausgehen (i, a) to go out, to start
ausgenommen except
ausgeschlossen impossible
ausgesprochen pronounced
ausgestalten to form, to develop
die Ausgestaltung, -en development, forming
der Ausgleich compensation
ausgleichen (i, i) to compensate
die Ausgrabung, -en excavation
der Ausläufer, — runner
auslösen to set free
das Ausmaß, -e degree, proportion
ausmerzen to eradicate
die Ausnahme, -n exception
ausnutzen to use fully, to utilize
ausprägen to coin, to delineate
die Ausreise, -n departure
ausrotten to eradicate
die Ausrottung eradication
ausschlaggebend determining
ausschleudern to hurl out
ausschließen (o, o) to exclude
ausschließlich exclusively
aussehen (ie; a, e) to look like, to appear
das Aussehen appearance
außer except
außerdem besides
sich äußern to express oneself
außerordentlich exceptional
äußerst extreme
aussetzen to expose, to skip
die Aussicht, -en prospect
aussichtslos hopeless
die Aussonderung selection
ausspucken to expectorate
ausüben to practice
die Ausübung practice, exercise
die Auswahl choice
auswählen to choose
auswählerisch choosy
der Auswanderer, — emigrant
auswandern to emigrate
die Auswanderung, -en emigration
die Auswertung utilization, exploitation
sich auswirken to work out in practice
die Auswirkung effect
die Auszehrung consumption
sich auszeichnen to distinguish oneself

B

der Bach, ⸚e brook
der Backenknochen, — jawbone
der Bahnbrecher, — pioneer
der Ballast ballast
der Ballen, — ball (of the hand or foot)
der Bambus bamboo
der Band, ⸚e volume
die Barre, -n sand bar
der Bauer, -n peasant
der Baustein, -e building stone
beachten to consider
der Beamte, — official
die Beantwortung reply
das Beben, — quaking, shaking
das Becken, — basin, pelvis
bedacht sein auf to be considerate of
der Bedarf need
bedenken (a, a) to consider
bedeuten to mean
bedeutend important
die Bedeutung, -en meaning, importance
sich bedienen to use
bedingen to cause
die Bedingung, -en condition
beeinträchtigen to influence
die Beere, -en berry
befallen (ä; ie, a) to affect
sich befassen mit to occupy oneself with
befestigen to attach, to make firm
sich befinden (a, u) to be
die Befreiung liberation
befruchten to fertilize

der Befund, –e state in which a thing is found, inventory
sich begeben auf (i; a, e) to go
die Begebenheit, –en event
begegnen to meet, to encounter
der Beginn beginning
beglaubigen to attest to
begleiten to accompany
die Begleiterscheinung, –en accompanying phenomenon
beglücken to surprise, to make happy
das Begrasen grazing
die Begrenzung, –en limitation
begründen to base upon
der Begründer, — founder
die Begründung, –en establishment, foundation
begünstigen to favor
behandeln to treat
sich behaupten to assert oneself
die Behauptung, –en assertion
die Behausung, –en housing
beherbergen to shelter
beherrschen to dominate
beibehalten (ä; ie, a) to retain
beiläufig contributory
beiseite aside
das Beispiel, –e example
der Beistand assistance
der Beitrag, ⸚e contribution
beiträglich contributory
bekämpfen to fight
die Bekämpfung fighting
bekanntlich as known
das Bekenntnis, –sse confession
die Belaubung foliage
sich belaufen auf (äu; ie, au) to amount to
beleben to be crowded by, populated
beleuchten to illuminate
beliebig any
bemächtigt controlled, secured
bemerkbar perceptible
bemerkenswert noteworthy
das Bemühen endeavoring
die Bemühung, –en endeavor
benachbart neighboring
benutzen to use, to utilize
die Benutzung use, utilization
beobachten to observe
der Beobachter, — observer
die Beobachtung, –en observation
berechenbar calculable
berechnen to calculate
berechtigt justified, justifiable
die Berechtigung, –en justification
der Bereich, –e reach, sphere, extent
bereichern to enrich
bereiten to prepare
bereitstellen to make ready
bergen (i; a, o) to shelter, to contain
berichten to report
berücksichtigen to consider
der Beruf, –e profession
beruflich professional
das Berufswesen professionalism
beruhen auf to be based upon
die Beruhigung quiescence
berühmt famous
berühren to touch
die Beschaffenheit condition
sich beschäftigen mit to occupy oneself with
die Beschäftigung, –en occupation
der Bescheid information
beschießen (o, o) to bombard
die Beschießung, –en bombardment
beschleunigen to accelerate
die Beschleunigung acceleration
beschränken to limit
beschreiben (ie, ie) to describe
die Beschwerde, –n complaint
beschwerlich difficult
die Beschwörung, –en conjuring
beseitigen to eliminate
der Besitz possession
besitzen (a, e) to possess

besonder special
besprechen (i; a, o) to discuss
die Besprechung, –en discussion
die Besserung, –en improvement
der Bestand, ¨e stand
der Bestandteil, –e component part
bestätigen to confirm
die Bestätigung, –en confirmation
bestechen (i; a, o) to bribe
die Bestechlichkeit corruption
bestimmen to determine
die Bestimmung, –en determination
das Bestreben endeavor
sich beteiligen an to participate in
betonen to emphasize
die Betonung emphasis
betrachten to consider
die Betrachtung, –en consideration
betragen (ä; **u, a**) to behave, to amount
betreiben (ie, ie) to carry on
betreffen (i; a, o) to refer to
betreffend respective
betreuen to care for
beurteilen to judge, to estimate
bevorzugen to prefer
sich bewähren to be found sound
bewandert versed (in)
der Beweggrund, ¨e motive
beweglich movable, motile
der Beweis, –e proof
beweisen (ie, ie) to prove
bewerkstelligen to accomplish
bewerten to evaluate
die Bewertung evaluation
bewirken to effect
bewohnbar habitable
bewußt conscious
das Bewußtsein consciousness
bezeichnen to designate
bezeichnend characteristic of
sich beziehen auf (o, o) to refer to
die Beziehung, –en reference
bezüglich in reference to
bilden to form, to shape
Bildhauerei statuary, sculptor's art
die Bindekraft, ¨e binding force
das Blatt, ¨er leaf, sheet
der Blitzkrieg, –e lightning war
der Block, ¨e block
bloß mere
das Blut blood
die Blüte, –n blossom
blutig bloody
der Blutkreislauf, ¨e circulatory system
die Blutzelle, –n blood cell
der Boden, ¨ soil
der Bogen, ¨ arch, curve
die Bombe, –n bomb
borgen to borrow
bösartig vicious
der Brauch, ¨e custom
brauchen to need
der Brite, –n British (*noun*)
der Bruch, ¨e break
die Brücke, –n bridge
die Brust, ¨e breast, chest
der Brustkorb, ¨e thoracic cavity
der Brutschrank, ¨e incubator
die Buchführung bookkeeping
die Bucht, –en bay
der Buckel, — hump
das Bündel, — bundle
der Bürger, — citizen
der Bürgerkrieg, –e civil war

C

charakterisieren to characterize
die Chloressigsäure chloroacetic acid
das Chlorhydrin hydrochloride
christlich Christian

D

dagegen on the other hand
dahinschreiten (i, i) to progress
dahinschwinden (a, u) to disappear

damalig at that time
Dämon, –e demon
dämonisch demoniacal
das Damwild cloven-hoofed game
die Dankbarkeit gratitude
der Darm, ⸚e intestine
darnach accordingly
darstellen to represent, to make
die Darstellung, –en representation, production
dasein to be present
das Dasein presence, existence
das Datum, Daten date
der Dauerzustand, ⸚e permanent condition
der Daumen, — thumb
die Decke, –n cover, ceiling
decken to cover
sich decken in to agree with
dementsprechend correspondingly
demgegenüber in the face of this
demgemäß accordingly
dennoch nevertheless
dergestalt in such a way
das Derivat, –e derivative
deshalb therefore
deswegen therefore
deuten to interpret
die Deutlichkeit clearness
der Diamant, –en diamond
dicht dense
die Dichte density
der Dichteausgleich equalization of density
dienstbar serviceable
dienstlich by way of service
diesbezüglich in this respect
das Ding, –e (–er) thing
diskutieren to discuss
disloziert dislocated
die Donau the Danube
das Dorf, ⸚er village
dreiwertig trivalent
die Dringlichkeit urgency
der Druck pressure
die Druckerschwärze printer's ink
die Drüse, –n gland
der Dualismus dualism
dualistisch dualistic
dulden to suffer
das Düngemittel, — fertilizer
der Dünger, — fertilizer
durchaus basically, entirely
das Durchgangsmedium medium of transit
durchlässig permeable
durchlaufen (äu; ie, au) to pass through
der Durchmesser, — diameter
die Durchschlagskraft power of penetration
durchweg entirely
der Durchzug, ⸚e transit
sich durchsetzen to assert oneself
der Durst thirst

E

ebenfalls likewise
ebengenannt just mentioned
das Echo echo
der Edelstein, –e gem
ehren to honor
das Ei, –er egg
die Eiche, –n oak
eigen proper, own
die Eigenart, –en characteristic
eigenartig peculiar, characteristic
die Eigenschaft, –en property
eigentlich real, actual
das Eigentum, ⸚er property
die Eigentümlichkeit, –en peculiarity
das Einbalsamieren embalming
einbegreifen (i, i) to include
eindringen (a, u) to enter by force, to penetrate
der Eindruck, ⸚e impression
eindrucksvoll impressive
einengen to limit
einfach simple
die Einfachheit simplicity

einfallen in (ä; ie, a) to invade
der Einfluß, ⸗sse influence
einführen to import, to introduce
der Eingeborene, –n native
eingehen auf (i, a) to enter into
eingehend in detail, detailed
eingesessen native
eingestehen (a, a) to admit
die Eingeweide (*pl.*) intestines, bowels
eingliedern to arrange, to line up
eingreifen in (i, i) to interfere with
der Eingriff, –e interference
einheimisch native
die Einheit, –en entity, unity, oneness
einheitlich uniform
sich einigen auf to agree in
einigermaßen to some extent
die Einimpfung, –en vaccination, inoculation
einleiten to introduce
einleuchtend to be clear
einmalig once
die Einreibung, –en massage
die Einreihung, –en arrangement
einrichten to arrange
die Einrichtung, –en arrangement, institution
einritzen to scratch into
die Einschätzung estimation
sich einschieben in (o, o) to insert oneself into
einschließen (o, o) to include, to inclose
einschließlich inclusive
einschneiden in (i, i) to cut into
einschneidend incisive
einschränken to limit
die Einschränkung, –en limitation
einseitig one-sided
einsetzen to set in, to estimate, to begin
einsichtlich clear
einstellen to adjust
die Einstellung, –en adjustment
der Einsturz, ⸗e fall, slide, cave-in
einteilen to divide
die Einteilung, –en division, distribution
der Eintritt entrance
einverleiben to embody
der Einwanderer, — immigrant
die Einwanderung, –en immigration
die Einzelheit, –en detail
einzeln individually, singly
einziehen (o, o) to draft
einzig only
einzwängen to limit
die Eisenbahn, –en railroad
das Eisenoxydhydrat ferric hydroxide
der Elefant, –en elephant
das Elendsquartier, –e slum(s)
die Emaille enamel
empfangen (ä; i, a) to receive
empfehlen (ie; a, o) to recommend
empfinden (a, u) to sense
die Empfindlichkeit sensitivity
empirisch empirical, by experience
empor up, upwards
emporbrechen (i; a, o) to break forth
emporschnellen to shoot forth
endgültig final
die Energie, –n energy
eng narrow
entarten to degenerate
entdecken to discover
die Entfaltung development
sich entfernen to leave
entgegengesetzt contrary, opposite
entgehen (i, a) to escape
enthalten (ä; ie, a) to contain
entheben (o, o) to relieve
erhöhen to elevate
die Entladung, –en discharge
entlassen (ä; ie, a) to dismiss
entleeren to empty
entlehnen to borrow
entnehmen (i; a, o) to take from

sich entscheiden (ie, ie) to decide
die Entspannung relaxation
entsprechen (i; a, o) to correspond
entstehen (a, a) to come into being, to originate
die Entstehung coming into being, origin
die Enttäuschung, –en disappointment
entvölkern to depopulate
entweichen (i, i) to escape
entwickeln to develop
die Entwicklung, –en development
die Entzündung, –en inflammation
die Epoche, –n epoch
erblich hereditary
das Erdbeben, — earthquake
der Erdboden soil
die Erde earth
erdrücken to choke
sich ereignen to occur, to happen
das Ereignis, –sse event
erfahren (ä; u, a) to experience
die Erfahrung, –en experience
erfahrungsgemäß by experience
erfassen to comprehend, to seize
erfinden (a, u) to invent
der Erfolg, –e success
erfordern to require
erforschen to explore
die Erforschung exploration
erfreulich happy
erfüllen to fulfill
das Ergänzungsfach, ⸚er supplementary course
sich ergeben aus (i; a, e) to result from
ergeben devoted
das Ergebnis, –sse result
ergiebig rich
sich ergießen in (o, o) to empty into
ergreifen (i, i) to seize
erhalten (ä; ie, a) to obtain, to conserve, to preserve
die Erhaltung conservation, preservation
erheben (o, o) to raise; **sich erheben** to rise
erheblich considerable
die Erhitzung heating, warming up
erkennen (a, a) to recognize
die Erkenntnis, –sse knowledge, recognition, fact
erklären to explain
erlangen to obtain, to attain to
erlassen (ä; ie, a) to pass, to remit
erlauben to allow
das Erleben experience
das Erlebnis, –sse experience
die Erleichterung, –en relief, facilitation of
ermöglichen to make possible
ernstlich serious
erobern to conquer
erörtern to discuss
errechnen to figure, to calculate
erregen to incite, to stimulate
der Erreger, — inciter, exciter
die Erregsamkeit excitability
erreichen to reach, to obtain
errichten to erect
die Errichtung, –en erection, construction
die Errungenschaft, –en achievement
die Erschaffung, –en creation
erscheinen (ie, ie) to appear
die Erscheinung, –en appearance, phenomenon
erschließen (o, o) to disclose, to unlock
die Erschöpfung exhaustion
die Erschütterung, –en shock, quaking
ersetzen to replace
ersichtlich clear
erstehen (a, a) to rise
erstmalig once
erstreben to strive for, to attain to
sich erstrecken auf to extend to
der Ertrag, ⸚e yield, result
erwachen to awake

der Erwachsene, –n adult
erwähnen to mention
erwarten to expect
die Erwartung, –en expectation
sich erwehren to defend oneself against
sich erweisen (ie, ie) to prove oneself
erweitern to enlarge
die Erweiterung, –en enlargement
erwerben (i; a, o) to acquire
das Erwerbswesen professional life
das Erz, –e ore
erzeugen to produce
das Erzeugnis, –sse product
die Erziehung education
erzielen to obtain
die Essigsäure acetic acid
etwaig probable, possible, some
eventuell sometime
ewig eternal
das Experiment, –e experiment

F

die Fabrik, –en factory
der Facharbeiter, — expert
fachgemäß expertly
die Fachleute (*pl.*) experts
fachmännisch expert (*adj.*)
der Faden, ⸚ thread
die Fähigkeit, –en capacity
der Faktor, –en factor
der Fall, ⸚e fall, case
der Fang, ⸚e catch
färben to dye
der Farbstoff, –e dyestuff
die Farm, –en farm
die Fäulnis decay
fehlen to be lacking in, to miss
der Fehler, — mistake
fehlschlagen (ä; u, a) to fail
feindlich inimical, hostile
der Felsen, — rock
fern distant
fertig ready, complete
fesselnd absorbing, gripping
fest solid, firm
das Festland, ⸚er continent
die Festlandbrücke, –n continental bridge
die Festnahme arrest
sich festsetzen to settle
feststellbar determinable
feststellen to determine
der Fettansatz deposit of fat
feucht moist
das Feuer, — fire
fiberhaft feverish
der Film, –e film
der Fisch, –e fish
flach flat, low
die Fläche, –n plane, surface
das Flachland, ⸚er lowland
die Flechte, –n moss
der Fleck, –en spot
die Fledermaus, ⸚e bat
das Fleisch flesh, meat
der Flieger, — aviator
fliehen (o, o) to flee, to escape
die Flocke, –n flake
das Flugzeug, –e aeroplane
die Flur, –en floor, open field, meadow
die Flüssigkeit, –en liquid
das Flußpferd, –e hippopotamus
die Flutwelle, –n tidal wave
die Folge, –n consequence, sequence
folgerichtig logical
die Folgerichtigkeit logic
folgern to reason
folglicherweise consequently
fordern to require, to demand
die Forderung, –en requirement, demand
die Form, –en form, shape
die Formel, –n formula
die Formierung, –en formulation
formulieren to formulate
der Forscher, — scientist

der Forstmann, ⸚er forester
forstwirtschaftlich forest management
sich fortbegeben (i; a, e) to go away
das Fortkommen livelihood
fortlaufend current
fortnehmen (i; a, o) to take away
sich fortpflanzen to propagate
die Fortpflanzung propagation
die Fortschaffung elimination
der Fortschritt, –e progress
fortschrittlich progressive
fortsetzen to continue
der Franzose, –n Frenchman
französisch French
der Freihandel free trade
die Freiheit freedom
das Freiwerden liberation
fremd strange, alien
friedlich peaceful
frieren (o, o) to freeze
die Front, –en front
der Frosch, ⸚e frog
fruchtbar fruitful
der Fuchs, ⸚e fox
fühlbar perceptible
die Fülle abundance
der Fund, ⸚e find, a thing found
die Furcht fear
das Futter fodder, feed

G

die Gabe, –n gift
sich gabeln to fork, to divide
der Gang, ⸚e walk, corridor
die Ganzheit totality
gänzlich entirely
die Gärung fermentation
die Gattung, –en species
die Geantiklinale anticline
die Gebärmutter, ⸚ uterus
das Gebiet, –e territory, region, field
das Gebilde, — formation
die Gebirgskette, –n mountain chain
die Geborgenheit security
der Gebrauch, ⸚e custom, use
die Geburt, –en birth
das Gedächtnis memory
der Gedanke, –n thought
gedanklich mental
gedeihen (ie, ie) to thrive
die Gefahr, –en danger
gefährden to endanger
das Gefälle drop
das Gefängnis, –sse prison
das Gefäß, –e vessel, container
das Gefolge following
gefrieren (o, o) to freeze
das Gefühl, –e feeling
die Gegend, –en region
der Gegensatz, ⸚e contrast
der Gegenstand, ⸚e object, subject
das Gegenteil opposite
gegenüberstellen to place opposite to, to contrast
gegenwärtig present
der Gegner, — opponent
geheim secret
das Geheimnis, –sse secret
der Gehilfe, –n helper, assistant
das Gehirn, –e brain
das Gehölz, –e woods
der Geist, –er mind, spirit, intellect
die Geisteswelt, –en abstract world
gekünstelt artificial
das Geld, –er money
die Geldanleihe, –n loan of money
die Gelegenheit, –en opportunity
das Gelenk, –e joint
gelingen (a, u) to succeed
gelockert loosened
gelten (i; a, o) to be worth, to refer, to hold true of
gemäß according to
gemäßigt moderate
gemeinsam in common

die Gemeinschaft, -en community
das Gemüse, — vegetable
das Gemüt, -er mind
genau exact
die Genauigkeit exactness
das Genick, -e neck
genießen (o, o) to enjoy
Genüge: zur — sufficiently
genügen to suffice
das Gepräge imprint, character
geradewegs straight
geraten (ä; ie, a) to get into, to turn out
das Geräusch, -e noise
das Gericht, -e court of law
gerichtlich lawful, legal
gering slight, little
der Germane, -n Teuton, German
germanisch Teutonic, Germanic
gesamt all, total
das Geschäftsleben business life
geschehen (ie; a, e) to happen
das Geschehnis, -sse event
geschichtlich historical
das Geschlecht, -er sex, generation
geschlechtlich sexual
der Geschmack taste
das Geschöpf, -e creature
das Geschoß, -sse bullet, projectile
die Geschwindigkeit, -en velocity, speed
die Geschwulst, ⸚e swelling, tumor
das Geschwür, -e ulceration, tumor
die Gesellschaft, -en society, company
das Gesetz, -e law
gesetzlich legal
gesetzmäßig in accordance with law
der Gesichtspunkt, -e viewpoint
das Gestade, -n shore, bank, beach
die Gestalt, -en figure, shape, form
gestalten to shape, to form
die Gestaltung, -en development, shaping
gestatten to permit
das Gestein, -e stone, rock
das Gestirn, -e constellation, star
gesund sound, healthy
das Gesundbad, ⸚er watering place, spa
das Gesunden recovery
die Gesundheit health
gesundheitlich from the standpoint of health
das Geviert, -e square
das Gewächs, -e vegetation, plant growth
die Gewalt, -en force, power
gewaltig powerful, forceful
gewaltsam forcibly
das Gewebe, — tissue, fiber
das Geweih, -e antlers
das Gewicht, -e weight
die Gewohnheit, -en habit
gewöhnlich usual, customary
gezwungenerweise forcibly
glänzend glittering, splendid
das Glas, ⸚er glass
glatt smooth
das Gleichgewicht equilibrium
gleichmäßig equally
gleichsam as it were
gleichstellen to equalize
die Gleichung, -en equation
die Gleichwertigkeit equivalence
der Gletscher, — glacier
die Gliedmaße, -n member, limb
der Globus globe, sphere
glücken to succeed
die Göttin, -nen goddess
der Graben, ⸚ ditch
der Grad, -e degree
granulieren to granulate
grasen to graze
grau grey
greifbar tangible
grenzen to border on

der Grieche, –n Greek (*noun*)
großartig broadly, magnificent
die Größe, –n size, magnitude
großenteils largely
der Grund, ⸚e reason
gründen to found, to establish
grundfalsch basically wrong
die Grundlage, –n basis
grundlegend basic to
gründlich thorough
die Grünernte, –n forage crop
die Gruppe, –n group
sich gruppieren um to group around
gültig valid
günstig favorable
der Gürtel, — girdle, belt
das Gut, ⸚er large farm, estate, property

H

sich habilitieren to establish oneself
der Hafen, ⸚ harbor
das Haff, –e marine lake
halber for the sake of
die Halbkugel, –n hemisphere
die Hälfte, –n half (*noun*)
die Haltung, –en attitude
hämmern to hammer
das Handbuch, ⸚er handbook
der Handel trade
die Handelsmarine, –n commercial fleet
die Handhabe, –n handle
die Handlung, –en act, action
handwerklich by way of trade, skilled
die Harke, –n hoe
die Härte hardness
der Haß hatred
sich häufen to pile up, to accumulate
häufig frequent
die Häufigkeit frequency
hauptsächlich chiefly, mainly
die Hauptstadt, ⸚e capital city
das Hausgerät, –e domestic furnishings
der Haushalt, –e household
das Haustier, –e domestic animal
heben (o, o) to raise, to lift
das Heer, –e army
sich heften an to attach oneself to
das Heidekraut, ⸚er heather
der Heilgott, ⸚er healing divinity
heilig holy, sacred
die Heilkunde medical science
die Heilmittellehre, –n medical theory
die Heilung, –en healing
die Heimat homeland
heimsuchen to afflict
der Helfer, — helper, assistant
hemmen to hem in, to prevent
herabsetzen to decrease
die Herabsetzung decrease
herannahen to approach
herantreten an (i; a, e) to approach
heranwachsen (ä; u, a) to grow up
sich heranwagen an to undertake
heranziehen an (o, o) to draw near to
herausarbeiten to work out
herausbilden to develop
herausgeben (i; a, e) to edit, to issue, to publish
sich herausstellen to prove to be, to turn out to be
herausziehen (o, o) to draw out
herbeiführen to bring about
herbeischaffen to produce
der Herd, –e hearth, seat
die Herkunft origin
die Herrschaft rule, domination
herrschen to rule, to dominate
der Herrscher, — ruler
herrühren to originate, to come from
herstellen to produce, to manufacture

die Herstellung production
hervorbringen (a, a) to produce
hervorgehen (i, a) to come from, to originate
hervorheben (o, o) to emphasize
hervorragend prominent
hervorspringen (a, u) to come from, to originate
sich hervortun (a, a) to distinguish oneself
das Herz, –en heart
die Heuschrecke, –n grasshopper, locust
heutig present-day
heutzutage present day, today
die Hilfe help
das Hilfsmittel, — means of aid, auxiliary
der Himmel, — heaven, firmament
hindern to hinder, to prevent
sich hineindrängen to push oneself into
hineinragen to protrude into
hineinreichen to project into
hinreichend sufficient
der Hintergrund background
das Hinterland hinterland
hinweisen (ie, ie) to point to
sich hinziehen zu (o, o) to extend to
hinzufügen to add
die Hirnsprachstudie, –n the study of cerebral speech centers
der Hirsch, –e stag
das Hochholz, ⸚er tall forest
die Hochschule, –n high school
die Hoffnung, –en hope
die Höhle, –n cave, cavity
der Hohlraum, ⸚e cavity, empty space
das Holz, ⸚er wood
der Holzschnitt, –e wood engraving
der Holzschnitzer, — wood carver
die Hüfte, –n hip
der Hügel, — hill
der Hund, –e dog, hound
die Hungersnot, ⸚e famine
der Husten cough
die Hysterie hysteria
hysterisch hysterical

I

das Ideal, –e ideal
immerwährend continually
imstande capable of
der Inbegriff, –e concept, idea
der Indianer, — Indian (*noun*)
das Indien India
das Individuum, –en individual (*noun*)
infolge in consequence of
der Inhalt content
der Inhaltstoff, –e content, subject matter
das Inhaltsverzeichnis, –sse table of contents
das Innere interior (*noun*)
die Inselbrücke, –n island bridge
inwiefern in how far
inzwischen in the meantime
irgendwelche some, any
irgendwie somehow
irisch Irish (*adj.*)
die Irrenanstalt, –en institution for the insane
der Irrtum, ⸚er error
italienisch Italian (*adj.*)

J

das Jagdtier, –e wild game
jahrelang for years
das Jahrhundert, –e century
das Jahrzehnt, –e decade
jedenfalls in any case
jedermann everybody
jedweder each one
jeglich each, any
jeweilig at any given time
der Jochbogen, ⸚ zygomatic arch

der **Jude, –n** Jew

die **Jugend** youth

der **Jünger, —** disciple

K

der **Kaktus, –een** cactus

der **Kalkstein, –e** limestone

der **Kampf, ¨e** combat, battle

der **Kampfplatz, ¨e** battlefield

der **Kanal, ¨e** canal, channel

die **Kappe, –n** cap

kathartisch cathartic

die **Keilschrift, –en** cuneiform writing

der **Keim, –e** germ

keineswegs in no wise, by no means

die **Kenntnis, –sse** knowledge

das **Kennzeichen, —** characteristic

kennzeichnen to characterize

der **Kern, –e** nucleus, kernel

die **Kette, –n** chain

die **Kinderheilkunst** pediatrics

die **Kinderlähmung** infantile paralysis

das **Kirchendogma, –en** church dogma

kirchlich ecclesiastical

die **Klage, –n** complaint

die **Klarheit** clearness, clarity

die **Kleidung** clothing

der **Klumpen, —** lump

der **Kohlenstoff** carbon (C)

der **Kollege, –n** colleague

konstatieren to notice, to determine

kontinuierlich continually

kontrollierbar controllable

der **Korb, ¨e** basket

das **Korn, ¨er** grain

der **Körper, —** body

der **Körperbau** structure of the body

die **Kosten** (*pl.*) costs

die **Kraft, ¨e** force, power, strength

kräftig vigorous, strong

krankhaft sickly, pathological

die **Krankheit, –en** illness, disease

das **Krankheitsbild, –er** aspect of disease

der **Krater, —** crater

der **Kratzer, —** scratcher

das **Kraut, ¨er** weed, plant

der **Krebs, –e** crab, cancer

der **Kreis, –e** circle

kreisen to circle

die **Kreuzung, –en** crossing

der **Krieg, –e** war

die **Kriegsführung** practice of warfare

die **Kritik, –en** criticism

kritisch critical

die **Krone, –n** crown

die **Kröte, –n** toad

der **Krumenpacker, —** soil packer

die **Kruste, –n** crust

die **Kuhmilch** cow's milk

sich kümmern um to concern oneself with

kund geben (i; **a, e**) to notify, to publish, to make something known

kund tun (**a, a**) to let something be known

die **Kunde, –n** news, science

künftig future (*adj.*)

die **Kunst, ¨e** art

kunstgerecht in conformity with the rules of art

die **Kurzwelle, –n** short wave

die **Küste, –n** coast

die **Küstenlinie, –n** coast line

L

laden to charge

die **Lage, –n** position, place

das **Lager, —** storage, position, camp

die **Lagerpflanze, –n** creeping plant

die **Lähmung** paralysis

landesweit countrywide
die Landkarte, –n map
die Landschaft, –en landscape
die Landstrecke, –n expanse of land
der Landstrich, –e piece of land
die Landwirtschaft agriculture
landwirtschaftlich agricultural
die Länge, –n length
langwierig patient
lasten to burden
der Lauf, ⸚e course
die Laune, –n whim
die Laus, ⸚e louse
laut accordingly
lauten to read, to say
das Leben, — life
lebendig alive, living
die Lebenshaltung, –en standard of living
der Lebensunterhalt means of subsistence, livelihood
das Lebewesen, — creature
lebhaft vivid, wide-awake
leer empty
der Lehm loam, clay
die Lehre, –n theory, doctrine
lehren to teach
der Lehrer, — teacher
das Lehrgebäude, — science
lehrreich instructive
der Leibesreiz, –e physical stimulus
leiden (i, i) to suffer
leihen (ie, ie) to lend, to loan
der Leiher, — lender
die Leistung, –en achievement
leiten to guide
die Leitung, –en conduit, guidance, direction
der Leming, –e lemming
lenken to guide, to direct
letztlich lastly
leugnen to deny
liefern to furnish, to deliver
die Linie, –n line
die Liste, –n list
das Loch, ⸚er hole
locken to entice; **anlocken** to attract
das Lockmittel, — bait
das Lohn, ⸚e wages; **der Lohn** reward
sich lohnen to be profitable, to be worth while
lohnend profitable
die Löhnung, –en wages
der Losbruch, ⸚e breaking away, fracture
lösen to solve, to dissolve
loslassen (ä; ie, a) to let go, to set free
die Lösung, –en solution
der Löwe, –n lion
lückenhaft defective, incomplete
die Luft, ⸚e air, atmosphere
die Lunge, –n lung
lustig gay
der Lustige, –n gay person

M

mächtig mighty, powerful
machtlos powerless
der Magen, ⸚ stomach
magmatisch magmatic
die Mahlzeit, –en meal
malen to paint
die Malerei, –en painting
mancherlei of various sorts
manchmal sometimes
der Mangel, ⸚ deficiency, lack
mannigfaltig varied, various
die Mannigfaltigkeit, –en variety
männlich male, masculine
der Mantel, ⸚ coat, overcoat, covering
der Markt, ⸚e market
die Maske, –n mask
die Masse, –n mass
der Maßstab, ⸚e ruler, rule, criterion, scale

die Maus, ⸗e mouse
das Medikament, –e medicine, medicament
medizinisch medical
das Meer, –e ocean, sea
der Meeresgrund, ⸗e ocean bottom
mehrfach several(ly), repeated(ly)
meinen to mean, to say
die Meinung, –en opinion
der Meister, — master
melden to announce
die Menge, –n crowd, a large number of
der Mensch, –en human being, man
die Menschheit mankind
menschlich human
das Merkmal, –e characteristic
messen (i; a, e) to measure
das Messer, — knife; **der Messer** measuring instrument
die Messung, –en measurement
das Meter, — meter
milchig milky
das Militärwesen military affairs
minderwertig inferior
die Mischung, –en mixture
das Mißverständnis, –sse misunderstanding
der Mitarbeiter, — collaborator
mitgeben (i; a, e) to give a person something to take along with him
mitgenommen affected
die Mithilfe cooperation
die Mitleidenschaft sympathy, common suffering
der Mitmensch, –en fellow human being
das Mittelalter Middle Ages
der Mittelpunkt, –e center
mittels by means of
der Mittelwald, ⸗er forest of medium height
mittler average (*adj.*)
die Mitwelt environment
die Moderne modern times
die Möglichkeit, –en possibility
möglicherweise possibly
der Mond, –e moon
monistisch monistic
das Moor, –e moor
der Mörder, — murderer
das Morgenland Orient
die Müdigkeit fatigue
die Mündung, –en opening, mouth of a river
das Muster, — pattern

N

der Nachfolger, — successor
nachfragen to inquire
nachlassen (ä; ie, a) to temper, to slacken, to relax
die Nachricht, –en news
nachweisbar provable
die Nachwelt posterity
die Nadel, –n needle
sich nähern to approach
die Nahrung nutrition, food
das Nahrungsmittel, — provisions, victuals
der Namensvetter, –n namesake
die Narbe, –n scar
naß wet
die Natur, –en nature, constitution, temperament
der Naturforscher, — natural scientist
naturgemäß naturally
natürlich naturally
das Nebenfach, ⸗er supplementary course
der Neger, — Negro
neigen to incline
die Neigung, –en inclination
nennen (a, a) to name
die Nervenanregung, –en nerve stimulus
der Nervenarzt, ⸗e neurologist
das Netz, –e net
neuerdings recently

die Neuerung, –en improvement
die Neuzeit modern times
neuzeitlich modern
nichtsdestoweniger nevertheless
nieder lower, down
niedergehen (i, a) to go down
der Niederwald, ⸚er low forest
die Niere, –n kidney
der Nil the Nile
das Niveau level
der Nomade, –n nomad
notwendig necessary
notwendigerweise necessarily
die Notwendigkeit, –en necessity
die Null, –en zero
die Nummer, –n number
nunmehr now
nutzbar useful
die Nutzbarmachung utilization
der Nutzen use

O

die Oberfläche, –n surface
oberflächlich superficial
obig above (*adj.*)
das Obst fruit
offenbar evidently
offenbaren to reveal
öffentlich public
ohnehin besides
ordnen to arrange
der Ort, –e (⸚er) place

P

passend suitable
der Pelz, –e fur, pelt
die Persönlichkeit, –en personality
der Pfad, –e path
das Pferd, –e horse
die Pflanze, –n plant
der Pflanzenwuchs plant growth
pflanzlich vegetable (*adj.*)
die Pflege care
pflegen to attend to, to cultivate, to administer
die Pflicht, –en duty
der Pflug, ⸚e plow
pflügen to plow
die Pforte, –n portal, door
der Plan, ⸚e plan
planmäßig according to plan
der Pilz, –e mushroom, fungus
die Platte, –n plate
der Platz, ⸚e place
plötzlich suddenly
das Polizeiwesen police department
das Polster, — upholstery
die Pore, –n pore
prächtig splendid, magnificent
das Praktikum practice
das Priesteramt, ⸚er priesthood
die Problematik problematics
der Prozentsatz, ⸚e percentage
prüfen to test, to check, to try
die Prüfung, –en test, examination
die Psyche soul, mind
die Pufferung, –en buffing
der Puls pulse
der Punkt, –e point, dot, period
punktartig like a dot

Q

das Quadrat, –e square
die Quelle, –n source, spring
die Quote, –n quota

R

das Rad, ⸚er wheel, bicycle
das Radar radar
der Rahmen, — frame
die Rakete, –n rocket
der Rand, ⸚er edge
die Rasse, –n race
raten (ä; ie, a) to advise
die Ratlosigkeit confusion
ratsam advisable

die Ratte, –n rat
das Raubtier, –e predatory animal
rauchen to smoke
der Raum, ⸚e space, room
die Raupe, –n caterpillar
rechnen to figure, to calculate
die Rechnung, –en bill; — **tragen (ä; u, a)** to account for
das Recht, –e right, law, justice
die Rede, –n speech
das Reelle real (*noun*)
rege active, moving, astir
die Regel, –n rule
die Regelmäßigkeit, –en regularity
der Regen, — rain
die Regierung, –en government
das Reh, –e roe, small deer
die Reiberei, –en friction, conflict, riot
reibungslos smooth, frictionless
das Reich, –e realm
reichhaltig abundant, rich
reichlich richly, abundant
der Reichtum, ⸚er riches, wealth
reifen to mature
die Reihe, –n row, series
rein pure
reinigen to clean, to purify
der Reinwald, ⸚er forest of predominantly one species, pure stand
reißen (i, i) to tear, to rip, to shred
reißend violent
der Reiz, –e stimulus
reizvoll stimulating, charming
der Rest, –e remains, residue
das Rezept, –e prescription, receipt
sich richten an to address, to turn to; — **nach** to follow
richtig correct, right
die Richtung, –en direction
der Riese, –n giant
riesig gigantic, huge
das Rind, –er cattle
der Ring, –e ring, circle
das Rinnsal, –e rill, small watercourse
die Rippe, –n rib
der Riß, –sse tear, break
roh raw, coarse
die Röhre, –n pipe
die Rolle, –n role
rollen to roll
das Rotkehlchen, — redbreast, robin
der Rücken, — back (*noun*)
der Rückgang, ⸚e recession
das Rückgrad, –e spine, backbone
die Rückkehr return
der Rückschlag, ⸚e rebound, recoil
die Rücksicht, –en consideration
der Ruf reputation
die Ruhe rest
rührig active
rund round, about
der Rundlauf, ⸚e circulation, circular course
russisch Russian

S

die Saat, –en seed
die Sache, –n matter, thing
die Sachlage, –n state of affairs
der Saft, ⸚e sap, juice
saftig juicy
die Sage, –n tale, story, legend
der Salpeter saltpeter
salpetrig nitrous
salzig salty
das Salzlager, — salt deposit
sammeln to gather, to collect
das Sammelwerk, –e collected works
die Sammlung, –en collection
der Sand sand
der Satz, ⸚e sentence, statement
die Sauberkeit cleanliness
sauer sour
der Sauerstoff oxygen
saugen to suck

das Säugetier, -e mammal
die Säure, -n acid
der Schädel skull
der Schaden, ⸚ damage
die Schädigung, -en injury
das Schaf, -e sheep
schaffen (u, a) to create
der Schall, -e sound
die Scham shame, modesty, chastity
scharfsinnig keen, incisive
schätzen to estimate
scheinbar seemingly
der Scheinwerfer, — searchlight
der Schelf, -e shelf
schenken to give
scheu shy, retiring
die Schicht, -en layer
die Schichtung, -en layering
schicken to send
das Schicksal, -e destiny
das Schiff, -e ship
das Schilf reed
die Schlacht, -en battle
der Schläfer, — sleeper
der Schlamm mud, slime
die Schlange, -n snake
schlechthin simply, merely
die Schleife, -n loop
schleimig slimy, muddy
schlichten to arbitrate
schließen (o, o) to close, to conclude
schließlich finally
der Schlüssel, — key
der Schnee snow
der Schnitt, -e cut
scholastisch scholastic
die Scholle, -n soil, acre, clod
die Schönheit, -en beauty
die Schöpfung, -en creation
der Schorf, -e scab
der Schornstein, -e chimney
schottisch Scottish
der Schrecken, — fright
der Schrei, -e cry
die Schrift, -en script
der Schritt, -e step
die Schuld, -en debt, guilt
der Schüler, — pupil, student
die Schulter, -n shoulder
das Schüttergebiet, -e region of quake
der Schutz protection
schützen to protect
der Schwamm, ⸚e sponge
schwanken to vary, to wave, to oscillate
schwärzen to blacken
der Schwarzwald the Black Forest
das Schweden Sweden
der Schwefel sulphur (S)
das Schweigen silence
der Schweiß perspiration
die Schwerkraft force of gravity
der Schwerpunkt, -e center of gravity
der Schwiegervater, ⸚ father-in-law
die Schwierigkeit, -en difficulty
schwimmen (a, o) to float
die Schwindsucht consumption, tuberculosis
schwingen (a, u) to oscillate, to swing
die Schwingung, -en vibration
der See, -n lake; **die —** ocean, wave
das Seebeben, - seaquake
die Seele, -n soul
die Seelenheilkunde psychiatry
die Seelenkunde psychology
die Seelenlehre psychology
seelisch psychic
der Seetank seaweed
seewärts seaward
segensreich prosperous, blessed
die Seife, -n soap
das Selbstbewußtsein self-consciousness
selbstredend naturally
selbstständig independent

die Seuche, –n epidemic
die Sicherheit security
sichern to secure
sichtbar visible
das Sichtfeld, –er field of vision
das Sichübervölkern overpopulating
das Sickerwasser, — drainage water
siegreich victorious
der Sitzplatz, ⸚e seat
sieden to simmer, to boil
die Siedlung, –en settlement
der Siegel (das —), — seal
die Silbe, –n syllable
der Sinn meaning, sense
das Sinnesorgan, –e sense organ
der Sitz, –e seat, hearth
skizzenhaft sketchy
die Skizzierung, –en sketch
sofort at once
sogar even
der Soldat, –en soldier
sonst else
sonstig otherwise
sonstwie otherwise
sorgen dafür to take care of
sorgfältig carefully
sorgsam carefully
die Spur, –en trace, trail
somit thus, therefore
die Spalte, –n crack
spanisch Spanish
die Spannung, –en tension, potential
der Speer, –e spear
der Sperling, –e sparrow
das Sperma sperm
das Spiel, –e play, game
die Spitze, –n tip, point
der Sport sport, variation, mutation
die Sprache, –n language, speech
die Sprengkraft, ⸚e explosive force
der Sproß, ⸚sse sprout
der Sprung, ⸚e crack
der Staat, –en state
das Staatsgeheimnis, –sse state secret
der Stab, ⸚e staff, rod
der Stachel, –n thorn, spine
das Stadtviertel, — section of a town
der Stamm, ⸚e stem, trunk
der Stand, ⸚e stand, class
im Stande sein to be capable of
ständig steady, constant
der Standpunkt, –e standpoint
der Star, –e blackbird, starling
die Stärke strength, force
stattfinden (a, u) to take place
der Staub dust
die Staude, –n shrub, bush
staunen to be astonished
staunenswert remarkable
stecken to stick, to be
steigen (ie, ie) to rise
steigern to increase, to raise
der Stein, –e stone
die Stelle, –n place, spot
stellenweise in places
die Stellung, –en position
die Stempelkissentinte stamping ink
der Stengel, — stem
die Steppe, –n steppe
der Sterndeuter, — astrologer
stetig steady, constant
Stich halten (ä; **ie, a**) to be valid
das Stichwort, ⸚er slogan
das Stocken interruption
das Stockwerk, –e story, layer
der Stoff, –e stuff, substance
stofflich material (*adj.*)
die Störung, –en disturbance
stoßen (ö; **ie, o**) to push, to ram
die Stoßkraft, ⸚e ramming power
die Strafe, –n penalty
straff strict, taut, rigid
der Strahl, –en ray
die Strapazen (*pl.*) exertions
der Strauch, ⸚er shrub

streng strict
der Strom, ⸚e stream
die Studie, –n study
die Stufe, –n step
die Stufenreihe, –n series of steps
der Sturm, ⸚e storm
sich stützen auf to lean on, to base oneself on
der Schützengraben, ⸚ trench
die Suche search
der Sumpf, ⸚e swamp
sumpfig swampy
die Summe, –n sum
sündlich sinful
sympatisch sympathetic

T

die Tafel, –n table, list
das Tal, ⸚er valley
der Tastsinn sense of touch
der Täter, — doer, actor
die Tatsache, –n fact
der Tatsachenbestand, ⸚e facts of the case
tatsächlich actual
der Taubenschwarm, ⸚e flock of pigeons
der Teer tar
der Teich, –e pond
der Teil (das —), –e part
teilnehmen (i; a, o) to take part in
teils partly
das Tetraeder tetrahedron
der Teufel, — devil
die Tiefe, –n depth
das Tiefland, ⸚er lowland
das Tier, –e animal
tierisch animal-like
die Tiersektion, –en animal dissection
der Tiger, — tiger
das Tischgerät, –e tableware
der Todesfall, ⸚e (case of) death, decease
der Ton clay; **der —, ⸚e** tone, sound
töten to kill
trachten to strive, to seek
die Tragweite importance, range of significance
der Trank, ⸚e drink, potion
die Traube, –n cluster (*as of grapes*)
der Traum, ⸚e dream
der Träumer, — dreamer
treiben (ie, ie) to carry on (out)
trennen to separate
die Trennung separation
die Triade, –n triad
der Trichter, — funnel
trocken dry
die Trommel, –n drum
der Trommler, — drummer
der Tropfen, — drop
das Tuch, ⸚er cloth, fabric

U

üben to practice
überall everywhere
überaus extremely, very
der Übeltäter, — evildoer
überblicken to survey
übereinstimmen to agree
überflüssig superfluous
der Übergang, ⸚e transition
sich übergeben (i; a, e) to surrender oneself to
übergehen (i, a) to skip, to go over
übergreifen (i, i) to go over to
überhaupt at all, as such
überkommen traditional (*adj.*)
sich überlagern to impose itself upon, to deposit over
die Überlandbahn, –en transcontinental train
überliefern to surrender, to hand down
überraschend surprising
die Überredung persuasion
der Überrest, –e remains

überschreiten zu (i, i) to go over to
der Überschuß, ¨sse excess
überschwemmen to flood
übersehen (ie; a, e) to overlook, to oversee, to survey
die Übersetzung, –en translation
übertragen (ä; u, a) to carry over, to transfer
die Übertragung, –en transfer
übertreffen (i; a, o) to surpass
die Überweisung, –en transfer
überwinden (a, u) to overcome
überzeugen to convince
die Überzeugung, –en conviction
üblich customary
übrig remaining
das Ufer, — shore, bank
die Uhr, –en clock
die Umänderung, –en change, transformation
der Umbau, –ten rebuilding, reconstruction
umfangreich abundant, comprehensive
umfassend comprehensive
die Umgebung surroundings, environment
umgehen (i, a) to go around, to circumvent
umgekehrt conversely
umgrenzen to limit, to outline
umhin: nicht — können (o, o) not to be able to do otherwise
umreißen (i, i) to sketch, to outline
der Umriß, –sse outline
der Umschlag, ¨e envelope
umschließen (o, o) to encompass, to enclose
umschreiben (ie, ie) to circumscribe
die Umsetzung, –en transformation
umstreiten (i, i) to question, to debate
unangenehm disagreeable
unbegrenzt unlimited
unbekannt unknown
unbewußt unconscious
uneben uneven
unedel low, base
uneingeschränkt unlimited
die Unendlichkeit infinity
unerheblich inconsiderable
unerreichbar unobtainable
der Unfall, ¨e accident
ungefähr about, approximately
ungeheuer immense
ungemein uncommon
die Ungleichheit, –en inequality
unheilvoll foreboding
die Unklarheit, –en vagueness, haziness, indistinctness
die Unmasse, –n large mass
die Unmenge, –n immense number *or* quantity
unmöglich impossible
die Unregelmäßigkeit, –en irregularity
die Unruhe restlessness
unruhig restless
unschädlich harmless
die Unschuldigkeit innocence
unsichtbar invisible
die Unterart, –en subspecies
die Unterbrechung, –en interruption
unterdrücken to suppress
unterhalten (ä; ie, a) to entertain, to promote, to sustain
unterlassen (ä; ie, a) to omit, to forget, to neglect
unterlegen inferior
unternehmen (i; a, o) to undertake
das Unternehmen, — undertaking
unterordnen to subordinate
unterrichten to instruct
der Unterschied, –e difference
unterschiedlich different
die Unterschrift, –en signature, subscript

das Unterseeboot, –e submarine
unterseeisch submarine (*adj.*)
unterstreichen (i, i) to emphasize, to underline
unterstützen to support
untersuchen to investigate
die Untersuchung, –en investigation
untertauchen to submerge
unterwerfen (i; a, o) to subject to
unübersehbar boundless, immense, vast
unumgänglich absolutely
unveränderlich unchangeable
unverdaulich indigestible
unvollkommen incomplete
unvorhersehbar unpredictable
unvorteilhaft disadvantageous
unwissend ignorant
unzählig countless
unzweideutig clear, plain, simple
ur– original, primitive
das Uran uranium (U)
urbar tillable, arable
die Ursache, –n cause
der Ursprung, ⸚e origin
ursprünglich original
die Urzeugung spontaneous generation

V

verabfolgen to deliver, to consign, to hand over
die Verallgemeinerung, –en generalization
veralten to age
veranlagt disposed
die Veranlagung, –en giftedness, disposition, talent
veranlassen to cause
die Veranlassung, –en cause
veranschaulichen to realize, to imagine
verantwortlich responsible
verarmen to become poor
verbergen (i; a, o) to hide
die Verbesserung, –en improvement
die Verbindlichkeit, –en kindness, favor, obligation
die Verbindung, –en combination, compound
verboten forbidden
der Verbrauch consumption
das Verbrechen, — crime
der Verbrecher, — criminal
die Verbreitung distribution
die Verbrennung combustion, burning
verbringen (a, a) to spend, to pass
verdanken to owe
verdaulich digestible
die Verdauung digestion
die Verdichtung packing, condensation
verdienen to earn, to deserve
das Verdienst earning, salary, wage
verdorben spoiled
die Verdrängung crowding
der Verein, –e club, group, union
vereinbar reconcilable, combinable, harmonizing with
die Vereinigten Staaten the United States
die Vereinigung, –en union
vereinzelt singly
verehren to honor, to revere
vererben to bequeath
das Verfahren, — procedure
der Verfasser, — author
verfechten (i; o, o) to fight for, to defend
der Verfechter, — proponent
sich verfilzen to mat
verflossen past
verfolgen to pursue
die Verfolgung, –en pursuit, persecution
die Verfügung availability, disposition

vergangen past (*adj.*)
die Vergangenheit past (*noun*)
sich vergegenwärtigen to realize, to imagine
vergessen (i; a, e) to forget
vergleichen (i, i) to compare
das Verhalten behavior
sich verhalten wie (ä; ie, a) to behave like
das Verhältnis, -se condition, relation, ratio
verhältnismäßig relatively
verhängnisvoll ominous, fateful
verheeren to devastate
die Verhütung prevention
der Verkauf, ⸚e sale
der Verkehr traffic
verknüpfen to connect
die Verknüpfung, -en connection
verkörpern to embody
verkrüppelt crippled
verlangen to demand
verlängern to lengthen, to elongate
verlangsamen to slow down
der Verlauf course
sich verlegen auf to change to
verleihen (ie, ie) to lend, to bestow, to give
die Verletzung, -en injury
verlieren (o, o) to lose
der Verlust, -e loss
sich vermehren to increase
die Vermehrung increase
die Verminderung decrease
die Vermittlung, -en intervention, mediation
vermögen (a; o, o) to be able to
vermuten to suspect
vernehmen (i; a, o) to perceive, to hear
vernichten to destroy
die Vernichtung destruction
die Vernunft reason
veröffentlichen to publish
die Veröffentlichung, -en publication
verpflanzen to transplant
verpöhnen to penalize, to prohibit
verraten (ä; ie, a) to betray
verrichten to accomplish, to do
verschaffen to procure
verschärfen to emphasize, to sharpen
sich verschieben (o, o) to displace, to shift
verschieden different
verschiedenartig different
die Verschiedenheit, -en difference
verschmelzen (i; o, o) to fuse
die Verschmelzung fusion
verschmutzen to soil
die Verschmutzung soiling
verschonen to spare
verschreiben (ie, ie) to prescribe
(ver)schwächen to weaken
verschwinden (a, u) to disappear
verschwindend minute (*adj.*)
versehen mit (ie; a, e) to supply with
versetzen to place, to displace
die Versicherung, -en assurance, insurance
versinken (a, u) to sink away
die Versklavung enslavement
verständig reasonable, understanding
das Verständnis understanding
verstärken to strengthen, to fortify
verstehen (a, a) to understand
verstumpfen to become dull
der Versuch, -e attempt, experiment
versuchen to attempt, to experiment
versuchsweise experimentally
die Verteidigung defense
die Verteilung distribution
sich vertiefen in to be deeply engaged in
vertraut intimate, familiar
die Vertrautheit familiarity
vertreiben (ie, ie) to drive away

vertreten (**i; a, e**) to represent
der Vertreter, — representative
verursachen to cause
die Verurteilung condemnation
die Verwaltung, –en administration
verwandeln to change
verwandt related
die Verweichlichung weakening, effeminacy
verwerten to utilize
verwesen to decay
die Verwesung decay (*noun*)
die Verwickeltheit, –en complexity
die Verwicklung, –en complication
die Verwirrung, –en confusion
verwunderlich strange, astonishing
verzehren to consume, to eat
verzeichnen to register
verzerren to distort
die Verzerrung, –en distortion
verzweigen to branch out
die Verzweigung, –en branching
das Vieh cattle, livestock
die Viehzucht cattle raising
vielfach often, varied
die Vielheit, –en variety
der Vogel, ⸗ bird
das Volk, ⸗er nation, people
völkisch popular, national
der Volkswissenschaftler, — sociologist
vollbringen (**a, a**) to accomplish
völlig completely, fully
vollkommen perfect, complete
die Vollkommenheit completion, perfection
vorangehen (**i, a**) to proceed
voraussetzen to assume
der Vorbehalt reservation
sich vorbereiten to prepare oneself
vorbeugen to prevent
das Vorbild, –er model
der Vorderarm, –e forearm
der Vordergrund, ⸗e foreground
vordringen (**a, u**) to advance
vorfinden (**a, u**) to find
vorführen to produce, to stage, to demonstrate
die Vorführung, –en demonstration, production
der Vorgang, ⸗e procedure, process
vorgeburtlich prenatal
vorgehen (**i, a**) to proceed, to advance
die Vorgeschichte, –n prehistory
vorgeschichtlich prehistoric
vorhanden present, available
das Vorhandensein presence, availability
vorher previously
vorhergehen (**i, a**) to precede
vorherig preceding
vorherrschen to predominate
vorig previous
vorkommen (**a, o**) to occur
vorlagern to deposit in front of
der Vorläufer, — predecessor
die Vorlesung, –en lecture
die Vorliebe propensity, liking
vornehmen (**i; a, o**) to undertake
vornehmlich especially
die Vorrichtung, –en arrangement
der Vorschlag, ⸗e proposal, suggestion
vorschlagen (**ä; u, a**) to propose, to suggest
vorschreiten (**i, i**) to advance, to progress
vorsichtig careful
vorstellen to imagine
die Vorstellung, –en production, idea
vorstellungshaft imaginary
die Vorstellungskraft, ⸗e power of imagination
vorstoßen (**ö; ie, o**) to advance
vorweg beforehand, in advance of
vorübergehend temporary
vorurteilslos unprejudiced
vorwiegend predominantly

die Vorzeit prehistoric times, early times
der Vorzug, ⸗e preference
vulkanisch volcanic

W

die Waare, –n merchandise
wachsam watchful
das Wachsein watchfulness
wachsen (ä; u, a) to grow
das Wachstum growth
der Wachzustand state of being awake
die Waffe, –n weapon
wählen to choose
wählerisch choosy
wahren to guard, to preserve
die Wahrheit, –en truth
wahrnehmen (i; a, o) to perceive
die Wahrscheinlichkeit, –en probability
der Wald, ⸗er forest
die Waldstrecke, –n extent of forest
der Waldstrich, –e forest tract, forest area
die Walze, –n roller
die Wanderung, –en migration
die Wärme heat
die Wechselbeziehung, –en mutual relation
wecken to awaken
weiblich feminine, female
weichen (i, i) to yield, to retreat
der Weichteil, –e vital part
die Weide, –n pasture
der Weise, –n wise man, sage
weitaus by far
weiter further, on
weiterhin furthermore
weitgehend far-reaching
weitläufig extensive
die Welle, –n wave
die Welt, –en world
die Welterschaffung creation of the world
der Weltruf world reputation
der Weltteil, –e quarter of the globe
der Wendepunkt, –e turning point
die Wendung, –en turn (*noun*), change
der Werdegang development
das Werk, –e work, achievement
das Werkzeug, –e tool
der Wert, –e value, worth
die Wertigkeit, –en valence
wertvoll valuable
das Wesen, — existence, essence, entity, substance, mode of existence
wesentlich essential
westlich western
das Wetter, — weather
der Wettlauf, ⸗e race
wichtig important
die Wichtigkeit importance
widerspiegeln to reflect
der Widerstand, ⸗e resistance
die Widerstandskraft, ⸗e power of resistance
widerwillen against one's will
widmen to devote
die Widmung, –en dedication
wiederauffangen (ä; i, a) to catch again
die Wiedergabe, –n reproduction
wiedergeben (i; a, e) to reproduce
wiederholen to repeat
wiederkehren to return
wiederum again
die Wiese, –n meadow
das Wild game (*animals*)
die Wildschar, –en herd of game
das Wildschwein, –e wild boar
die Willenskraft, ⸗e will power
der Wirbel, — vertebra
die Wirbelsäule, –n spinal column
die Wirklichkeit, –en reality
wirksam effective

das Wissen knowledge
die Wissenschaft, –en science
der Wissenschaftler, — scientist
wissenschaftlich scientific
die Witterung weather, scent
die Woche, –n week
das Wohl welfare
das Wohlergehen welfare, well-being
der Wohnsitz, –e residence, settlement
der Wolf, ⸚e wolf
der Wuchs growth, stature
die Wunde, –n wound
das Wunder, — wonder, miracle
wünschenswert worth-while, desirable
der Wurm, ⸚er worm
die Wurzel, –n root
wüst desolate, forsaken
die Wüste, –n desert

Z

zahlenmäßig statistical
der Zahlenwert, –e numerical value
zahlreich numerous
zähmen to tame
die Zähmung taming, domestication
die Zahnheilkunde dentistry
der Zaum, ⸚e bridle
das Zebra, — zebra
das Zedergeholz, ⸚er cedar thicket, grove, *or* woods
die Zehenspitze, –n tip of the toe
das Zeichen, — sign, indication
zeigen to show
das Zeitalter, — era
zeitigen to produce
zeitlich timely, in time, early
die Zeitspanne, –n span of time, interval
die Zelle, –n cell
das Zentrum, –en center
zerfallen (ä; ie, a) to decay, to fall apart
zerfetzen to tear to shreds
sich zergliedern in to dismember into, to be classified
die Zerlegung, –en analysis, separation
zerschleißen (i, i) to rip apart
die Zerstörung destruction
zerstreuen to scatter
zertrümmern to destroy by heavy blows
die Zertrümmerung destruction
zerwühlen to uproot
die Zeugung generation
ziehen (o, o) to draw, to pull, to move; **nach sich —** to have as its consequence
das Ziel, –e aim, goal
ziemlich rather
der Zinsfuß, ⸚e percentage
zitieren to cite
die Zivilbevölkerung civil population
die Zivilisation, –en civilization
der Zivilist, –en civilian
die Zone, –n zone
die Zucht breeding, discipline, cultivation
die Züchtung breeding, stock, culture
der Zucker sugar
zudem moreover, in addition to this
der Zudrang crowding to
der Zufall, ⸚e accident, chance
zufällig accidental
der Zufluchtsort, –e (⸚er) place of refuge
zufrieden satisfied
zufriedenstellend satisfactory
der Zug, ⸚e trait, train, migration
zugänglich accessible
zugeben (i; a, e) to admit, to add
sich zulegen to take, to acquire
zumeist mostly

zunächst first, next
zunehmen (i; a, o) to increase
zurückführen to trace back
zurückgreifen (i, i) to go back to
zurückkehren to return
zurückweisen (ie, ie) to refuse, to reject
zusagen to agree, to promise
zusammenballen to agglomerate, to make into a ball
zusammenfassen to summarize
die Zusammengehörigkeit feeling of belonging together
zusammenhalten (ä; ie, a) to hold together
der Zusammenhang, ⸚e connection, relationship
zusammenhanglos disconnected, without connection
die Zusammensetzung composition
zusammenstürzen to collapse
der Zusatz, ⸚e addition
zuschreiben (ie, ie) to ascribe
der Zustand, ⸚e condition
zustande kommen (a, o) to come about
zuteilen to distribute, to allot, to impart
zutreffen (i; a, o) to agree, to come true
zuverlässig dependable
sich zuwenden (a, a) to turn to
zuwider contrary to
der Zwang force, compulsion
zwar to be sure
der Zweck, –e purpose
zwecks for the purpose of
zweifeln to despair
zweifelsohne doubtless
der Zweig, –e branch
die Zwergföhre, –n scrub pine
der Zwischenraum, ⸚e interval, intervening space